STRIVING FOR QUALITY IN HEALTH CARE

R. Heather Palmer
Avedis Donabedian
Gail J. Povar

STRIVING FOR QUALITY IN HEALTH CARE

An Inquiry into Policy and Practice

 Health Administration Press
Ann Arbor, Michigan 1991

95 94 93 92 91   5 4 3 2 1

Library of Congress Cataloging-in-Publication Data

Palmer, R. Heather (Ruth Heather), date.
  Striving for quality in health care : an inquiry into policy and practice / R. Heather Palmer, Avedis Donabedian, Gail J. Povar ; with an introduction by Kathleen N. Lohr.
     p.   cm.
  Papers originally prepared for an Institute of Medicine study.
  Includes bibliographical references and index.
  ISBN 0-910701-69-5 (soft : alk. paper)
  1. Medical care—United States—Quality control. 2. Quality assurance—United States. I. Donabedian, Avedis. II. Povar, Gail J. III. Institute of Medicine (U.S.) IV. Title.
  [DNLM: 1. Ethics, Medical—United States. 2. Medicare. 3. Quality of Health Care—standards—United States. W 84 AA1 P168s]
  RA399.A3P33   1991   362.1'0973—dc20
  DNLM/DLC for Library of Congress   91-7024 CIP

The paper used in this publication meets the minimum requirements of American National Standard for Information Sciences—Permanence of Paper for Printed Library Materials, ANSI Z39.48-1984 ∞ ™

Health Administration Press
A division of the Foundation of the
  American College of Healthcare Executives
1021 East Huron Street
Ann Arbor, Michigan 48104-9990
(313) 764-1380

Contents

Introduction

Quality of Health Care: An Introduction to Critical Definitions, Concepts, Principles, and Practicalities. ix

Kathleen N. Lohr

Part I

Considerations in Defining Quality of Health Care. 1

R. Heather Palmer

    Introduction 3

    Defining Quality. 4
        Origins of the Physician Role in Setting Standards
        The Traditional Physician Perspective on Good Medical Care
        Physician Definitions of Quality of Care
        Expansion of Government's Role in Defining Quality
        Defining Appropriate Use
        Definition of Quality from the Government Perspective
        Evidence for Inefficient Provision of Services to Populations
        Cost Containment in the 1980s: The Competition Strategy
        Defining Accessibility of Care
        Expansion of the Consumer's Role in Defining Quality
        Patient and Consumer Definitions of Quality
        Physician Satisfaction
        Inclusive Definition of Quality of Care

    Quality Measurement and Assurance 28
        Data for Quality Measurement
        Standards for Quality Measurement

Quality Assurance Interventions
Quality Measurement Techniques Developed in the 1970s
Examples of Quality Measurements Based on Different Data Types
Strategies for Quality Assurance in the 1990s

Conclusion 41

Glossary. 54

Part II

Reflections on the Effectiveness of Quality Assurance 59

Avedis Donabedian

Introduction 61
The Subject
The Method

The Larger Environment 71
Social Commitment to Quality
The Organization of Care
The Organization of Financing
The Legal Environment

The Intraorganizational Environment 79
Distinctiveness
Relevance
Features

The Medical Profession. 84
Introduction
Some General Features of the Medical Profession
Some Special Features of the Medical Profession
Some Features of Intrainstitutional Practice

The Nature of Professional Work and Its Product. 92
Professional Work
The Science of Technical Care
The Science of Interpersonal Care

The Method of Assessing Performance. 95
The Definition of Quality and the Objectives of Assessment
Approaches, Targets, and Timing
Particularization and Individualization
The Criteria and Standards of Quality
Information about Care

Organization of the Monitoring Enterprise 101
    Organizational Leadership and Authority
    Intraorganizational Linkages
    Internal Structure of the Monitoring Function
    Extraorganizational Linkages

Methods of Obtaining Behavioral Change 106
    Direct Intervention
    Reminders
    Feedback
    Education and Training
    Incentives and Disincentives
    Some Organizational Adaptations
    Using Consumers to Influence Practitioners

The Role of Consumers 113
    Consumers as Contributors to Quality Monitoring
    Consumers as Targets of Monitoring
    Consumers as Users of Monitoring Information

Summary and Conclusions 118

Part III

What Does "Quality" Mean? Critical Ethical Issues
for Quality Assurance 129

Gail J. Povar

    Introduction 131

    Medical Ethics: A Review...................................... 132
        The Case of tPA
        Principles of Medical Ethics
        The Case of Prostatic Surgery
        The Principles Revisited

    Implications for Quality Assurance in Medicare 150
        Beneficence and Nonmaleficence
        Autonomy
        Justice
        Fidelity

    Whither Quality Assurance for Medicare? 156
        What Do We Mean by Quality?
        Who Should Define the Social Optimum?

What Elements of Care Are Critical?
He Who Pays the Piper Calls the Tune

Conclusion 162

Index.. 169
About the Authors 175

Quality of Health Care: An Introduction to Critical Definitions, Concepts, Principles, and Practicalities

Kathleen N. Lohr

THE INSTITUTE OF MEDICINE STUDY

In 1986, the Congress of the United States asked the National Academy of Sciences for assistance in answering a broad set of questions about quality of care in the Medicare program. The questions facing Congress in the mid-1980s appeared to stem from a confusing picture of the health care sector: state-of-the-art health care technology and generally satisfied patients and consumers, *but* extremely expensive health care that consumes nearly 12 percent of the nation's gross national product; 12 percent or more of the citizenry lacking adequate (or any) health insurance to cover those expenses; discouraging figures for standard indicators of health status such as life expectancy and infant mortality; and many doubts about current or future levels of quality of care.

As to the last, many observers were raising (and continue to raise) alarms about trends in costs and utilization of health services, possible harmful effects of more stringent cost-containment efforts, intrusive administrative bureaucracies to review medical care, and generally the capacity of the nation, or more particularly the Medicare program, to ensure adequate and appropriate health care for its members. In short, following a decade or more (the 1960s and 1970s) concerned with access and a decade or two (the 1970s and 1980s) concerned with costs, the 1990s appear to be bringing quality of care to the fore, even as the nation continues to be troubled about both access and costs. The real possibility exists, in fact, for concerted attention to quality of care to begin to provide some answers to the access and cost questions, even as it improves the ability of providers and consumers to reach for and attain higher levels of quality of care.

The congressional commission to the National Academy of Sciences, in the Omnibus Budget Reconciliation Act of 1986, called for an ambitious, challenging, and long-range plan to assess and assure the quality of health care for the elderly during the next decade. The call was taken up by the Academy's Institute of Medicine (IOM), with funding from the Health Care Financing Administration of the U.S. Department of Health and Human Services, in a study to "design a strategy for quality review and assurance in Medicare." The study, begun in late 1987 and completed in mid-1990, is documented in a two-volume report, *Medicare: A Strategy for Quality Assurance.*[1]

The IOM committee under whose direction the project was conducted first defined quality of care and developed a related conceptual framework for the strategy. It examined contemporary methods for measuring and assuring the quality of health care, including the current Medicare Peer Review Organization (PRO) program, and advanced a broad agenda of research in and capacity-building for quality assurance and related efforts. Finally, it proposed a fundamentally new approach to quality review and assurance for Medicare.

This new strategic plan is, first of all, grounded in a clear definition of quality of care. That definition, adopted only after appreciable debate among the IOM committee members, reads as follows: "Quality of care is the degree to which health services for individuals and populations increase the likelihood of desired health outcomes and are consistent with current professional knowledge."

The new program also seeks to be responsive to a changing health care environment. It is intended to have enough flexibility to prevent, detect, and correct problems in all settings in which the elderly receive care, and it is meant to be able to adapt to coming health care needs of the elderly population, to unpredictable results of the incentives of new financing and reimbursement schemes both within and outside of Medicare, and to unforeseen social realities of the 1990s.

The new approach to quality assurance emphasizes professionalism and internal quality improvement over regulation and external inspection. It gives more attention to patient and consumer concerns and decision making and, in particular, to very broadly defined health outcomes. This increased regard for health status and health-related quality of life reflects in part a concern for the complex interactions of quality assurance and ethical principles such as autonomy, beneficence, and justice.

This new plan accentuates the need to generate new knowledge from clinical practice and to return that information to providers in a timely way that improves their own decision making. That is, it places considerable emphasis on changing providers' behaviors and performance, not just on measuring quality of care. It draws more attention to systems of care (rather than individual providers) and to continuity and episodes of care (rather than single events). In this connection, it moves more aggressively into settings and types of care not usually subjected to formal quality assurance, such as ambulatory care in physician offices and home health care. Finally, the new program would become far more accountable through extensive public oversight and rigorous evaluation.

In conducting their work, the IOM committee and staff carried out many different activities: They convened periodically for intensive deliberations, gathered background information, consulted broadly with groups across the country, and acquired or produced technical documents. Among the study tasks completed were the establishment of two sets of focus groups (eight among elderly Medicare beneficiaries and eight among practicing physicians); the creation of a public hearing process with two formal public meetings; many site visits across the country; the creation of a special panel to develop criteria by which quality-of-care criteria, such as clinical practice guidelines, might be evaluated; and many consultations with experts in both the public and private sectors.

To complete these tasks, the IOM committee relied heavily on papers and studies commissioned for the project. Among these, the three works featured in this book, by Heather Palmer, Avedis Donabedian, and Gail Povar, stood out. They dealt with core issues of the study: the definition of quality of care; the conceptual framework and practical considerations of a comprehensive effort both to measure quality of care and to improve it through behavior change on the part of practitioners and institutions; and the perplexing conflicts in putting a functioning quality assurance program into place while optimizing important ethical principles of medicine and health. In all three cases, the authors' treatments of the subjects at hand were fresh, extensive, and scholarly, and the IOM committee believed itself well served with these efforts. Readers will find the book of great value, as it provides a solid understanding of the subject, significant insights into key conceptual and practical issues, and graceful exposition of appeal to many different audiences.

DEFINING QUALITY OF CARE

The IOM study committee devoted much time and energy to defining quality of care. A critical source of background information and history concerning the definition of quality of care was a lengthy paper by R. Heather Palmer of the Harvard School of Public Health, which appears in revised form as Part I of this book.

Palmer defines quality of health care as a means of advancing our understanding of how to *measure* quality, taking into account the perspectives of various parties at interest, such as practitioners and providers, government, and patients and consumers. Using a historical logic, Palmer moves from a definition of quality generated by the concerns of practitioners, chiefly physicians, through one prompted by concerns of government, to one reflective of concerns of patients.

Originally, a physician-oriented definition of care can be seen to have been motivated by two main ethical obligations: patients were owed the best possible care (as defined by physicians), and society was owed some assurance as to the competence of members of the profession. From these ideas would devolve implied definitions based on provider or physician competence, such as ones centering on the ability of physicians to improve the health of individual patients. The concentration on individual patients, rather than groups, populations, or society, was evident.

Government's role in defining quality was prompted in part by concerns with access (a quarter of a century ago) and with health care costs and expenditures (more recently). To the extent that the vast outlays of public sector dollars on expenditures cover some amount of unnecessary and inappropriate care, a view now widely held, the core of quality of care from the government's perspective became appropriate care in relation to cost of care. That is to say, a progression of sorts was made from a notion of balancing the probability of benefit to a patient and the probability of harm (or at least no benefit)—the idea of appropriateness, pure and simple—to the idea of appropriateness of health care services weighed against their costs. Furthermore, government policymaking is less concerned with individuals qua individuals; its touchstone, rather, is the benefits of care received by populations and the consequent justification of expenditures in the aggregate.

Government, however, is not society, and more recently, consumers have had a role in defining quality. In addition to traditional concerns with access and provider competence, patients and consumers have introduced (to some extent unwittingly) ideas of personal values and preferences. That is, health care should be readily available, not constrained by financial considerations (but also not overpriced), and rendered by well-trained, skillful practitioners "who care about their patients"; it should also be acceptable care, producing the improved health outcomes and levels of satisfaction desired by patients.

In weaving these themes together, with many threads of empirical data and conceptual reasoning, Palmer arrives at an "inclusive" definition of quality of care that incorporates the perspectives of all three parties: "the production of improved health and satisfaction of a population within the constraints of existing technology, resources, and consumer circumstances" (p. 27). This definition and the IOM committee's definition have several elements in common: an emphasis on health and health outcomes (not medical care or patient outcomes, for instance); a focus on populations (not just individuals); and a recognition of the limits of the existing professional knowledge base. What makes them dissimilar is Palmer's inclusion of resource constraints in her definition—a component deliberately excluded from the IOM's definition in the belief that quality of care, in an era of increasingly constrained public and private means, should not be defined in terms of available resources.

Using key elements of her definition—provider competence, accessibility, and acceptability—Palmer proceeds in her work to discuss the measurement of quality of care. Measurement of quality of care is, in her view, the comparison of data describing care received to standards (i.e., criteria indicating appropriate services for a particular patient or class of patients, together with the threshold value for compliance with those criteria that will trigger further investigation or corrective action). She touches on the multiplicity of factors that must be taken into account when measuring quality, largely using Avedis Donabedian's paradigm of structure, process, and outcome as the organizing framework.

For a complete view of quality of care, one must move beyond quality measurement to quality assurance. Quality assurance is at base an effort to find and overcome problems with quality—that is, to change the performance and behaviors of practitioners, institutions, and systems toward those that are more appropriate and acceptable (in terms of health outcomes, or expenditures, or both). Palmer briefly reviews the historical progress made in data, standards, and interventions, concluding that with the right context and design of a quality assurance strategy, such programs can be effective.

BARRIERS TO QUALITY ASSURANCE

Most experts in the quality-of-care field agree that defining and measuring quality of care is far easier than improving or assuring quality. The mechanisms for quality assurance can be catalogued and described, but little empirical evidence demonstrates whether such mechanisms really work. Perhaps partly for that reason, some authorities in the area contend that one can never "assure" the quality of health care, in the absolutist sense of guaranteeing exemplary performance (i.e., good science applied in compassionate ways). The best one can do is strive to improve performance, preferably *continually* to improve, as the proponents of "continuous quality improvement" and similar models would have it. Nevertheless, the concepts of quality assurance and the phrase itself have a long tradition, and the IOM study ultimately did not abandon that terminology.

The major issues in quality assurance are those of finding effective means of changing professional and organizational behavior. Knowledge in this area is scanty, in part because factors that encourage change and impediments that delay or frustrate change are not well understood. To overcome this gap in its understanding, the IOM committee asked Avedis Donabedian to reflect on barriers to constructive quality assurance. His scholarly and philosophical essay appears as Part II of this volume.

If one accepts the view that changing the actions of providers—physicians, nurses, and other individual caregivers, as well as the institutions and systems within which they function—is the key to quality assurance, then one must consider what attributes of providers, especially individual professionals, facilitate or impede behavior change. Donabedian's thought-provoking treatise argues, in this vein, that one must appreciate several special characteristics of the medical profession, it being the principal target of most quality assurance efforts today. Only with an understanding of those characteristics can one proceed more confidently in the effort of changing professional behavior.

Among the many features of the medical profession that Donabedian identifies as relevant to quality assurance, the tension between professional autonomy in the practice of medicine and accountability for its quality may count among the most important. Indeed, professing fidelity to certain obligations and rules established by one's peers is the hallmark of a profession. Society, in granting the medical profession responsibility for quality of care, has acknowledged the special expertise needed to determine what constitutes quality, but it has also looked for the profession to demonstrate a reasonable degree of public accountability. The contrapuntal pressures of professional autonomy and accountability probably account for much of the difficulty encountered in organized quality assurance programs. The IOM study, therefore, was much concerned with the question of how to strengthen the practical applications of professionalism while still holding quality assurance programs accountable for their actions and outcomes.

Donabedian highlights two other related characteristics of medicine that have significant implications for quality assurance: processes of recruitment, training, and socialization of members of the profession, and the preference for informal rather than formal quality assurance interventions. He then moves to examine externally imposed efforts, noting the alienating effect (from the physician perspective) of formal, external efforts that emphasize identification of individual malfeasance rather than improvement of ordinary performance. When the search for so-called outliers (i.e., those performing significantly below acceptable levels) becomes the raison d'être for a quality assurance program, it is not surprising that monitoring is resisted, if not undermined completely. The IOM study committee, in response to these factors, decided to emphasize a more broadly based, and more internally driven, quality assurance effort—a program, in other words, that would provide positive benefits for all members of the profession.

Another factor, often overlooked, that impedes quality assurance is the sheer unfamiliarity of physicians with the concepts, methods, and tools of quality assessment and quality assurance. This lack of understanding makes it difficult for members of the profession to exert leadership in quality assurance, and it underscores the need for educational reform and for efforts to increase the capabilities of professionals to act in this role with knowledge and confidence. Donabedian suspects, in his words, that "fundamental reform in medical education must occur before monitoring becomes fully acceptable and effective" (p. 89). Reflecting that view, the IOM study committee included as one of its ten major recommendations a specific call for "capacity building" and training among the nation's health professionals.

Donabedian examines with great insight other issues related to changing professional behavior. Among the approaches he discusses are educational interventions, directives, incentives and disincentives, and various forms of organizational adaptations that may facilitate professional growth and change, routinize behaviors, or bypass recalcitrant individuals together.

Turning then from the professional to the consumer, Donabedian explores in his concluding section the important role of consumers in quality assurance. Here he sees informed consumers as contributing in at least three ways. Consumers can help set standards, through their participation in articulating an understandable and operational definition of quality of care. They can act as evaluators, by expressing clearly their satisfaction or dissatisfaction with care, and as informants, by acting as sources of information about what they have experienced in the process of care and what their outcomes have been. Consumers have a further role in quality of care to the extent that they are "coproducers of care," to use Donabedian's term, and to the extent that they are users of information produced by quality assurance programs. Again, the IOM study committee reflected these ideas in at least two ways: its call for improving clinical decision making between patient and provider, and its strong endorsement of getting information on outcomes of care from patients or from persons empowered to speak for them.

THE ETHICAL CONSIDERATIONS OF QUALITY ASSURANCE

As implied or stated directly by both Palmer and Donabedian, health care rendered by physicians and other professionals, to be considered of high quality, must conform to a clear set of philosophical and moral principles and concepts. Although the specifics of such a code may differ across professions and perspectives, several core concepts seem to form a framework that most commentators agree constitutes the corpus of duties of health care professionals.

In Part III of this book, Gail Povar defines these bedrock ethical principles and explores their implications for collective quality assurance. She highlights the ways in which a quality assurance program has ethical obligations paralleling those of the health care professional and alerts us to the possible conflicts between certain of these duties, depending upon whether the perspective taken is of individual patients or populations. The interweaving of bioethical reasoning with the practicalities of measuring and assuring quality of care—using contemporary health care questions (for instance, "the case of tissue plasminogen activator") as the foil—makes this essay a unique contribution to the literature on quality assurance.

The central precepts of bioethics are to prevent harms ("nonmaleficence"), to promote good care ("beneficence"), and to consider first one's patients and clients ("fidelity"). In addition, the duty to respect persons ("autonomy"), in its application to health care, refers to the duty to respect the right of self-determination regarding choices about lives, minds, and bodies. Finally, the duty not to discriminate on the basis of irrelevant characteristics ("justice") or—the more commonly invoked version—the duty to distribute health care resources in ways that are fair and not capricious ("distributive justice") is a key maxim that requires thinking about health care from the perspective of society, not just the individual.

What sorts of conflicts are perceived to exist among these duties? From the point of view of good quality care, beneficence (and nonmaleficence) may conflict with distributive justice if a decision is made not to provide a highly sophisticated therapy in situations (e.g., rural hospitals) where potential negative side effects could not be properly managed. Would assuring good quality then require health care providers to upgrade the latter situations, at potentially high costs to society as a whole, or to deny certain patients a potentially beneficial therapy on the grounds that possible harms must be avoided? Another example is the potential clash of obligations to patient autonomy and to beneficence/nonmaleficence, for instance in situations in which competent patients appear to make "irrational" choices that nonetheless conform with their own values and priorities. How, then, is a quality assurance program to assess the process or outcomes of medical care when the course of events accords with the (documented) wishes of well-informed patients exercising their powers of decision making but does not accord with normative professional criteria about preferred medical interventions or expected outcomes?

Povar advances some ideas about how health care professionals, and society more generally, might begin to resolve some of these conflicts. For instance, in trying to balance the goals of distributive justice against (collectively) those of beneficence, nonmaleficence, and autonomy, she observes that criteria for quality (and hence for quality assurance) might be developed in alternative ways—from the perspective of benefits to populations as against benefits to individuals, or with regard to, or irrespective of, the costs of care.

In the end, society may have to choose between equally deserving but seemingly incompatible ethical principles underpinning a quality assurance program, at least in the public sector. Adopting a definition of quality of care, setting goals for a quality assurance program, and articulating criteria by which the performance of health care professionals and systems shall be judged will all require consideration of relevant theories of beneficence, autonomy, and justice. As Povar says, "this moral reference point will require public discussion if the quality assurance program is to be susceptible to moral evaluation by the public it serves" (p. 160). The IOM committee underscored this view by stating its belief that a quality assurance program should acknowledge the ethical dimensions of health care, particularly the "art of care," the fiduciary relationship between patients and clinicians, their mutual respect for dignity and freedom, and the practice of humanism in health care.

CONCLUDING COMMENT

The Institute of Medicine study revealed an exceptional diversity of challenges to maintaining and improving the quality of health care for the elderly (indeed, for all in society). It demonstrated the necessity for all involved with health care for the elderly—patients, providers, and social agents alike—to participate in a comprehensive strategy for quality review and assurance if those challenges are to be met. In devising that strategy, the study committee drew heavily on the scholarship and humanism of many experts and contributors to the study. The three works compiled in this volume exemplify the quality of the writings with which the study was endowed. The insights provided for the Institute of Medicine study should prove equally rewarding to readers of this book.

ACKNOWLEDGMENTS

The author wishes to acknowledge the efforts and insights of the Institute of Medicine study committee in the conduct and completion of the project, of which this book is an outgrowth (Mark R. Chassin, Leo M. Cooney, Robert B. Copeland, Charles J. Fahey, Paul F. Griner, William S. Hoffman, Robert L. Kane, Harold S. Luft, Maxwell J. Mehlman, Marie Michnich, Marilyn Moon, James D. Mortimer, Albert G. Mulley, Edward B. Perrin, Margaret D. Sovie, and Loring W. Wood) and to express particular appreciation to the committee chairman, Steven A. Schroeder. An additional debt is owed to her IOM study colleagues, Molla S. Donaldson, Jo Harris-Wehling, and Allison J. Walker, for their professional, collegial, and personal exertions. In addition, the contributions of Theresa Nally and Thelma Cox, the study's secretaries, must be given the greatest commendation.

The study was supported by the Health Care Financing Administration under Cooperative Agreement No. 17-C-99170/3; Harry L. Savitt was the exemplary project officer for the government. The views expressed are those of the author and do not necessarily represent those of the Institute of Medicine, the National Academy of Sciences, or the Department of Health and Human Services.

NOTE

1. Institute of Medicine, *Medicare: A Strategy for Quality Assurance, Volume I* and *Volume II: Sources and Methods,* ed. Kathleen N. Lohr (Washington, DC: National Academy Press, 1990).

Kathleen N. Lohr, Ph.D., is the Deputy Director of the Division of Health Care Services at the Institute of Medicine, National Academy of Sciences, where she has responsibility for a cluster of clinical evaluation activities involving quality of care, outcomes and effectiveness research, clinical practice guidelines, and technology assessment and innovation. In her previous role as Senior Professional Associate with the IOM, she served as the study director for a congressionally mandated study to design a strategy for quality review and assurance in Medicare.

Part I

Considerations in Defining Quality of Health Care

R. Heather Palmer

"When I use a word," said Humpty Dumpty in a rather scornful tone, "it means just what I choose it to mean—neither more nor less."

"The question is," said Alice, "whether you can make words mean different things."

"The question is," said Humpty Dumpty, "which is to be master— that's all."

—Lewis Carroll, *Through the Looking Glass*

INTRODUCTION

Words may have different meanings—which we choose depends upon our purpose. The purpose of this chapter is to define quality of health care in order to determine how to measure it. We therefore need a definition that relates readily to a means of measurement. In fact, a single definition will not suffice because methods of measurement vary according to their intended use, and there are many potential uses of measurements of quality of health care. We must include those measurable constructs that fit the perspectives of various users. The principal users are the various parties concerned with assuring the quality of care received by patients.

We will therefore approach definition of quality of health care through the evolution of mechanisms to assure quality and through the perspectives of the various parties concerned. In the first half of the chapter we will consider important concepts in defining quality of health care. Definitions for these concepts are listed, along with definitions for other technical terms, in the glossary at the end of this section of the book. The parties whose perspectives will be considered are providers (physicians, hospitals, and health plans), governments and other third party payers, and patients and other consumers. The second half

3

of this chapter is concerned with issues of quality measurement and assurance. In order to keep the discussion within reasonable bounds, we will focus primarily on physicians and on hospital care.

DEFINING QUALITY

Origins of the Physician Role in Setting Standards

For more than a hundred years physicians have been entrusted with maintaining standards of quality for health care. Now physician dominance is being eroded. In order to understand the implications of this development, it is essential to examine briefly why physicians came to dominate the provision of health care.[1]

For goods and services sold through markets, customers make their own determination of quality. Presumably they choose the highest quality available for the price they are willing to pay (best value). In some situations governments intervene to protect consumers from imperfect knowledge of quality by establishing an inspection system to enforce a threshold for quality consonant with public safety. Consumer organizations may also publish standards, test products, and distribute information on product quality and safety to the public. Government bureaus of standards and consumer associations are not concerned about products or services *exceeding* standards. It is up to individual consumers to decide if they are willing to pay for further degrees of quality.

Commodities regarded as essential to life, such as food and shelter, often receive special handling. Most societies provide for those who lack money to enter these markets.[2] In support of such interventions it is argued that the public has an interest in having a productive citizenry, or that the public prefers to be part of a society that accepts responsibility for the financially needy. Even a conservative administration accepts the legitimacy of public expenditures on a safety net for the truly needy. Some cultures encourage direct provision through charity. Modern industrialized societies, like the United States, tend to prefer tax funding of income redistribution to enable the financially needy to enter the market. Vendors prefer this approach because it eliminates competition from free distribution and provides more paying customers. Needy customers who are given funds to enter the market exercise their own preferences in choosing the quality and quantity of food and shelter they can afford.

Health care distribution has a different history. It used to consist mostly of personal caring by relatives and, for those with no relatives and no resources, by charities. Patients with sufficient resources could choose services from a variety of schools of practice and sets of nostrums according to their beliefs. Since there was no objective evidence to support the value of any of these services, there was little justification for regulating them or providing them through public means.

During the nineteenth century, medical science advanced to the point where interventions clearly could be life saving, but also dangerous if misapplied. Concern arose about these effective interventions being in unqualified hands. State governments adopted the idea that scientific medicine was valuable, and only scientifically trained professionals could be trusted to provide it or to judge quality of performance. They therefore deliberately restricted the market. They set up medical licensure boards dominated by physicians to administer laws that limited practice to qualified practitioners. In return, they obligated physicians to adopt a fiduciary relationship with patients, namely, to act in the patient's best interest and to accept responsibility for maintaining standards of quality within the profession.[3]

Licensing boards relied upon standards set by physician organizations to control the structure for provision of health care. Various physician organizations controlled the prerequisites for licensure by accrediting medical school education and administering examinations for medical school graduates. Other physician organizations accredited residency training programs and examinations for certification of specialists. State medical societies maintained standards for the moral and financial behavior of their members and occasionally recommended to state medical boards revocation of the license of a physician guilty of some gross offense.

By the mid–twentieth century in the United States, private health insurance plans were developed in collaboration with physician groups to help individuals pay for the increasing number of medical interventions that could substantially improve health. These plans covered services that were prescribed by physicians, primarily hospital care and physician services performed in hospitals.

As objective evidence for effectiveness of tests and treatments mounted, there was public pressure to make them available to those who could not obtain insurance, as an essential for life (like food and shelter). When public funding for health care was first introduced in the United States in the 1960s, a means had to be found to determine what services to provide. Individuals need different amounts and types of health care at different points in time, depending upon their health status. Special expertise and a case-by-case judgment is needed to determine an individual's health status and whether he or she will benefit from health care. When they became third party payers through the Medicare and Medicaid programs, the federal and state governments followed health insurance companies in allowing physicians to determine the need for service on a case-by-case basis. Governments would only pay for care prescribed by physicians and given in hospitals accredited by a body initiated and dominated by physicians, the Joint Commission on Accreditation of Hospitals (JCAH) (Joint Commission on Accreditation of Healthcare Organizations, or JCAHO, since 1987).

The Traditional Physician Perspective on Good Medical Care

From the 1930s through the 1960s the prevailing perception of good medical care was that espoused among physicians. It is particularly important to understand this perspective because it remains predominant among physicians, and as divergent views increasingly gain hold in public opinion, serious tensions are created.

First, physicians perceived their role as defining for a patient what care was needed. The patient presented with complaints of illness: the physician first took a history, in which the patient's idiosyncratic presentation was translated into standardized constructs called symptoms; then examined the patient to elicit signs of disease; and, finally, ordered tests to confirm or refute hypotheses as to the cause of the symptoms. When this diagnostic process was complete, the physician prescribed any effective treatment that was available. From the traditional professional perspective, it was the physician's duty and sole prerogative to determine the workup and treatment that a patient needed.

To the extent that physicians used the term "demand," it had a negative connotation of giving in to patient requests for unnecessary or ineffective care. For instance, as recently as 1960, sociologists observed that physicians practicing in isolation from professional contacts were vulnerable to loss of professional respect by succumbing to client demands for services, which the physician should have known were unnecessary or useless.[4]

A second component of the professional perspective was a general preference, when faced with uncertainty as to need, for doing something rather than nothing. In other words, the guiding principle, if you could not be sure of need for treatment, was to err in the direction of assuming that disease was present and that treatment would be effective.[5]

A third component was that physicians felt an obligation to the needs of their own patients only, and not to those of a target population. Outreach to convince members of the population that they needed service was seen as close to drumming up business—a form of advertising, which was believed to be unethical. Given the preference just described for errors of commission rather than of omission, there was a tendency for physicians to overuse resources for members of the population who sought services, and to ignore those who did not, although they might be equally likely to benefit from similar services.[6]

Physician Definitions of Quality of Care

Efforts to measure and assure quality of health care began primarily among physicians.[7] They were motivated by their twin obligations: to patients, to give the best possible care, and to society, to ensure the competence of all members of the profession. Although few of these pioneers formally defined quality of care, we can infer definitions from the measures they used. We can also observe that these definitions were constrained, as one might expect, by the traditional physician perspective on health care described above.

For instance, in 1916 Codman published his studies of the end results of care for his patients one year after he had performed surgery.[8] This and subsequent early studies based on outcomes implied that quality of care could be measured by the production of improved health of a patient. The physician preference for concentrating on individual patients rather than populations is evident. There is also a bias in assuming that physician interventions, rather than effectiveness of existing technology and the severity of illness, are the primary determinants of the patient's health status after care. In later, more sophisticated studies of quality, these factors are taken into account, yielding an implied definition that "quality of care is measured by the production of improved health of a patient after adjustment for the constraints of existing technology and severity of the patient's illness."[9]

Other investigators chose to measure quality by studying whether physicians' decisions matched expert professional opinion as to effective diagnostic and treatment practices for given types of patients. In this case, the implied definition of quality is based on provider (physician) competence, or "the ability of the provider (physician) to coordinate available technology, skill, and judgment to improve the health of patients."[10] Again we note the tendency to focus on patients and not populations, on physician contributions, and on change in health status as the goal. Few studies until the 1970s broadened this definition by including in the concept of provider competence contributions of other health professionals such as nurses and technicians, or issues of implementation of physician decisions by managers and support staff. Most studies of provider competence focused on technical rather than interpersonal skills of physicians and, within technical skills, on decision making and recording rather than perceptual or manual skills.[11]

Expansion of Government's Role in Defining Quality

In the United States in the 1960s, government was committed to the idea that "more care is better." To the generous funding of biomedical research and hospital building that had begun in the 1950s were added funds to provide personal health care for those who could not afford it via the Medicare, Medicaid, and Title V programs.[12] For Medicare and Medicaid, which affected the greatest numbers of patients and providers, beneficiaries were permitted to purchase services in the same way as privately funded individuals. As we noted earlier, this method of provision for the financially needy is preferred by providers. Reimbursements to the providers of services were generally open-ended. Physicians received fee-for-service reimbursement based on "usual and customary" charges. Hospitals were paid fee-for-service with charges set retrospectively on the basis of reported costs. Only in some Medicaid programs were limits set on benefits, which in turn limited provider reimbursements.

This influx of funds led to substantial increases in physician, nursing, and technician supply, and the supply of hospital-based technologies. In addition, the federal government began, and many state governments increased, direct funding of medical education to promote physician supply more directly. The federal government also started Regional Medical Programs to encourage the diffusion of new technologies to all physicians and hospitals so that all patients might benefit. Technologies that the government sought to disseminate included new surgical procedures and treatment programs, not just new types of equipment.

These policies worked well. There was enormous growth of health care technology, diffusion of this technology to the public, and increased access to technology for the poor. The United States built a health care system that delivered more sophisticated technology to more people than any other in the world. There was, however, a problem. The costs substantially exceeded expectations and continue to do so today.[13] State governments and the federal government were forced to control costs.

Policymakers became convinced that excessive application of new health care technologies was a major determinant of the acceleration in costs of care. In considering the introduction of a new technology, economists portray the relationship between dollars available for this technology and benefit accruing to patients as a benefit-cost curve.[14] When available funds are too low, some benefits are not realized. The quality of care is poor. As more dollars are spent on health care, more benefits are conferred and quality of care is improved, until a plateau is reached where further expenditures produce no gain. Finally, as more is spent, services are provided to less and less seriously ill patients until the risks and discomforts of the services exceed the benefits. On this downward slope, excessive use of services has actually caused a decline in the quality of care. The problem is compounded when many new technologies are introduced in a short period of time, particularly if they are added to, and do not replace, older technologies.

In the late 1970s, some economists argued that decisions made by U.S. physicians and hospitals had placed many patients receiving particular technologies at least on the plateau of the benefit-cost curve, if not on the downward slope. This implied that costs could be decreased without sacrificing or even while improving quality.

Physicians could agree that unnecessary care was a disbenefit to patients; as we noted earlier, that was a component of the traditional physician view of good medical practice. Physicians were therefore willing to collaborate on reducing unnecessary care. Several state Medicaid programs contracted with physician groups who used the labor-intensive method of case-by-case utilization review to detect unnecessary use of bed days, for which payment would be denied.[15] Following the same argument that cutting unnecessary care was a means to improve quality, the federal government in 1974 launched its quality assurance initiative, the Professional Standards Review Organization (PSRO) program.[16] PSROs were organizations of locally practicing physicians who were given government grants to ensure that services provided to beneficiaries of the Medicare, Medicaid, and Title V health programs were medically necessary, of a quality that met locally determined professional standards, and given at the least costly appropriate level of care.

Some state governments also sought to contain costs by requiring review of the appropriateness of health care facilities' plans to expand or to purchase expensive new technologies.

Defining Appropriate Use

Physician groups and government policymakers agree that one important component of quality of care is appropriate use of health care technology. However, the speedy diffusion of many new technologies, which contributes to the dramatic increases in costs of care, makes it difficult to determine what is appropriate.[17] Given the traditional preference for doing something rather than nothing, as physicians become familiar with a new test or treatment and more confident of its safety, they tend to apply it for less and less seriously ill patients. A striking example is the dissemination of renal dialysis under the federal End-Stage Renal Disease Program. It is not easy to know when the limit of appropriateness is reached.

Determining whether use is appropriate requires a careful assessment of the properties of a technology in terms of efficacy, effectiveness, and safety. The congressional Office of Technology Assessment (OTA) defines efficacy as "the probability of benefit to individuals in a defined population from a medical technology applied for a given medical problem under *ideal* conditions of use."[18] The preferred method for measurement of efficacy is a randomized clinical trial under tightly controlled conditions. If the term "benefit" is modified to "net benefit"—benefit minus any disbenefit caused by ill effects of the technology—then measurement of safety is integrated with measurement of efficacy. Effectiveness is defined as the probability of benefit to individuals in a defined population from a medical technology applied under *average* conditions of use.[19] Measurement of effectiveness by a randomized controlled trial requires enrolling patients who are at risk to receive a technology in the usual course of their medical care.

There is a subtle bi-directional relationship between technology assessment and quality measurement. Technology assessment is intended to identify properties of a technology so that one can generalize from the study population to predict net benefits that the technology will produce in other similar populations. However, in any particular trial of effectiveness, the net benefit to the study population depends, in part, upon the quality of performance of the providers who give them care. Strictly speaking, the estimate of net benefit can only be generalized to similar populations who are under similar resource constraints, and who *receive care of equivalent quality*.[20] Assessments of effectiveness therefore require knowledge about the quality of care given to the study population.

Quality measurement, on the other hand, requires knowledge of effectiveness of technologies. Quality measurement is intended to measure quality of care given by actual providers and received by actual patients under usual operating conditions. Findings of technology assessments are needed for process measures of quality of care, since these should measure whether effective care is given to those who can benefit and not to those who cannot. Findings of technology assessments are also needed for outcome measures of quality of care, since these should control for severity of illness and for the effectiveness of available technology, in order to determine whether any observed change in patient's health status is attributable to provider intervention.

Unfortunately, technology assessments are not available for most tests and treatments. If they are available, they do not provide clear direction for many of the combinations of patient circumstances that a physician may encounter or many of the details on which a physician must decide. In assessing appropriateness, therefore, expert physician judgments are used to extrapolate from existing knowledge about effectiveness.

Decision making that yields appropriate care can be classified as part of the technical component of physician competence, which was defined earlier as the ability of the physician to coordinate available technology, skill, and judgment to improve the health of patients.

Definition of Quality from the Government Perspective

As government policymakers became involved in third party payment for health care, it became clear that their perspective on quality of care differed from the traditional physician view. The preceding discussion of appropriateness dealt solely with issues of benefit and disbenefit to patients. This framework is acceptable to physicians because determining appropriateness in these terms is simply a sophisticated version of the older concept of defining clinical "need." Purchasers of care, however, are interested in appropriateness in relation to the cost of care. They begin with an assumption of limits on the funds available for health care.[21] As prudent purchasers for the public, the federal and state governments are concerned with the opportunity costs of spending on health care when the same resources might yield more valued benefits if spent on other goods and services. They must consider quality not in absolutist terms, but as a desirable attribute whose worth must be weighed against its cost.

Another important difference from the traditional physician perspective emerges in the OTA definitions of efficacy and effectiveness, which refer to the probability of benefit to populations, rather than to individual patients. Government policymakers want proof that costs are justified by the benefits received by the whole population. They must resist increased spending to deliver high-quality services for those already inside the health system when some individuals with equal or greater need have not gained access to services at all.[22]

The weighing of the quality of a product against cost is captured in the concept of efficiency. Efficiency can be expressed either in terms of obtaining a product of the desired quality at the lowest possible cost or in terms of obtaining the highest possible quality for a given cost. The traditional physician perspective fits best with the first form. A standard is set for quality, and efficient providers are those who achieve this standard at lower cost. When payments are fixed prospectively, there is a subtle reversal. The measure of efficiency is now the level of quality that is achieved for a fixed cost. The idea that more or less quality might be purchased depending upon the resources available is still unfamiliar and uncomfortable to many people in the United States.[23]

There are several levels for consideration of efficiency. "Production efficiency" is the provision of a unit of service, such as a laboratory test or a bed day, of the highest possible quality for the fixed cost.[24] This is the responsibility of managers of health care facilities. At a higher level of aggregation, "clinical efficiency" is the combination of individual units and bundles of service to provide the maximum net benefit to a particular patient for the fixed cost.[25] Appropriate physician decision making is required for efficient bundling of services and for designing efficient strategies to meet a particular patient's clinical needs. Finally, "utilization efficiency" occurs when the maximal net medical benefit from application of a procedure to the population is achieved at a cost that is less than or equal to the opportunity costs. The issue of equitable access is subsumed into efficiency when the latter is considered at the level of the whole population.[26] Although utilization efficiency is greatly affected by physician decisions, it remains primarily a concern of large-scale purchasers and providers of health care.

We have defined quality of care, above, solely in terms of benefit to patients. When resources to pay for health care are limited, however, the clinical strategy that a physician adopts may need to be changed in order to maximize a given patient's benefit. For instance, declining resources may constrain staffing levels for an expensive surgical procedure so that safety features, such as the frequency of postoperative monitoring of patients, are weakened. At some point in declining staffing ratios, it becomes preferable for the patient to forgo the procedure rather than face the risk of errors in its implementation. In this sense, physicians must tailor their recommendations to the economic realities in order to obtain the best quality of care (best outcomes) for their patients.[27]

We can modify our definition of quality from the physician perspective to accommodate the economic perspective on quality as follows: Quality of care is measured by the production of improved health of a population after adjustment for the constraints of existing resources, technology, and burden of illness within the population.

Evidence for Inefficient Provision of Services to Populations

During the 1970s and 1980s, analyses of care received by federal beneficiaries revealed substantial variations in the rates of use of medical and surgical procedures for populations in different geographical areas of the United States.[28] Differences in the burden of illness seemed insufficient to explain the magnitude of variation observed. It was also evident that greater variations were observed for "discretionary" procedures, which lacked clear-cut indications about appropriate use. It was widely supposed that areas experiencing high use must be receiving more inappropriate services than areas experiencing low use. Government policymakers were understandably concerned that there might be inequitable use of health care resources.

An interpretation of this situation based on economic theory was widely adopted in proposing solutions. It goes as follows. Physicians, like all producers, try to maximize their profits. Unlike other producers, physicians control the demand for health care procedures since they decide whether patients need them. When payment is by fee-for-service, and when reimbursements exceed costs, physicians have a financial interest in creating patient demand for physician-performed procedures. For conditions where the clinical indications are not clear-cut, physicians favor overutilization because it is financially advantageous. They are particularly likely to overprescribe their services when there is an oversupply of physicians.[29] To account for variations in use of services, physicians in high-use areas are assumed to be more aggressive income maximizers than their colleagues in low-use areas. A leading health economist has pointed out that there is too little evidence to choose between this and other plausible explanations for the observed variations in use of services.[30] Nevertheless, policymakers took hold of the idea that areas with high usage rates must also be areas with high rates of unnecessary use.

Economic theory was also used to appraise overutilization of services that provide no direct financial advantage to physicians, such as laboratory tests in a hospital. Third party reimbursement makes services appear to be "free" to the beneficiaries on whose behalf physicians act, thus artificially stimulating demand. However, these services are not really free; they have opportunity costs. Physicians who ignore these opportunity costs are acting irresponsibly in spending the public's money on health care.[31]

These analyses suggested a simple solution: Focus on high-utilizing physicians and persuade them to behave like their more responsible low-using colleagues.

Studies done in 1987 and 1990 show that the phenomenon of geographic variations in utilization is more complex than the arguments above suggest.[32,33] In the 1990 study, criteria formulated by physician experts were used to assess the appropriateness for procedures in which large geographic variations were observed. This revealed a substantial amount of inappropriate care in both high-use and low-use areas. Contrary to prevailing belief, however, the proportion of care that was inappropriate did not parallel the large differences in utilization between high-use and low-use areas. At least in the judgment of their expert colleagues, physicians apparently do not always discriminate between necessary and unnecessary care. The study did not determine whether there was underutilization in low-use areas, although this seems likely in view of the findings.

This study shows that government concern about inefficient utilization is warranted, as is physician concern about the disbenefits of unnecessary care to patients. However, the problem cannot be solved by focusing attention only on high-use areas because populations in low-use areas receive inappropriate care in similar proportions. Evidently, eradicating inappropriate care will be more difficult than originally supposed.

Cost Containment in the 1980s: The Competition Strategy

During the late 1960s, the state and federal governments, in their role as third party payers, formed partnerships with physician groups to deny payment for inappropriate care. Throughout the 1970s, these joint efforts were concentrated in the federal PSRO program. The program foundered partly because of the conflict in perceptions between physicians and policymakers. Physicians perceived the mission to be eradicating unnecessary care in order to promote quality, but the federal government wanted PSROs to eradicate unnecessary care to control costs. By 1980, when the minor impact of PSROs on costs became apparent, federal policymakers were disenchanted with the program and dissolved the partnership.[34]

During the 1980s, the federal Health Care Financing Administration (HCFA) sought a new approach for limiting funds spent on health care. The single most visible change was the introduction of prospective per-case payment for hospital admissions for Medicare beneficiaries.[35] Hospitals that use more tests, treatments, and bed days on average to complete an episode of admission may now suffer financial losses. The responsibility for eradicating inappropriate hospital care is therefore shifted to the hospitals themselves and their medical staffs. Hospitals have since internalized utilization review mechanisms like those previously used for external review by PSROs at government expense. Since hospitals could profit under per case payment by increasing their numbers of admissions or by transferring sicker patients, external utilization review of admissions and transfers was mandated.

In addition, economic advisers challenged prior assumptions about the special nature of health care, urging a reexamination of market mechanisms as a means to ensure efficient distribution of care at the population level. For instance, Enthoven proposed that consumers should "shop" for best value.[36] The unit of purchase would be a health care plan rather than a particular episode of care, since the latter is sought when the need is too urgent and the patient too distressed for considered choices. A market-oriented policy would treat health care as much as possible like any other business by letting plans compete for customers and letting consumers become prudent purchasers of health care plans. Plans would be forced to become more efficient producers of services lest they lose their customers to more efficient competitors. Patients and their physician advocates choosing clinical strategies would be forced to focus on best value—that is, production of acceptable quality at an acceptable price. Consumers would choose the level of investment in health care that they prefer. The financially needy would be permitted to choose among those health plans offering care at prices set by the government.

Guided by this argument, the Reagan administration took several bold initiatives.[37] The HCFA permitted Medicare beneficiaries in certain jurisdictions under pilot programs to choose between traditional fee-for-service care and enrolling for comprehensive health care in a managed health care plan of their preference.[38] The managed health care plans now accept the risk for costs of service in excess of the capitation payments they receive, which amount to 95 percent of average annual beneficiary cost. Managed plans can achieve efficiencies by varying the mix of institutional settings and types of staff used.

The HCFA also amended the Medicaid program rules to permit similar innovations.[39] Several states subsequently enrolled beneficiaries involuntarily in managed health care plans, which were chosen on the basis of competitive bidding to provide care for a fixed price.[40]

Federal policymakers made other changes designed to foster market conditions. By expanding coinsurance and deductibles in fee-for-service arrangements, they sought to increase consumer price sensitivity.[41] They also encouraged provision of provider price and quality information to consumers, removing constraints on provider advertising. Of these changes, coinsurance, deductibles, and fixing of prices yielded immediate savings in federal expenditures for Medicare.

Many corporate purchasers of health care followed the government lead by encouraging their employees to seek care from managed health care plans, by incorporating utilization review and coinsurance and deductibles into fee-for-service plans, and by offering coverage through contracts with preferred providers who provide services at a discount. Corporate benefits staffs have grown as they increasingly act as "prudent purchasers" for a portfolio of plans to be offered to employees.[42] Provided corporate purchasers are sensitive to the preferences of their employees, they have the economic leverage to set the investment in health care at a level that the public prefers.

During this same time period, the early 1980s, there was substantial growth in for-profit health care enterprises.[43] The rapid expansion of physician-owned and investor-owned health care corporations was undoubtedly fostered by the new pro-market climate created by government policies.

Critics of a market strategy for health care argue that the long-standing policy of protecting health care from market pressures was well-founded. Customers' inability to detect differences in quality limits their ability to choose plans.[44] Measuring quality in order to inform consumers of quality differences may cost even more than direct regulation of care because average consumers lack the sophistication of regulators in understanding quality-of-care measures. Meanwhile, providers will compete by diverting resources that might have been spent on health care to advertising. They will tend to market aspects of care that attract customers, even if these are not rational choices in terms of real health benefits.[45]

It is also argued that the quality of care received by consumers will suffer in a competitive market. Providers can more easily achieve savings by limiting spending on staff, equipment, and facilities than by increasing efficiency. Consumers, it is said, cannot detect their own health needs and so will not know when they do not receive services that could benefit them.[46] Therefore, the argument goes, costly regulation will still be needed to protect the public against underuse rather than overuse of services.

There are more subtle potential impacts on quality. For instance, in a competitive situation inefficient providers go out of business. Long-standing trust relationships between patients and doctors, and patients and health care institutions, are thereby disrupted. Yet continuity in care is an important component of quality of care and is valued by patients.[47]

There is evidence that competition has had some of the predicted effects on efficient delivery of health care. Health plans are devoting substantial resources to advertising and to law suits against one another's advertising campaigns. Unscrupulous providers have profited from capitated payments by selectively enrolling consumers least likely to demand services, by denying needed services to unwitting patients, and by providing care of extremely poor quality.[48]

It also appears that some consumers, when sensitized to cost, choose a level of investment in health care that is not in their own long-term interest. The RAND health insurance experiment showed that when the poor responded to higher coinsurance and deductibles by lowering demand, they did not discriminate well between effective and ineffective health services and particularly tended to forgo effective preventive services.[49]

A similar problem of underestimation of future needs can be expected to emerge in consumer decisions about purchase of a health plan. The problem that this underinvestment creates is peculiar to health care as opposed to other types of insurance. The insurance business is viable because customers purchase coverage before they are certain that they will suffer an accident, a fire, a disability, or an untimely death. Once the fire, accident, or untimely death has occurred, customers who wish they had purchased better coverage can haggle to obtain the largest possible payment, but whatever the size of the final payment, it cannot change the damage that was done. However, customers who purchase insufficient health care coverage and who then develop a serious treatable illness, may be able to reverse the damage if they receive appropriate treatment.[50] For so long as they remain untreated, they are likely to lobby, perhaps publicly, to receive services that might prevent still further decrements in health. Handling enrollee complaints of denial of service is a major problem for management of prepaid plans. The public sympathizes with individuals whose lives could be saved or changed by medical care, as many news stories attest. Health plans can find it impossible to resist such pressure without losing other customers.

Given the unpopularity of denying care from which individuals could benefit, few policymakers publicly advocate such rationing.[51] However, as more medical technology becomes available to ameliorate disease, rather than preventing or curing it, rationing will become inevitable. It could be deferred for some time by more efficient use of services,[52] but the RAND study of geographic variations in utilization shows that achieving better discrimination between necessary and unnecessary services will require a substantial effort.

Defining Accessibility of Care

Those concerned that quality of care will decline because of underprovision draw attention to that aspect of quality generally known as "accessibility," the extent to which appropriate care is equitably received by a population.

Accessibility must be considered at several levels. First, there is the level of the health care market: Can consumers purchase coverage for health services from which they will benefit? Market access is an issue for federal and state policymakers. They are obligated, at the very least, to ensure fair access to the market for acceptable plans for health care coverage, and to make such provision for the financially needy as is supported by public opinion.[53]

Second, there is access for the enrollee or beneficiary who has financial coverage: To what extent do they receive in a timely fashion promised services from which they could benefit?[54] Access at this level is the responsibility of providers, both managed care plans and individual institutions. Providers, however, are subject to a conflict of interest when operating in competitive conditions. In order to compete successfully, plans and institutions must prevent delivery of unnecessary services.[55] Inefficient plans may compete instead by making inadequate provision to serve the enrollee population, by flatly denying needed services, by permitting excessive queuing, or by erecting other bureaucratic barriers to services. In the case of hospitals, denial of access may take the form of forcing premature discharge of patients or transferring very sick patients to other facilities for financial reasons.[56] The elderly, the disadvantaged, the sick, and those with language difficulties are particularly vulnerable to such maneuvers. Governments therefore come under pressure from consumer groups to ensure that providers do not improperly deny access to beneficiaries.

There is a fine distinction between access and provider competence. If beneficiaries do not receive appropriate services because physicians do not detect need, there is a problem with provider competence. However, physicians justifiably become more conservative in judging need when there are limits on the services that are available. The concept of "triage" is based on such judgments. We can allow for this by defining provider competence as the ability of the physician to coordinate available technology skill and judgment within the constraints of available resources to improve the health of patients. The evaluator concerned with provider competence, then, studies physician decision making under comparable resource constraints, and counts underprovision as evidence of provider incompetence.

If services are not received because the plan budgets too tightly for staff, equipment, and facilities, or is overzealous in restricting utilization, then it is an issue of access. The evaluator concerned with access must set up controls for competent decision making by physicians, and then study such features as the enrollees' ability to obtain appropriate information when telephoning the plan; delays in obtaining appointments, including appointments for specialized diagnostic and treatment services and hospitalization; waiting time in the office, walk-in clinic, or emergency room; and failure to receive appropriate services for which coverage is promised. Note that poor access may occur because plans deliberately control utilization or because poor management permits delays, detours, and queues for enrollees seeking service.

Expansion of the Consumer's Role in Defining Quality

As the Reagan administration began to dissolve the PSRO program, the plan for a prospective payment system (PPS) for Medicare hospitalizations began to emerge. In Congress, which had previously supported dismantling the PSRO program, there arose concerns about the impact on quality of such strong cost-containment incentives. Congress therefore passed legislation tying the phaseout of PSROs to the phase-in of a replacement, the Peer Review Organization (PRO) program, which was designed specifically to maintain quality standards.[57] HCFA, which opposed spending tax dollars on regulatory programs, delayed implementation of the PRO program. The first round of contracts negotiated by HCFA in 1985 required PROs to devote most of their efforts to preventing hospitals from evading the cost-reducing incentives of the PPS, rather than preventing hospitals from denying services.

As PPS took effect, elderly consumers persistently complained to Congress that quality of care was declining, particularly through premature discharge of the sick elderly. As Medicare began at-risk contracts for competitive health care plans, concerns about denial of access to ambulatory care also emerged. Prodded by lobbying from the American Association of Retired Persons (AARP) and other such groups, Congress exerted steady pressure for PROs to conduct effective review of quality, even passing legislation setting deadlines for program implementation, mandating expansion of PRO quality review functions, and requiring that PROs be paid promptly and adequately. The second round of contracts negotiated in 1987 shifted PRO functions toward detecting poor quality of care rather than unnecessary care. The success of this lobbying effort was an indication of the determination of consumer groups to be involved in defining and controlling quality of care.

As consumer groups have become more vocal, their distinctive perspective on quality of health care has emerged. In their role as prospective patients, consumers are concerned with two familiar dimensions of quality that also concern physicians and governments: accessibility and provider competence.

Numerous polls confirm that consumers value highly access to effective technology. They want technology that could benefit health to be available without limits. Like physicians, they are uncomfortable with the notion that quality of care fluctuates depending upon the available resources. They are opposed to permitting cost considerations to limit access to care and are therefore unhappy with coinsurance and deductibles as means for cost control. However, they are not insensitive to health care costs. They believe that health care is too costly but that high costs are attributable to the fact that physicians and hospitals charge too much. They therefore favor cost control through limiting payments to hospitals and physicians, and through more efficient management of health care.[58]

Consumers also value provider competence; they want assurance that mistakes will not be made in their care. A superficial reading of patient surveys could lead to an opposite conclusion. When asked to rate their personal physicians, patients do not distinguish between personal qualities and technical competence.[59] They also tend to rate their own physician highly and physicians in general much less so.[60] These attitudes are often interpreted as an indication that consumers do not distinguish between competence and likability and do not consider professional competence important. An alternative explanation is that patients value competence so highly that they do not remain attached to a physician whose competence they do not trust. They limit the rating of their physician to personal qualities since belief in the competence of their own physician is a given. Their doubtful attitude about the competence of physicians in general is not an inconsistency. Rather, it reflects their fear of falling into the hands of an incompetent physician.

Consumer fears of incompetence derive from real situations. As PROs have switched their attention from issues of appropriateness, they have discovered substantial pockets of physician incompetence. Some PROs have responded by removing numbers of physicians from participation in Medicare. It is noteworthy that such sanctions may only be issued for "gross and flagrant violations of accepted standards of professional conduct."[61] PROs with low tallies of sanctioned physicians do not deny that any incompetent physicians exist, arguing instead that incompetent physicians should be reeducated or rehabilitated, with sanctions reserved only for the recalcitrant.[62]

Prior to this recent PRO activity, the most visible manifestation of physician incompetence was the increasing number and size of settlements in malpractice lawsuits. Although many factors contribute to this increase, the increase is founded upon a large number of genuine instances where patients were injured through incompetence.[63] At least one prestigious organization of U.S. physicians, the Council of Medical Specialty Societies, conceding that poor performance by physicians is a serious issue, has launched an educational program for physicians about the errors of omission and commission that lead to patient injury and successful malpractice claims.[64] There is even evidence that the problem is much larger than it appears from the number of successful suits. In the 1970s, the California Medical Insurance Feasibility Study concluded that 1 percent of hospital admissions resulted in patient injuries that would have won a legal award if a claim were made.[65] The proportion of patients who sue successfully is very much smaller than this. The Harvard Medical Practice Study of 1990 confirms and expands upon these findings.[66] It appears, therefore, that a majority of patients injured by negligence do not sue, although they would likely receive awards for malpractice injuries if they did.

It is noteworthy that the country whose health care is a model for excellence to the world should be the country most preoccupied with incompetence among providers. One force driving concerns about quality of care in the United States is the perception of a widening gap between the best available care and the care provided on average. As medical technology advances, remarkable improvements in health become possible, and patients' expectations rise. Unfortunately, the new technologies often are dangerous and demand great skill from physicians and hospitals. It is difficult for average physicians and hospitals to match what is achieved on the advancing edge of health care. Yet the average American patient is not willing to accept less than the best. Increasingly in malpractice suits, failure to match national rather than local standards of practice has become the test of negligence.

Physicians have responded to the difficulty of keeping up with advances in technology by specializing. Specialization makes it easier both to keep informed and to perfect skills through practice. The disadvantage is that specialists are more likely to make mistakes if the patient needs care that falls outside their expertise. Yet if the specialist defers on such matters to other specialists, care of the patient becomes fragmented, with no one responsible for the whole patient.[67] In such circumstances, there is an increased likelihood of errors of oversight. Malpractice awards now commonly concern damage done by such errors of omission as well as errors of commission.[68] Physicians are reported to respond defensively to the threat of malpractice suits by ordering tests and treatments for marginal indications, thus adding to the problem of inappropriate care.[69]

Patient and Consumer Definitions of Quality

Provider competence and access are dimensions of quality emphasized by physicians and governments, as well as consumers. To these, consumers add a new dimension of quality, namely, that health care received by patients should be in keeping with their personal values. This we can call the "acceptability of care," the degree to which health care satisfies patients.

There is a substantial literature that explores the origins and consequences of patient satisfaction.[70] Patients seek much more than access to technically correct health care. They want their physician to listen to them, care about them, and communicate to them. It is not just that interpersonal skills are appreciated; patients want a physician who relates to them as one human being to another. This attribute was called by one distinguished physician "samaritanism," in reference to the altruistic Samaritan who tended to a wounded stranger.[71]

Patients seek humanistic qualities as well as technical competence. It is common to equate the technical component with the science of care and the humanistic component with the art of care. But the parallel is not exact. Technical excellence depends not just on scientific knowledge but upon manual, perceptual, and judgmental skills that are more art than science. The humanistic caring that patients value is less a matter of art than of philanthropic attitude. Patients are also concerned with matters of comfort, convenience, and privacy, which can be grouped together as the "amenities" of care.[72]

To incorporate the consumer and patient perspective we can modify our definition as follows: Quality of care is the production of improved health and satisfaction for myself. By omitting mention of constraints of resources and technology, we incorporate the consumer preference for care to be given without limits.

In this definition, patient satisfaction is given equal status with improved health as a goal of medical care. There is a potential conflict here. As noted earlier, patient demand for care and a competent practitioner's assessment of need for care are not identical. In rating satisfaction with care given, patients may not know what medical interventions were appropriate for their condition; had they known, their preference might have been different. Similarly, in rating satisfaction with the outcome of care, patients know their preferences but may not fully apprehend their own health status. For instance, hypertensive patients may feel well, although objective measurement of their blood pressure reveals them to be doomed to deterioration in health unless treated. They may also have unrealistic expectations concerning the capacity of health care to improve their conditions. These differences are minimized to the extent that practitioners communicate effectively with their patients.

For some consumers, communication from a physician will not resolve conflicts in perception of quality since they reject the "medical model" altogether.[73] They would not accept that appropriateness of care should be determined by medical science, as physicians and governments appear to agree. Allowance for consumer preferences, and the lobbying of special provider groups, leads to such paradoxical situations as Medicare paying for chiropractic services when it refuses to pay for physician services that are not "medically necessary."

There are additional difficulties caused by the complex relationships between patient satisfaction and health status. Patients in poor health tend to be dissatisfied whether or not good care could have improved their health.[74] Also, satisfied patients are known to comply better with physician recommendations. Therefore, to the extent that the physician recommends effective care, satisfaction may produce improved health.[75]

Despite these difficulties, in the 1980s it is unthinkable to exclude acceptability to patients from the definition of quality of care. Patient satisfaction is then both a desired outcome, a measure of quality, and a predictor of patient behavior.[76]

Physician Satisfaction

As we have seen, the perspectives of physicians, governments and other third party payers, and consumers are different and to some extent in conflict. As consumers have become vocal on health care issues, legislators have responded to their concerns. Physicians have not been heard so well. Increasingly, they are distressed and disillusioned by government policy toward them and by negatively slanted public rhetoric about them. This trend has consequences for patient care: demoralized workers do not do good work.[77]

Some of this distress is common to all workers who fear real income decline over time, and who lose control over their own work process. Their sense of self-worth deteriorates. These feelings are exacerbated for physicians, who for so long have had substantial job security, autonomy, power, and prestige. Some other physician complaints are also common to other types of small businesses. For instance, physicians in private practice are particularly dissatisfied with the phenomenal increase in paperwork created by regulation. This consumes a higher proportion of their practice income than it does for their prepaid competitors, putting them at a competitive disadvantage.[78]

Policymakers are familiar with these types of complaints and with balancing the public interest against the interests of such special groups. They are less equipped by familiarity to understand sources of dissatisfaction that are peculiar to the practice of medicine. One major phenomenon peculiar to medicine is the "malpractice crisis," which causes many kinds of stress for physicians.[79] Engaged in the difficult job of trying to keep up with advances in medicine, physicians are squeezed between contradictory forces. If they do too much they are accused of venality or irresponsibility; if they do too little they risk a lawsuit for omission of indicated tests and treatments.[80] Physicians have also been troubled by shifts in legal theory that changed doctor/patient relationships after the fact. By alleging failure to obtain informed consent, plaintiffs' lawyers obtained awards for injured patients from sympathetic juries, even though the physician's care was not negligent.[81] Physicians had believed that patients preferred not to be worried by knowing in detail all the risks of medical care. They thought patients wanted them to weigh the risks and benefits and tell them what to do.[82] As a result, physicians now feel that an adversarial relationship with patients has emerged. They defend themselves by writing letters to patients to document their patients' knowledge of and consent for the care given, and by recording minute details of the warnings given to patients of potential complications of tests and treatments.

The increase in successful malpractice suits also affects physician incomes through increases in malpractice insurance premiums.[83] Since most insurers charge the same premiums to all physicians in the same specialty and geographic location, irrespective of their involvement in malpractice settlements, competent physicians are forced to pay higher premiums because of the poor performance of others. For this and other reasons, physicians have become more willing to engage in efforts to identify incompetent physicians and dangerous practices.[84] Yet involvement in peer review activities is itself a source of stress.[85]

One category of physicians who perform poorly are those with alcohol or drug addiction, or mental illness. The numbers of physicians concerned are hard to determine; estimates start at 1 percent. Many state medical societies now operate impaired physicians programs, which cooperate with state licensing boards to encourage physician colleagues with such problems to enter treatment programs as an alternative to losing their license to practice.[86]

Until recently, physicians received little encouragement for dealing with incompetent physicians because boards of licensure were not organized and funded to conduct the necessary investigations, and PSRO procedures for sanctioning physicians were extremely cumbersome.[87,88] Worse still, conscientious physicians who took part in peer review to detect and correct inadequate care were sometimes successfully sued for damages by the reviewee.[89] In part, this problem derived from the government's pro-competition policy. As market theory was applied to medical practice, professional self-discipline sometimes was adjudged to violate antitrust regulations. Among activities now deemed inappropriate were longstanding state medical society programs to prevent physicians from advertising or charging excessive fees, and some internal quality assurance programs that removed incompetent physicians from group practice.

The confrontation between the medical and economic models over the desirability of peer review is theoretically resolved if information about quality of care generated by peer review is given to consumers, rather than being used to remove practitioners from the market.[90] There is already a movement in this direction, but its success depends critically upon the accuracy of the quality information provided and the capacity of consumers to understand it.[91] Inaccurate information could lead consumers to make harmful choices.

A proposed solution for protection of peer review is the Health Quality Improvement Act of 1986, which coordinates efforts to deal with incompetent physicians.[92] The act provides immunity from lawsuit for damages for persons who report poor quality of care and reviewers who make judgments of poor quality of care, provided that the informant or peer reviewer acted in good faith and followed proper procedures. At the same time, the act requires that payers of malpractice claims, state licensing boards, health care institutions, and physician organizations report to a national data bank all actions they take because of malpractice or incompetence of a physician. Hospitals and health care institutions will be required to check with this data bank before permitting a physician to work in their facilities.

Congress also passed legislation in 1986 permitting PROs to share detailed evidence about poor quality of care with state licensing boards. When implemented, this will expedite removal of licenses from providers who have been found by the PRO to be giving poor care. Recently, many states have also instituted requirements for periodic relicensure of physicians, thorough checks of physicians' qualifications, requirements for reporting instances of potentially substandard care, and better organized procedures for acting upon physician incompetence.[93] These developments provide support for physicians who fulfill the traditional obligation to maintain quality standards within the profession.

The other obligation in the social contract between the profession and the public is physicians' fiduciary responsibility to patients. They must suppress their own interests in order to act in the best interest of the patient. For many physicians, the most disturbing concomitant of the commercialization of medical practice is that it destroys this traditional doctor/patient relationship.[94] This source of dissatisfaction should be taken the more seriously because it affects most strongly the most committed and altruistic physicians. They are genuinely outraged by the implication that their patients should be subject to the market doctrine of caveat emptor. They are deeply troubled by having thrust on them so overtly the role of rationer who must deny benefits to patients in order to adhere to cost constraints.[95] In particular, they reject, and believe their colleagues should reject, arrangements that reward physicians for denying services or for directing patient referrals to particular providers for financial reasons.[96] Also, those who watch poor and sick patients suffer from treatable causes when services are cut are saddened by the public's indifference to its most helpless members.[97]

It is legitimate for physicians to be concerned when a longstanding social contract is rapidly overturned, particularly when it is not obvious that the general public supports the change. The perspective from which physicians traditionally define quality of care is under attack. Until a new and acceptable social contract redefines what is desirable behavior, physicians are understandably bewildered about their role in assuring quality of care.

Inclusive Definition of Quality of Care

The perspective of the three parties considered above—providers, governments, and patients—can be combined to define quality of care as the production of improved health and satisfaction of a population within the constraints of existing technology, resources, and consumer circumstances. Note that this definition contains similar terminology to the definition of quality assurance adopted by an Institute of Medicine report in 1974.[98]

This omnibus definition, however, is not helpful as we proceed to discuss measurement of quality of care. For this discussion, we must identify which dimension of quality is to be measured and under what constraints. Three dimensions were considered above: provider competence, accessibility, and acceptability of care. The three constraints discussed were limitations in effectiveness of technology, limitation of resources, and differences in consumer circumstances. The three dimensions themselves can be broken down into smaller components. Components of provider competence included technical components (cognitive, manual, and perceptual skills) and interpersonal components. Accessibility was considered both at the market level and at the beneficiary or patient level. Components of acceptability, it was noted, vary according to the expectations of each individual consumer.

Despite the complexity that has emerged in defining quality of care, the discussion so far has been oversimplified because it has been restricted to only three of the parties concerned (providers, governments, and consumers), to only three types of providers (physicians, hospitals, and health plans), to the general population, and to the current state of affairs. Definition of quality needs also to be considered in relation to other parties, in relation to the situation of different kinds of patients, in relation to other health care settings, and in relation to the changing health care environment. However, it is beyond the scope of this chapter to do justice to the considerations that arise in these varied circumstances.

QUALITY MEASUREMENT AND ASSURANCE

Measurement is the assignment of a quantity to an attribute of a phenomenon by collecting observations of the attribute and comparing these observational data to objective standards. The value of measurement is that it permits comparisons between phenomena affecting events from different locations and different points in time. Quality of health care is measured by comparing data describing patients and the care they receive to standards. Quality measurement is commonly used for quality assurance, which is a cyclic activity; it requires measurement of quality and, if measurement reveals deficiencies in care, intervention to improve care, followed by remeasurement of quality to determine the success of the intervention. In this section we will first consider the two essential components of measurement: data and standards. We will then consider the component added for quality assurance: intervention to improve care. Finally, we will briefly review quality assurance strategies.

Data for Quality Measurement

Donabedian describes three types of data for measuring quality of health care: structure, process, and outcome.[99] Structural data describe features of health care facilities, equipment, professional and nonprofessional staff, and organization for delivery of care. Process data describe the things actually done to or for a patient. Outcome data describe the change in health status of a patient that is attributable to health care.

We can gain new insight into measuring quality of health care by drawing analogies between measures of product quality in industry and the classification developed independently by Donabedian for measuring quality of health care using structure, process, and outcome data. In a paper on the meaning of product quality in industry, Garvin lists different perspectives for measuring product quality, based on the product, the manufacturing approach, and the user.[100] Each perspective connects with a different type of data for quality measurement. Detailed comparison reveals that Garvin's observations about the corollaries of different measures of product quality in industry apply also to their health care counterparts.

In product-based definitions, says Garvin, higher quality is perceived as more of some desired measurable ingredient. For instance, more knots per square inch designate a higher-quality rug. Product-based definitions are quantitative and objective. They imply that quality for a given product must cost more. This perspective is allied to the measurement of quality of health care from structure. There is an implication with structural measurement, as with product-based perspectives, that more equipment, more spacious facilities, more and better-trained staff, and more organizational policies and procedures mean higher quality.

The manufacturing-based approach, as described by Garvin, is the perspective of the supplier. It equates quality with conformance to specifications. It is linked with the philosophy that "making it right the first time" will save money in the long run by preventing rework, repair, or replacement under warranty. A manufacturer will include in specifications those features for which deviations yield a high proportion of product failures. The provision of health care is a type of service industry. Given this perspective, a manufacturing-based approach is analogous to measurement of quality of health care from process data. Standards for process of health care specify what should be done in order to ensure the best possible outcome for the patient.[101]

There is an analogy in health care for the costs of not making it right the first time. These costs include excessive use of tests, treatments, bed days, and ambulatory care visits because of incompetence in decision making and delivery of care; the added costs of treating illness when delay or error in diagnosis or treatment has allowed progression to a more serious stage of disease; the costs of care associated with preventable iatrogenic injury, including drug reactions and nosocomial infections; and the costs of malpractice insurance.[102] As this list indicates, poor health care process is extremely costly.

In user-based definitions, quality is defined in terms of satisfying consumer preferences. It is easy to see that a counterpart of user-based definitions in health care is the concept of acceptability, which is measured by patient satisfaction with care. We argued earlier that both patient satisfaction with care and change in health status attributable to care are legitimate outcomes of health care. Furthermore, we argued that change in health status should be valued in terms of patients' preferences. Given these clarifications, user-based measures of product quality are analogous to outcome measures of quality of health care.

Garvin notes that to measure product quality in a market from the user perspective, some means must be found to aggregate individual subjective preferences. The usual approach is to equate quality with satisfying the majority of consumers. There is an obvious analogy here between user-based measurement of product quality and user-based measurement of quality of health care. Patients' preferences as to the care they receive vary.[103] For instance, some prefer a paternalistic physician, others prefer a more coequal relationship. Similarly, patient preferences as to the outcome of care are highly individualistic.[104] For instance, some may prefer death to continued existence in a helpless and pain-ridden condition. When quality of care is measured by severity-adjusted mortality rates an assumption is being made that a majority of patients prefer life to death, irrespective of the quality of life. When quality is measured using aggregations of patient ratings for satisfaction with care received, the tastes of the majority among those surveyed determine the result. For an objective comparison of two providers of care who serve different patient populations, one must adjust for differences in tastes.

Garvin describes another definition of product quality that is less easily related to measurement but is becoming prevalent among consumers: the value-based approach. Quality is defined in terms of performance at an acceptable price or conformance at an acceptable cost. Garvin calls this "affordable excellence." This concept is clearly analogous to that of efficiency in health care. It requires that any definition of quality in health care must be constrained by limits on health care costs. Without this constraint, the concept of excellence in health care at some point becomes irrelevant because it is inconceivable that anyone can be found to pay for so much excellence.

Structure, process, and outcome data all have a place in measurement of quality. Which data are used depends upon the circumstances. Structural measures are used to ensure that staff, facilities, equipment, and organizational features meet minimal necessary conditions for good care. Process measures are used for detailed and definitive judgments of care that lead to actions intended to improve care. Outcome data, adjusted for case severity, are used to screen large patient data bases for evidence of disproportionately bad outcomes that may indicate poor quality of care.

Standards for Quality Measurement

Data are essential components of measurement; the other essentials are standards. Like data, different forms of standards are suited to different circumstances.

Those JCAHO hospital standards that concern structure specify desired characteristics of the hospital. Presence of a particular characteristic results in passing the standard, and absence of the characteristic means failure.

Standards for measuring quality based on process of care are complex since many different actions make up a coherent package or sequence of care. A rule specifying a particular action is called a criterion; a set of criteria is the sequence of actions that is indicated for a particular class of patients. Criteria usually specify that an action must always be done for a given patient, or must never be done. This type of criterion is equivalent to a pass/fail standard in that each individual patient care episode either meets or does not meet the criterion. More sophisticated criteria distinguish between degrees of goodness. For instance, Lohr, Brook, and Kaufman developed criteria for ambulatory care episodes and set up a scale of minimal, acceptable, and high quality for measurement of process of care.[105]

When a group of patient care episodes are studied, the word "standard" is used to describe a threshold value for compliance with criteria that will trigger further investigation or corrective action. For instance, although the criterion states that all prenatal patients must have their blood pressure taken at their first visit, no action will be taken if this criterion is failed for only 2 percent of first prenatal patient visits. The standard is then said to be set at 2 percent compliance with the criterion.

For outcome data, it is unusual to try to set pass/fail standards for individual patients. More commonly, a standard is set as a threshold value for a group of patient care episodes; it specifies the percentage of patients experiencing a bad outcome above which care is deemed unacceptable.

Criteria and standards may be set in various ways. In the earliest attempts at quality measurement, respected physicians were asked to judge whether a particular episode of care was acceptable. Decisions about the actions that should be taken or the outcomes that should be achieved were all made within these individuals' minds; they were said to be using "implicit" criteria. If the desired actions or outcomes were specified in writing they were said to be "explicit" criteria.

Implicit criteria have the advantage that, without prior effort, physicians can be asked to judge care for any patient care episodes within their realm of expertise. The great disadvantage of measurements based on implicit criteria is that they are unreliably applied. Different judges frequently disagree upon whether a given case passes or fails. The same judge may give a different answer for the same case on a different occasion. In either case, obviously the criteria were changed between the two judgments. Even if implicit judgments were reproduced perfectly on each occasion, until the rationale is made explicit, no one but the judge knows specifically what it was about the process or outcome that was unacceptable. Measurements based on implicit judgments can be made more reliably if judges are trained carefully, if the aspect of care to be judged is narrowly defined, and if the findings of multiple judges for the same case are combined by consensus or by a suitable scoring method.

Explicit criteria and standards are reliable; the same criteria yield the same result when applied to the same episode of care.[106] However, explicit criteria and standards for process are difficult to construct because they must allow for the complex logic of medical decision making. To make the task manageable, criteria are usually designed for a limited category of patient care. To accommodate subgroups within this category, criteria must incorporate branching logic (e.g., if a patient's test result is positive, then that treatment should be given). Even so, it is inconceivable to construct explicit process criteria so complex that they apply infallibly to every combination of patient circumstances. For unusual cases, therefore, the measurements yielded by explicit criteria will be invalid.

A common practical solution to these difficulties evolved in the 1970s. Both types of criteria are now used in turn. Cases that fail to meet explicit criteria are reviewed implicitly to determine if some special patient circumstance justified variation from the expected course of action. The explicit criteria serve as a screen to detect cases with probable deficiencies in care, and the implicit review of these cases provides the definitive judgment. This has become the accepted procedure for quality measurements using process data.

Explicit criteria apply to a defined category of patient care. Donabedian calls this the "referent," that to which the criteria refer.[107] In earlier work on quality measurement, the referent for criteria was usually a diagnosis or operative procedure. Later, criteria were developed that referred to a type of therapy, such as antibiotics, or a diagnostic test, such as a pulmonary scan, or a particular patient need, such as management of the comatose patient. Whenever the referent is a feature of a defined subset of patients, the criteria are said to be specific.

In the 1980s, sets of criteria that apply to all patients irrespective of diagnosis, procedure, tests, or treatments came into widespread use. These generic criteria sets are simpler in structure, contain fewer individual criteria than specific criteria sets, and have a more limited purpose. They deal only with states or needs common to all patients. For instance, generic criteria referring to bad outcomes (so-called adverse events or sentinel events) are used in many hospitals to detect potentially recurring problems in patient care.[108] Other sets of generic criteria are in widespread use to measure the appropriateness of admissions or discharges. For instance, generic criteria for admission are used to determine whether the patient needed tests or treatments that could only be given in a hospital.

The preceding discussion of criteria and standards dealt exclusively with the kind of criteria and standards that prescribe what is or is not acceptable—that is, with statements that certain actions should or should not occur or that certain outcomes should or should not result. Both pass/fail criteria and threshold standards can be prescriptive (also called normative) in form.[109] As an alternative to prescribing what should be done or achieved, one can compare what *is* done or achieved in different settings. With this technique, data for one group of patients are compared to data from other groups. These comparative criteria (also called empirical criteria)[110] are particularly useful with outcome data. For instance, mortality rates for appendectomy, adjusted for case severity, are compared between all hospitals in a country. Using comparative criteria, one may simply report that one group of cases received better care than another. Alternatively, one can set an absolute standard by comparing each group of cases to the mean for the whole group, or comparing each group to the one group that is believed to give exemplary care.[111]

Quality Assurance Interventions

Measurements of quality have become a high priority because they are needed for quality assurance and cost control. Measurement is not the end in itself but a means of intervention in order to attain the desired trade-off between benefits and costs of health care. Different types of interventions for quality assurance and cost control are available to governments and other third party payers, and to professional groups.

Governments and other organizations that purchase health care in bulk can control access to technology, the privilege of delivering care, and the financial incentives under which care is given. The purchaser can refuse to pay for ineffective technologies and for care given by providers who are incompetent or wasteful. Governments also have a power unavailable to other third party payers, namely, the ultimate sanction of removing a provider's license to practice. During the last two years in the United States, numerous initiatives at both the national and state government levels have attempted to tighten mechanisms to invoke this sanction. Rearrangement of financial incentives has proved to be a powerful means for cost control but has raised concerns about the impact on quality. The impact of recent vigorous attempts to exclude ineffective technologies and incompetent providers is still to be determined.

The tools that professional groups can use to improve quality and cost control include education, peer pressure, and feedback on performance. Education is the means by which physicians are prepared for their responsibilities and kept up to date with advances in technology. The combination of feedback on performance and peer pressure has proved more effective than formal education as a means to change established physician behavior.[112]

Health care organizations can encourage their professional staff to control quality and cost, but they also have an additional tool. Administrators can limit acquisition and use of technology and can set limits on a professional's scope of practice that match the individual's current abilities. When used with discretion, these are effective means of control.

An increasing number of health care organizations are adopting the concepts of "total quality management," which are spreading within U.S. industry. The primary feature of total quality management is a radical change in organizational culture in which the leadership and all who work in the organization accept the goal of striving for continuous quality improvement. A second feature is an emphasis on dialogue between customers and suppliers of services through which the supplier learns how to meet the needs and expectations of the customer. A third major feature is an emphasis on designing organizational systems to facilitate high-quality work, monitoring system performance to detect quality problems, and when problems are encountered, intervening to solve them. This last feature, of course, is the closest to traditional quality assurance, although "total quality managers" draw on industrial models for their quality control and improvement efforts.[113] The movement for total quality management has brought a flood of fresh concepts, tools, and enthusiasm, which can revitalize internal quality assurance.

Quality Measurement Techniques Developed in the 1970s

Implementation of the PSRO program during the 1970s required combining data, standards, and interventions into quality assurance strategies. Three techniques were developed.[114] The term "medical care evaluation" applied to studies in which explicit prescriptive criteria were used to evaluate the process or outcome of care for specific categories of patients. Implicit review of all cases that failed to meet the explicit criteria was conducted by a physician. In the 1970s, this was the method most commonly used for measuring quality of care. This technique had many similarities to the medical audits that the JCAH required hospitals to perform from 1974 to 1978.[115]

The other two techniques, utilization review and profile analysis, were directed toward reducing unnecessary bed days and surgical procedures. For utilization review, the medical records of patients admitted to the hospital were promptly reviewed using explicit prescriptive criteria to determine if the admission was justified. If so, at a date determined by a comparative criterion (the regional average for length of stay for the diagnosis or procedure), the record was again reviewed using prescriptive criteria to determine if continued stay was justified. If the criteria were not met, a physician reviewer was contacted to make a final "implicit criterion" decision. If continued care was found to be unnecessary, the government would not pay for it.

Profile analysis (now often called profile monitoring or pattern analysis or pattern monitoring) was a form of exploratory data analysis. Data banks containing brief abstracts of hospital admission and discharge data were used to display patterns of hospital admissions and lengths of stay in order to determine which hospitals and physicians had apparently overused services, and for which diagnoses or procedures. This information could then be used to indicate where utilization review should be most intensively pursued. The same data banks used for profile analysis provided the comparative criteria for average lengths of stay that were used in utilization review.

The combination of profile analysis and utilization review was only marginally effective in reducing unnecessary services when used in the PSRO context. A formal evaluation in 1979 showed a benefit-cost ratio of 1.269.[116] Variations on these three techniques continue to be used widely in quality assurance programs in the 1990s.

Examples of Quality Measurements Based on Different Data Types

As noted above, data concerning structure, process, and outcome are each useful for different quality assurance strategies. Programs of licensure, accreditation, and certification were the earliest forms of quality assurance; they used structural data for quality measurement. For instance, in 1918 the American College of Surgeons began its Hospital Standardization Program, which compared hospitals to standards for plant safety and maintenance specifications, policies for supervision of laboratories and x-ray departments, qualifications of the medical staff, conduct of educational conferences for the medical staff, policies for quality of medical records, and policies for medical staff committees to review quality of medical records. This program grew in size and sophistication until it evolved in 1952 into the JCAH Hospital Accreditation Program.[117] Other examples of structural measurement are found in programs that certify physicians as specialists using standards for the content of their education, and their knowledge as tested by examination.

Structural data are relatively inexpensive to collect and review. Quality measurements using structural data are limited, however, because meeting structural standards, at least those currently used, does not ensure that patients will receive good care. The best quality standards we have may be necessary conditions, but not sufficient conditions to ensure the quality of care. It is also possible to set structural standards so high that access to care is restricted either by shortages of equipment, facilities, and staff that meet the standards, or by the cost of care that meets the standards. Some providers complain that structural standards increase administrative work, without improving the process or outcome of care. This criticism, for instance, has been made of prior JCAHO accreditation standards.[118]

Currently, the JCAHO is engaged in a major redesign of its structural standards.[119] This redesign is consonant with the emphasis in industry quality management on "quality by design." Quality management scientists argue that the best way to produce high quality is to design the organizational structure to promote high-quality work.

Process measurements usually focus on individual cases and use data from patients' medical records. The validity of the measurement then depends upon the quality of the medical record and upon recognition of the limits of medical records data when constructing standards. However, additional data for process measurements may come from an institution's management information systems or may be requested from the physician in charge of the case.

Many third party payers and the PRO program seek to promote appropriate process of care by requiring review and approval of decisions to admit a patient or to perform a surgical procedure upon a patient. Except in emergencies, approval is required before the admission or procedure occurs. Preadmission review is usually accomplished using explicit criteria. Preprocedure review may be accomplished either using explicit criteria or by requiring an opinion from a second surgeon, a form of implicit criteria review.

Review of the process of care for individual cases by a peer reviewer (i.e., implicit criteria review) is also the final step in many review processes that begin with identification of cases with adverse outcomes. For instance, many individual hospitals and the PRO program use generic criteria to screen medical records in order to find patients who experienced adverse events; these cases are then subjected to peer review of the process of care. Similarly, the PRO program applies peer review to case records for Medicare beneficiaries who experience readmission within 30 days after hospital discharge, in order to detect problems with premature discharge or inadequate postdischarge care.

Process-based measures are particularly useful for quality assurance, because failure to meet process standards immediately reveals what must be done differently to improve care. However, there are two serious obstacles to the use of process standards.

The first problem with process-based measurements of quality is the difficulty of knowing what should be done to or for patients. Ideally, process standards should specify performance only of effective medical care—that is, care that has been proven by scientific methods to improve patients' health. Unfortunately, as noted earlier, there is considerable uncertainty for much of health care as to what is effective. Patients and their diseases come in an infinite variety of forms so that extrapolation upon extrapolation is needed to apply the limited inventory of research findings about effectiveness of diagnostic and treatment strategies to particular cases. Despite this uncertainty, physicians must make judgments, and should do so using the best available knowledge. Process standards also have to be based on the best available knowledge.

The second problem is that few process standards can apply broadly to heterogeneous groups of patients. In order to evaluate important details of care, standards must differentiate among specific categories of patients. Such process measurements are difficult to design because they require the development of complex algorithms that allow for many different patient characteristics.

During the 1980s, the federal government developed two initiatives that will help in addressing these problems. First, the Health Care Financing Administration proposed a "medical effectiveness and outcomes initiative" to advance knowledge about the effectiveness of medical technologies.[120] The Omnibus Budget Reconciliation Act of 1989 then restructured the National Center for Health Services Research as the Agency for Health Care Policy Research and assigned to it the task of implementing this program. Named the Medical Treatment Effectiveness Program (MEDTEP), the program funds large research teams who use existing patient care data bases to extend knowledge of the effect of treatments on patient outcome.

Second, the new agency is charged to promote the development of practice guidelines that incorporate information on treatment effectiveness into specific protocols or algorithms to guide physician decision making.[121] The legislation also requires that the guidelines be translated into criteria for use in quality measurement. There are many independent groups, particularly physician organizations, also at work on practice guidelines. Those engaging in this activity now have at their disposal recent advances in synthesizing results of research, including improved techniques for expert group decision making,[122] meta-analysis and mathematical modeling,[123] and greatly improved capacities in computer hardware and software.

Quality measurements based on outcome data are appealing since they deal with the ultimate goal of health care: the improvement of patients' health. They also appear to bypass the difficulties of specifying the correct process of care. However, collecting outcome data is often difficult and expensive, since it should be done after an episode of care has ended, and an episode may last many years.

The more serious disadvantage of measuring quality of care based on patient outcomes is that patients' health status after receiving care is mostly determined by factors not under the control of the provider, such as the severity of disease, the presence of complications, patient age and resilience, patient willingness to comply with recommended therapy, and the effectiveness of the therapies available. In measuring the quality of care one must therefore distinguish how much of any change in a patient's health status is attributable to the health care given.

To date, outcome measures are usually based on data concerning bad outcomes, such as mortality or complication rates. Recently, more sophisticated measures of health status have made it possible to distinguish relative degrees of goodness of health and to address dimensions of health such as functional and emotional status.[124] If such measures are used in the future to monitor and manage quality of care, the emphasis will be placed on helping patients to feel and function better, rather than solely on preventing death.

During the 1970s and 1980s there was much argument about the relative value of measurements from process or outcome.[125] As a result of these early studies and arguments it is now much clearer how to measure quality. If process data are used, the criteria specify that only effective technology—as defined by the best available evidence—should be used. Specific criteria must usually incorporate branching logic to allow for differences between patients in clinical condition and severity of illness. Generally, process criteria should focus on care received by the patient—that is, on the completion of sequences of care rather than the physician's order for the sequence to begin.

If outcome data are used, criteria should measure those changes in a patient's health status that can be produced by existing health care technology. The measures must control for differences in the patient's clinical condition (case mix) and severity of illness (case severity), and for other concomitant conditions (comorbidity). Adjustments should allow for the patient's circumstances before care, and for changes occurring during, but independently of, care.

Adjustments for case characteristics can be done using epidemiological methods, either by observing patients with different outcomes in a case-control study, or by making observations of change in health status for patients in a cohort study. Alternatively, statistical adjustments can be used. For instance, for its annual publication of mortality rates for Medicare beneficiaries by hospital, the PRO program uses diagnosis-related groups (DRGs) as a first approximation for adjustment. However, DRGs are designed to adjust hospital payments for case mix and case severity differences. Other variables within the Medicare claims data base are used by the PRO program for further statistical adjustments of the mortality data. Several other techniques for adjustment for case mix and severity and comorbidity are now available; these generally require detailed clinical data, which must be obtained by abstraction from medical records.[126] The considerable controversy over the methods for adjustment of mortality rates, and over their interpretation, illustrates the difficulty in using outcome data to measure quality.[127]

None of these existing methods for adjustment of outcome data deals adequately with the tricky issue of adjusting appropriately for social and emotional circumstances that may affect outcomes. Similarly, explicit process criteria rarely allow adequately for patients' social and emotional circumstances.

Strategies for Quality Assurance in the 1990s

Research into and development of methods for quality assurance and cost control in health care have proceeded rapidly as increased funding has resulted from government interest in these issues. The basic components of measures described in this work are increasingly combined in a variety of strategies suited to different purposes and different circumstances. Internal quality assurance is used within a health care organization for quality and cost control. External quality assurance is used by a regulator, accreditor, or purchaser of health care to stimulate better internal efforts. As a last resort, government regulators may remove from practice those who cannot or will not meet acceptable standards. External agencies also may provide quality information to consumers.[128] The PRO publication of hospital mortality rates is one example.

For internal use, the current emphasis is on building programs of continuous quality improvement into ongoing operations, involving all personnel in efforts to find and solve problems promptly. In order to concentrate quality review efforts where the payoff is greatest, the JCAHO requires staff to monitor performance systematically, using specific quality indicators.[129] Once a problem with quality is identified, an intervention to improve care is devised, and performance is monitored until the desired improvement is achieved. For internal quality-control programs the mechanisms for intervention include education, feedback on performance, and administrative change.

Hospitals have also internalized the techniques of profile analysis and utilization review, which were deployed earlier in the PSRO program. For hospitals that have acquired internal management information systems, a sophisticated form of profile analysis can be used to screen for problems of inappropriate use and adverse outcomes.[130] The data base captures for each admission the physician, the diagnoses made, the services given, certain critical clinical findings and test results, and the patient's status on discharge. The clinical data are used to classify severity of illness using one of the newer, more sensitive measures of case severity. Comparative criteria can then be used to judge the appropriateness of services used for similar patients by different physicians and to screen for worse outcomes for similar patients, either of which may indicate problems with quality of care for certain physicians. Detailed, definitive review using explicit and implicit criteria is then focused in these problem areas.

In the external review mode, techniques for screening for problems in quality must accommodate huge numbers of providers. This is more readily accomplished by the establishment of a high-quality uniform data base that can be used to compare all institutions of a given type.[131] Two major developments of this kind are in progress. The PRO program has begun deployment of a Uniform Clinical Data Set (UCDS) for hospital patients.[132] It will contain a substantial amount of clinical detail and will be used for a variety of methods of quality review. The JCAHO is also developing a data system containing reports of clinical indicators. Hospitals will report their performance on these indicators to the JCAHO and will receive feedback comparing their performance to that of other similar hospitals.[133]

CONCLUSION

Great advances have been made in the last three decades in the essential components for quality assurance and cost control—data, standards, and interventions—and in the incorporation of these elements into strategies and programs. Much additional work is needed to refine measures, to extend their range of application, and to bring down their cost. Now, at the start of the 1990s, it appears that leaders in medicine and public policy have committed themselves to this effort. This commitment derives from a renewed application of an age-old duty, the obligation of physicians to serve the interests of their patients.[134]

ACKNOWLEDGMENTS

The author wishes to thank the anonymous reviewer of the draft for this work, members of the Institute of Medicine committee, and members of the Boston Area Seminar on Quality, especially Joseph Newhouse. The views expressed in this text are those of the author only.

NOTES

1. For a full discussion of the evolution of physician dominance, see P. Starr, *The Social Transformation of American Medicine* (New York: Basic Books, 1982).

2. The subsequent discussion of the nonmarket mechanisms for health care distribution relates to the classic discussion of this issue by K. J. Arrow, "Uncertainty and the Welfare Economics of Medical Care," *The American Economic Review* 53 (1963): 941–73.

3. Starr, *Transformation of American Medicine*; Arrow, "Economics of Medical Care."

4. See the discussion in E. C. Hughes, *Men and Their Work* (Glencoe, IL: The Free Press, 1958), 88–101; and E. Freidson, "Client Control and Medical Practice," *American Journal of Sociology* 65 (1960): 374–82. See also a recent example recounted by J. F. Burnum, "Medical Practice à la Mode: How Medical Fashions Determine Medical Care," *New England Journal of Medicine* 317 (1987): 1220–22. Note also S. O. Rhee, R. D. Luke, and M. B. Culverwell, "Influence of Client/Colleagues Dependence on Physician Performance in Patient Care," *Medical Care* 18 (1980): 829–41.

5. This point is elaborated by T. J. Scheff, "Preferred Errors in Diagnosis," *Medical Care* 22 (1984): 166–72.

6. See the discussion by H. H. Hiatt, "Protecting the Medical Commons: Who Is Responsible?" *New England Journal of Medicine* 293 (1975): 235–45.

7. Some authors trace quality assurance to the work of a nurse, Florence Nightingale, who conducted studies of mortality rates among wounded British soldiers in the Crimean War of the late 1850s, to demonstrate the need for measures to reduce the spread of infection and to prove that adoption of these measures reduced mortality. See K. N. Lohr and R. H. Brook, "Quality Assurance in Medicine," *American Behavioral Scientist* 27 (1984): 583–607.

8. E. A. Codman, *A Study in Hospital Efficiency: The First Five Years* (Boston: Thomas Todd, 1916).

9. For a detailed review of the development of measures of quality based on change in patient health status (changes in outcome), see P. J. Sanazaro, "Quality Assessment and Quality Assurance in Medical Care," *Annual Review of Public Health* 1 (1980): 37–68.

10. R. H. Palmer, "Quality Assessment: Definitions and Data," Chapter 2 in *Assuring Quality in Medical Care*, ed. R. Greene (Cambridge, MA: Ballinger, 1976), 11–60. For examples of this approach to quality measurement, see Sanazaro, "Quality Assessment and Assurance."

11. Palmer, "Quality Assessment," pp. 20–23.

12. Starr, *Transformation of American Medicine*. See also F. A. Wilson and D. Neuhauser, *Health Services in the United States* (Cambridge, MA: Ballinger, 1976).

13. L. Breslow, "Quality and Cost Control: Medicare and Beyond," *Medical Care* 12 (1974): 95–114.

14. See, for instance, A. C. Enthoven, "Cutting Cost without Cutting the Quality of Care," *New England Journal of Medicine* 298 (1978): 1229–38; and V. R. Fuchs, *Who Shall Live? Health, Economics, and Social Choice* (New York: Basic Books, 1974).

15. For a description of state utilization review programs, see M. R. Chassin,

"The Containment of Hospital Costs: A Strategic Assessment," *Medical Care* 16, suppl. (1978): 27–55.

16. M. J. Goran, "The Evolution of the PSRO Hospital Review System," *Medical Care* 17, suppl. (1979): 1–47.

17. For a brief discussion of this problem, see M. E. Avery and V. Chernick, "On Decision Making Surrounding Drug Therapy: A Continuing Dilemma," *New England Journal of Medicine* 296 (1977): 102–3.

18. U.S. Congress, Office of Technology Assessment, "Assessing the Efficacy and Safety of Medical Technologies," Office of Technology Assessment, Washington, DC, 1978.

19. Ibid.

20. R. H. Brook and K. N. Lohr, "Efficacy, Effectiveness, Variations, and Quality: Boundary-Crossing Research," *Medical Care* 23 (1985): 710–22.

21. The situation was forcefully described in Fuchs, *Who Shall Live?* See also L. C. Thurow, "Medicine versus Economics," *New England Journal of Medicine* 313 (1985): 611–14; and O. R. Bowen, "What Is Quality Care?" *New England Journal of Medicine* 316 (1987): 1578–80.

22. V. R. Fuchs, "The 'Rationing' of Medical Care," *New England Journal of Medicine* 311 (1984): 1572–73.

23. It is not, of course, an unfamiliar idea for physicians and patients in fixed-budget health systems such as the British National Health Service. See Commentary from Westminster, "Review of Expenditure in the Family Practitioner Service: Cash Limits in View?" *Lancet* 2 (31 July 1982): 281–82; and D. Owen, "Clinical Freedom and Professional Freedom," *Lancet* 1 (8 May 1976): 1006–9.

24. W. B. Schwartz and P. L. Joskow, "Medical Efficacy versus Economic Efficiency: A Conflict in Values," *New England Journal of Medicine* 299 (1978): 1462–64.

25. A. Donabedian, J. R. C. Wheeler, and L. Wyszewianski, "Quality, Cost, and Health: An Integrative Model," *Medical Care* 20 (1982): 975–92. See also H. Vuori, "Optimal and Logical Quality: Two Neglected Aspects of the Quality of Health Services," *Medical Care* 18 (1980): 975–85.

26. Schwartz and Joskow, "Medical Efficacy versus Economic Efficiency."

27. For a defense of this idea by a distinguished British physician, see D. Black, "Cui bono?" *British Medical Journal* 2, no. 6095 (1977): 1109–14.

28. Selected papers dealing with this issue include J. E. Wennberg, "Dealing with Medical Practice Variations: A Proposal for Action," *Health Affairs* 3, no. 2 (1984): 6–32; R. H. Brook, K. Lohr, M. R. Chassin, J. Kosecoff, A. Fink, and D. H. Solomon, "Geographic Variations in the Use of Services: Do They Have Any Clinical Significance?" *Health Affairs* 3, no. 2 (1984): 63–73; P. Caper, "Variations in Medical Practice: Implications for Health Policy," *Health Affairs* 3, no. 2 (1984): 110–19; J. Wennberg, "Which Rate Is Right?" *New England Journal of Medicine* 314 (1986): 310–11; M. R. Chassin, R. H. Brook, R. E. Park, J. Keesey, A. Fink, J. Kosecoff, K. Kahn, N. Merrick, and D. H. Solomon, "Variations in the Use of Medical and Surgical Services by the Medicare Population," *New England Journal of Medicine*

314 (1986): 285–90; J. F. Boyle, "Regional Variations in the Use of Medical Services and the Accountability of the Profession," *Journal of the American Medical Association* 254 (1985): 407; B. A. Barnes, E. O'Brien, C. Comstock, D. G. D'Arpa, and C. C. Donahue, "Report on Variation in Rates of Utilization of Surgical Services in the Commonwealth of Massachusetts," *Journal of the American Medical Association* 254 (1985): 371–75; B. Pasley, P. Vernon, G. Gibson, M. McCauley, and J. Andon, "Geographic Variations in Elderly Hospital and Surgical Discharge Rates, New York State," *American Journal of Public Health* 77 (1987): 679–84.

29. For further reading on theories of physician-induced demand, see J. E. Harris, "How Many Doctors Are Enough?" *Health Affairs* 5 (1986): 73–83; H. S. Luft and P. Arno, "Impact of Increasing Physician Supply: A Scenario for the Future," *Health Affairs* 5 (1986): 31–47; U. E. Reinhardt, "The Theory of Physician-Induced Demand: Reflections After a Decade," *Journal of Health Economics* 4 (1985): 187–93; V. R. Fuchs, "The Supply of Surgeons and the Demand for Operations," *The Journal of Human Resources* 13 (1978): 35–56.

30. M. V. Pauly, "What Is Unnecessary Surgery?" *Milbank Memorial Fund Quarterly* 57, no. 1 (1979): 95–117.

31. V. R. Fuchs, "Supply of Surgeons"; A. S. Relman, "The Allocation of Medical Resources by Physicians," *Journal of Medical Education* 55 (1980): 99–104; J. M. Eisenberg and A. J. Rosoff, "Physician Responsibility for the Cost of Unnecessary Medical Services," *New England Journal of Medicine* 299 (1978): 76–80.

32. M. R. Chassin, J. Kosecoff, R. E. Park, C. M. Winslow, K. L. Kahn, N. J. Merrick, J. Keesey, A. Fink, D. H. Solomon, and R. H. Brook, "Does Inappropriate Use Explain Geographic Variations in the Use of Health Care Services? A Study of Three Procedures," *Journal of the American Medical Association* 258 (1987): 2533–37. See also L. L. Leape, R. E. Park, D. H. Solomon, M. R. Chassin, J. Kosecoff, and R. H. Brook, "Does Inappropriate Use Explain Small-Area Variations in the Use of Health Services?" *Journal of the American Medical Association* 263 (1990): 669–72.

33. N. P. Roos, L. L. Roos, and P. D. Henteleff, "Elective Surgical Rates—Do High Rates Mean Lower Standards? Tonsillectomy and Adenoidectomy in Manitoba," *New England Journal of Medicine* 297 (1977): 360–65; J. P. Logerfo, "Variation in Surgical Rates: Fact vs. Fantasy," *New England Journal of Medicine* 297 (1977): 387–89.

34. For a more detailed analysis of the demise of the PSRO program, see M. J. Goran, "The Evolution of the PSRO Hospital Review System," *Medical Care* 17, suppl. (1979); A. R. Nelson, "Perceptions on PSRO," *Western Journal of Medicine* 131 (1979): 451–54; H. L. Smits, "The PSRO in Perspective," *New England Journal of Medicine* 305 (1981): 253–59.

35. J. K. Iglehart, "The New Era of Prospective Payment for Hospitals," *New England Journal of Medicine* 307 (1982): 1288–92.

36. A. C. Enthoven, *Health Plan: The Only Practical Solution to the Soaring Cost of Medical Care* (Reading, MA: Addison-Wesley, 1980).

37. For detailed accounts of the Reagan administration pro-competitive approach, see R. N. Rubin, "The New Federalism for Health: Shifting Responsibilities and Reducing Costs into the 80s," *Journal of the American Medical Association* 247 (1982): 2911–22; J. K. Iglehart, "Drawing the Lines for the Debate on Competition," *New England Journal of Medicine* 305 (1981): 291–96; J. K. Iglehart, "The Administration Responds to the Cost Spiral," *New England Journal of Medicine* 305 (1981): 1359–64.

38. J. K. Iglehart, "Medicare Turns to HMOs," *New England Journal of Medicine* 312 (1985): 132–36.

39. J. K. Iglehart, "The Reagan Record on Health Care," *New England Journal of Medicine* 308 (1983): 232–36.

40. See, for instance, E. P. Melia, L. M. Aucoin, L. J. Duhl, and P. S. Kurokawa, "Competition in the Health-Care Marketplace: A Beginning in California," *New England Journal of Medicine* 308 (1983): 788–92.

41. L. H. Aiken and K. D. Bays, "The Medicare Debate—Round One," *New England Journal of Medicine* 311 (1984): 1196–1200.

42. B. Dowd, R. Feldman, and J. Klein, "What Do Employers Really Want in a Health Plan?" *Business and Health* 4 (January 1987): 44–48.

43. A. S. Relman, "Investor-Owned Hospitals and Health-Care Costs," *New England Journal of Medicine* 309 (1983): 370–72; B. H. Gray and W. J. McNerney, "For-Profit Enterprise in Health Care: The Institute of Medicine Study," *New England Journal of Medicine* 314 (1986): 1523–28; A. S. Relman, "The New Medical-Industrial Complex," *New England Journal of Medicine* 303 (1980): 963–70.

44. L. Wyszewianski, J. R. C. Wheeler, and A. Donabedian, "Market-Oriented Cost-Containment Strategies and Quality of Care," *Milbank Memorial Fund Quarterly* 60 (1982): 518–50.

45. E. Ginzberg, "The Grand Illusion of Competition in Health Care," *Journal of the American Medical Association* 249 (1983): 1857–59; E. Ginzberg, "The Destabilization of Health Care," *New England Journal of Medicine* 315 (1986): 757–60.

46. Wyszewianski et al., "Cost-Containment Strategies and Quality."

47. B. C. Vladeck, "The Market vs. Regulation: The Case for Regulation," *Milbank Memorial Fund Quarterly* 59 (1981): 209–23; K. L. Grazier, W. C. Richardson, D. P. Martin, and P. Diehr, "Factors Affecting Choice of Health Care Plans," *Health Services Research* 20, no. 6 (1986): 659–82.

48. J. K. Iglehart, "Second Thoughts about HMOs for Medicare Patients," *New England Journal of Medicine* 316 (1987): 1487–92.

49. K. N. Lohr, R. H. Brook, C. J. Kamberg, G. A. Goldberg, A. Leibowitz, J. Keesey, D. Reboussin, and J. P. Newhouse, "Use of Medical Care in the RAND Health Insurance Experiment: Diagnosis- and Service-Specific Analyses in a Randomized Controlled Trial," *Medical Care* 24, suppl. (1986). See also N. Lurie, N. B. Ward, M. F. Shapiro, and R. H. Brook, "Termination from Medi-Cal—Does It Affect Health?" *New England Journal of Medicine* 311 (1984): 480–84; N. Lurie, N. B. Ward, M. F. Shapiro, C. Galtege, R. Vaghaiwalla, and R. H. Brook, "Termination of Medi-Cal Benefits: A

Follow-up Study One Year Later," *New England Journal of Medicine* 314 (1986): 1266–68.

50. For a detailed argument that different considerations apply to health insurance, see Vladeck, "Market vs. Regulation." See also L. D. Brown, "Competition and Health Cost Containment: Cautions and Conjectures," *Milbank Memorial Fund Quarterly* 59 (1981): 145–89.

51. It is argued that health care has always been rationed in the United States, but because rationing was "implicit" it attracted little attention. It is explicit rationing that is now under discussion and that arouses controversy. See Fuchs, " 'Rationing' of Medical Care"; and D. Mechanic, "Cost Containment and the Quality of Medical Care: Rationing Strategies in an Era of Constrained Resources," *Milbank Memorial Fund Quarterly* 63 (1985): 453–75.

52. R. H. Brook and K. N. Lohr, "Will We Need to Ration Effective Health Care?" *Issues in Science and Technology* 3, no. 1 (1986): 68–77.

53. For a discussion of current concerns about governmental responsibility for access, see H. Darling, "The Role of the Federal Government in Assuring Access to Health Care," *Inquiry* 23 (1986): 286–95; R. Curtis, "The Role of State Governments in Assuring Access to Care," *Inquiry* 23 (1986): 277–85. For a discussion of the reduced access of the poor to health care resulting from market-oriented government health policy, see J. K. Iglehart, "Medical Care of the Poor—A Growing Problem," *New England Journal of Medicine* 313 (1985): 59–63; M. O. Mundinger, "Health Service Funding Cuts and the Declining Health of the Poor," *New England Journal of Medicine* 313 (1985): 44–47; The Robert Wood Johnson Foundation, "Access to Health Care in the United States: Results of a 1986 Survey," Special Report Number 2, The Robert Wood Johnson Foundation, 1987.

54. This has been called "realized access." See R. M. Andersen, A. McCutcheon, L. A. Aday, G. Y. Chin, and R. Bell, "Exploring Dimensions of Access to Medical Care," *Health Services Research* 18 (1983): 50–74. For an elaborate schema for the concept of access, see R. Penchansky and J. W. Thomas, "The Concept of Access: Definition and Relationship to Consumer Satisfaction," *Medical Care* 19 (1981): 127–40.

55. The special considerations of timely access to managed care plans is discussed by A. I. Mushlin, "Testing an Outcome-Based Quality Assurance Strategy in Primary Care," *Medical Care* 18, suppl. (1980): 43–63.

56. This practice, nicknamed "patient dumping," is reviewed by D. A. Ansell and R. L. Schiff, "Patient Dumping: Status, Implications, and Policy Recommendations," *Journal of the American Medical Association* 257 (1987): 1500–1502.

57. See U.S. Congress, Office of Technology Assessment, *Medicare's Prospective Payment System: Strategies for Evaluating Cost, Quality, and Medical Technology,* OTA-H-262 (Washington, DC: U.S. Government Printing Office, 1985), especially Appendix G: 202–5.

58. R. J. Blendon and D. E. Altman, "Public Opinion and Health Care Costs," in *Health Care and Its Cost,* ed. C. Schramm (New York: W.W. Norton, 1987), 49–63.

59. J. E. Ware and M. K. Snyder, "Dimensions of Patient Attitudes Regarding Doctors and Medical Care Services," *Medical Care* 13 (1975): 669–82; J. E. Ware, M. K. Snyder, W. R. Wright, and A. R. Davies, "Defining and Measuring Patient Satisfaction with Medical Care," *Evaluation and Program Planning* 6 (1983): 247–63.

60. R. D. Hays and J. E. Ware, "My Medical Care Is Better Than Yours: Social Desirability and Patient Satisfaction Ratings," *Medical Care* 24 (1986): 519–25.

61. See Chapter 6 in K. N. Lohr, ed., *Medicare: A Strategy for Quality Assurance, Vol. 1* (Washington, DC: National Academy Press, 1990), especially pp. 163–69, 189.

62. A. H. Webber, "A PRO Report Card," *The Internist* 27, no. 6 (1986): 7–9.

63. U.S. General Accounting Office, *Medical Malpractice: No Agreement on the Problems or Solutions*, GAO/HRD-86-50 (Washington, DC: U.S. Government Printing Office, 1986). See also American Medical Association, "Response of the American Medical Association to the Association of Trial Lawyers of America Statements Regarding the Professional Liability Crisis," AMA Special Task Force on Professional Liability and Insurance, August 1985.

64. Council of Medical Specialty Societies, *Courtrooms Are for Lawyers, Not Doctors* (Lake Forest, IL: Council of Medical Specialty Societies, 1984), 35mm slide/sound program script.

65. California Medical Association and California Hospital Association, *Report on the Medical Insurance Feasibility Study* (San Francisco: Sutter Publications, 1977). See also A. R. Meyers, " 'Lumping it': The Hidden Denominator of the Medical Malpractice Crisis," *American Journal of Public Health* 77 (1987): 1544–48.

66. T. A. Brennan, A. R. Localio, L. L. Leape, et al., "Identification of Adverse Events Occurring during Hospitalization," *Annals of Internal Medicine* 112 (1990): 221–26; L. L. Leape, T. A. Brennan, N. Laird, et al., "The Nature of Adverse Events in Hospitalized Patients: Results of the Harvard Medical Practice Study II," *New England Journal of Medicine* 324 (1991): 377–84.

67. R. H. Palmer and M. C. Reilly, "Individual and Institutional Variables Which May Serve as Indicators of Quality of Medical Care," *Medical Care* 17 (1979): 693–717.

68. U.S. General Accounting Office, *DOD Health Care: Better Use of Malpractice Data Could Help Improve Quality of Care* (Washington, DC: U.S. Government Printing Office, 1987).

69. J. E. Harris, "Defensive Medicine: It Costs, But Does It Work?" *Journal of the American Medical Association* 257 (1987): 2801–2.

70. See, for instance, Ware et al., "Defining and Measuring Patient Satisfaction"; and Ware and Snyder, "Dimensions of Patient Attitudes." Also see J. E. Ware, W. R. Wright, M. K. Snyder, and G. C. Chu, "Consumer Perceptions of Health Care Services: Implications for Academic Medicine," *Journal of Medical Education* 50 (1975): 839–48. Also T. R. Zastowny, K. J. Roghmann, and A. Hengst, "Satisfaction with Medical Care: Replications and Theoretic Reevaluation," *Medical Care* 21 (1983): 294–322.

71. W. McDermott, "Medicine: The Public Good and One's Own," *Perspectives* 21, no. 3 (1977): 15–24; W. McDermott, "Absence of Indicators of the Influence of Its Physicians on a Society's Health: Impact of Physician Care on Society," *American Journal of Medicine* 70 (1981): 833–43.

72. A. Donabedian, *The Definition of Quality and Approaches to Its Assessment* (Ann Arbor, MI: Health Administration Press, 1980).

73. For radical critiques of the "medical model," see I. Illich, *Medical Nemesis: The Expropriation of Health* (New York: Random House, 1975); and R. Carlson, *The End of Medicine* (New York: Wiley, 1975).

74. D. L. Patrick, E. Scrivens, and J. R. H. Charlton, "Disability and Patient Satisfaction with Medical Care," *Medical Care* 21 (1983): 1062–75.

75. J. E. Ware and A. R. Davies, "Behavioral Consequences of Consumer Dissatisfaction with Medical Care," *Evaluation and Program Planning* 6 (1983): 291–97; M. S. Marquis, A. R. Davies, and J. E. Ware, "Patient Satisfaction and Change in Medical Care Provider: A Longitudinal Study," *Medical Care* 21 (1983): 821–29.

76. H. Vuori, "Patient Satisfaction—An Attribute or Indicator of the Quality of Care?" *Quality Review Bulletin* 13 (1987): 106–8.

77. Note, for instance, from a study of nursing staff/client interaction that staff satisfaction was associated with client satisfaction, which was in turn associated with client acceptance of staff advice. See C. S. Weisman and C. A. Nathanson, "Professional Satisfaction and Client Outcomes: A Comparative Organizational Analysis," *Medical Care* 23 (1985): 1179–92; R. D. Hays and K. White, "Professional Satisfaction and Client Outcomes: A Reanalysis," *Medical Care* 25 (1987): 259–64.

78. R. Berrien, "What Future for Primary Care Private Practice?" *New England Journal of Medicine* 316 (1987): 334–37; G. L. Glandon and J. L. Werner, "Physicians' Practice Experience during the Decade of the 1970s," *Journal of the American Medical Association* 244 (1980): 2514–18.

79. American Medical Association, "Response to Professional Liability Crisis"; B. H. Mawardi, "Satisfactions, Dissatisfactions, and Causes of Stress in Medical Practice," *Journal of the American Medical Association* 241 (1979): 1483–86.

80. R. A. Reynolds, J. A. Rizzo, and M. L. Gonzalez, "The Cost of Medical Professional Liability," *Journal of the American Medical Association* 257 (1987): 2776–81. See also Harris, "Defensive Medicine."

81. W. J. Curran, "Informed Consent in Malpractice Cases: A Turn toward Reality," *New England Journal of Medicine* 314 (1986): 429–31.

82. F. J. Ingelfinger, "Arrogance," *New England Journal of Medicine* 303 (1980): 1507–11; H. M. Schoolman, "The Role of the Physician as a Patient Advocate," *New England Journal of Medicine* 296 (1977): 103–5.

83. Reynolds et al., "Medical Professional Liability."

84. J. J. Coury, "Physicians' Fundamental Responsibility," *Journal of the American Medical Association* 256 (1986): 1005–6; American Medical Association Board of Trustees, "AMA Initiative on Quality of Medical Care and Profes-

sional Self-Regulation," *Journal of the American Medical Association* 256 (1986): 1036–37.

85. Mawardi, "Stress in Medical Practice."
86. G. D. Talbott, K. V. Gallegos, P. O. Wilson, and T. L. Porter, "The Medical Association of Georgia's Impaired Physicians Program: Review of the First 1000 Physicians: Analysis of Specialty," *Journal of the American Medical Association* 257 (1987): 2927–30; J. M. Brewster, "Prevalence of Alcohol and Other Drug Problems among Physicians," *Journal of the American Medical Association* 255 (1986): 1913–20.
87. A. S. Relman, "Professional Regulation and the State Medical Boards," *New England Journal of Medicine* 312 (1985): 784–85; R. J. Feinstein, "The Ethics of Professional Regulation," *New England Journal of Medicine* 312 (1985): 801–4.
88. Webber, "PRO Report Card." See also Lohr, ed., *Medicare,* p. 89.
89. W. J. Curran, "Medical Peer Review of Physician Competence and Performance: Legal Immunity and the Antitrust Laws," *New England Journal of Medicine* 316 (1987): 597–98; L. C. Dolin, "Antitrust Law versus Peer Review," *New England Journal of Medicine* 313 (1985): 1156–57; H. A. Waxman, "Medical Malpractice and Quality of Care," *New England Journal of Medicine* 316 (1987): 943–44.
90. K. N. Lohr, "Commentary: Professional Peer Review in a 'Competitive' Medical Market," *Case Western Reserve Law Review* 36 (1986): 1175–89.
91. M. S. Marquis, D. E. Kanouse, and L. Brodsley, *Informing Consumers about Health Care Costs: A Review and Research Agenda,* R-3262-HCFA (Santa Monica, CA: RAND Corporation, 1985).
92. J. K. Iglehart, "Congress Moves to Bolster Peer Review: The Health Care Quality Improvement Act of 1986," *New England Journal of Medicine* 316 (1987): 960–64.
93. For example, see Feinstein, "Professional Regulation."
94. P. R. Alper, "Medical Practice in the Competitive Market," *New England Journal of Medicine* 316 (1987): 337–39; S. Levey and D. D. Hesse, "Bottom-Line Health Care?" *New England Journal of Medicine* 312 (1985): 644–46; V. R. Fuchs, "The Counterrevolution in Health Care Financing," *New England Journal of Medicine* 316 (1987): 1154–56; D. Blumenthal, "The Social Responsibility of Physicians in a Changing Health Care System," *Inquiry* 23 (1986): 268–74.
95. M. D. Reagan, "Physicians as Gatekeepers: A Complex Challenge," *New England Journal of Medicine* 317 (1987): 1731–34.
96. D. F. Levinson, "Toward Full Disclosure of Referral Restrictions and Financial Incentives by Prepaid Health Plans," *New England Journal of Medicine* 317 (1987): 1729–31; A. S. Relman, "Dealing with Conflicts of Interest," *New England Journal of Medicine* 313 (1985): 749–51; A. L. Hillman, "Financial Incentives for Physicians in HMOs: Is There a Conflict of Interest?" *New England Journal of Medicine* 317 (1987): 1743–48.
97. Lurie et al., "RAND Health Insurance Experiment." See also D. O. Nutter,

"Medical Indigency and the Public Health Care Crisis: The Need for a Definitive Solution," *New England Journal of Medicine* 316 (1987): 1156–58.

98. Institute of Medicine, *Advancing the Quality of Health Care: A Policy Statement* (Washington, DC: National Academy of Sciences, 1974).

99. Donabedian, *Definition of Quality*.

100. D. A. Garvin, "What Does 'Product Quality' Really Mean?" *Sloan Management Review* 26, no. 1 (1984): 25–43. For another interesting comparison of product standards to quality of health care standards, see D. Hemenway, "Editorial: Thinking about Quality: An Economic Perspective," *Quality Review Bulletin* 9 (1983): 321–27.

101. Note, however, that the best possible outcome is achieved only if the fewest possible tests and treatments are used, because unnecessary tests and treatments raise risks of harm without adding benefits.

102. Obviously, malpractice insurance costs under the present system, which is not experience-rated, will only decline if quality of care improves overall, causing malpractice claims to decline.

103. An illustration of this effect is provided in a study by L. S. Linn, M. R. DiMatteo, B. L. Chang, and D. W. Cope, "Consumer Values and Subsequent Satisfaction Ratings of Physician Behavior," *Medical Care* 22 (1984): 804–12.

104. See, for instance, B. J. McNeil, R. Weichselbaum, and S. G. Pauker, "Speech and Survival: Tradeoffs between Quality and Quantity of Life in Laryngeal Cancer," *New England Journal of Medicine* 305 (1981): 982–87.

105. K. N. Lohr, R. H. Brook, and M. A. Kaufman, "Quality of Care in the New Mexico Medicaid Program (1971–1975): The Effect of the New Mexico Experimental Medical Care Review Organization on the Use of Antibiotics for Common Infectious Diseases," *Medical Care* 18, suppl. (1980): 1–129.

106. A. Donabedian, "Advantages and Limitations of Explicit Criteria for Assessing the Quality of Health Care, *Milbank Memorial Fund Quarterly* 59 (1981): 99–106.

107. A. Donabedian, *The Criteria and Standards of Quality* (Ann Arbor, MI: Health Administration Press, 1982).

108. J. Craddick, *Medical Management Analysis: A System for Controlling Losses and Evaluating Medical Care* (San Francisco: Marsh & McLennan, Professional Liability Division, 1978); D. D. Rutstein, W. Berenberg, T. C. Chalmers, C. G. Child, A. P. Fishman, and E. B. Perrin, "Measuring the Quality of Medical Care: A Clinical Method," *New England Journal of Medicine* 294 (1976): 582–88.

109. Donabedian uses the term "normative," but the term is frequently confused with "norms," which are set by comparison to other providers rather than prescriptively. See Donabedian, "Assessing the Quality of Health Care."

110. Ibid. Donabedian uses the term "empirical," but this is frequently confused with prescriptive (normative) criteria because prescriptive criteria should be based on evidence of effectiveness, which comes from empirical research.

111. W. E. McAuliffe, "On the Statistical Validity of Standards Used in Profile Monitoring of Health Care," *American Journal of Public Health* 68 (1978): 645–51.

112. Methods to change physicians' utilization behavior are reviewed by J. M. Eisenberg and S. V. Williams, "Cost Containment and Changing Physicians' Practice Behavior: Can the Fox Learn to Guard the Chicken Coop?" *Journal of the American Medical Association* 246 (1981): 2195–2201; R. M. Grossman, "A Review of Physician Cost-Containment Strategies for Laboratory Testing," *Medical Care* 21 (1983): 783–802; L. P. Myers and S. A. Schroeder, "Physician Use of Services for the Hospitalized Patient: A Review, with Implications for Cost Containment," *Milbank Memorial Fund Quarterly* 59 (1981): 481–507.

113. D. M. Berwick, "Continuous Improvement as an Ideal in Health Care," *New England Journal of Medicine* 320 (1989): 53–56; G. Laffel and D. Blumenthal, "The Case for Using Industrial Quality Management Science in Health Care Organizations," *Journal of the American Medical Association* 262 (1989): 2869–73.

114. M. J. Goran, J. S. Roberts, M. A. Kellogg, J. Fielding, and W. Jessee, "The PSRO Hospital Review System," *Medical Care* 13, no. 4, suppl. (1975): 1–33.

115. Joint Commission on Accreditation of Hospitals, *The Pep Primer and Other Materials* (Chicago: Joint Commission on Accreditation of Hospitals, 1975).

116. Health Care Financing Administration, "Professional Standards Review Organization 1979 Program Evaluation," HCFA Pub. No. 03041 (Washington, DC: U.S. Government Printing Office, 1980).

117. J. S. Roberts, J. G. Coale, R. R. Redman, "A History of the Joint Commission on Accreditation of Hospitals," *Journal of the American Medical Association* 258 (1987): 936–40.

118. G. Dunea, "Inspecting the Hospitals," *British Medical Journal* 284 (1982): 890–91.

119. R. D. Lehmann, "Joint Commission Sets Agenda for Change," *Quality Review Bulletin* 13 (1987): 148–50. Note that concurrently with this change in strategy, the organization changed its name on 29 August 1987 from the Joint Commission on Accreditation of Hospitals to the Joint Commission on Accreditation of Healthcare Organizations; Joint Commission on Accreditation of Healthcare Organizations, *Primer on Indicator Development and Application Measuring Quality in Health Care* (Oakbrook Terrace, IL: Joint Commission on Accreditation of Healthcare Organizations, 1990).

120. W. L. Roper, W. Winkenwerder, G. M. Hackbarth, and H. Krakauer, "Effectiveness in Health Care: An Initiative to Evaluate and Improve Medical Practice," *New England Journal of Medicine* 319 (1988): 1197–1202; K. A. Heithoff and K. N. Lohr, eds., *Effectiveness and Outcomes in Health Care: Proceedings of an Invitational Conference by the Institute of Medicine Division of Health Care Services* (Washington, DC: National Academy Press, 1990).

121. M. J. Field and K. N. Lohr, eds., *Summary: Clinical Practice Guidelines: Directions for a New Program,* Committee to Advise the Public Health Service on Clinical Practice Guidelines, Institute of Medicine (Washington, DC: National Academy Press, 1990).

122. N. J. Merrick, A. Fink, R. E. Park, R. H. Brook, J. Kosecoff, M. R. Chassin, and D. H. Solomon, "Derivation of Clinical Indications for Carotid Endarterectomy by an Expert Panel," *American Journal of Public Health* 77 (1987): 187–90.

123. D. M. Eddy, "The Challenge," *Journal of the American Medical Association* 263 (1990): 287–90; D. M. Eddy, "Practice Policies: What Are They?" *Journal of the American Medical Association* 263 (1990): 877–80; D. M. Eddy, "Practice Policies: Where Do They Come From?" *Journal of the American Medical Association* 263 (1990): 1265–75; D. M. Eddy, "Practice Policies: Guidelines for Methods," *Journal of the American Medical Association* 263 (1990): 1839–41; D. M. Eddy, "Guidelines for Policy Statements: The Explicit Approach," *Journal of the American Medical Association* 263 (1990): 2239–43.

124. A. L. Stewart, J. E. Ware, and R. H. Brook, "Advances in the Measurement of Functional Status: Construction of Aggregate Indexes," *Medical Care* 19 (1981): 472–88; K. N. Lohr and J. E. Ware, eds., "Proceedings of the Advances in Health Assessment Conference," *Journal of Chronic Disease* 40, suppl. 1 (1987): 1–193. See also D. Riesenberg and R. M. Glass, "The Medical Outcomes Study," *Journal of the American Medical Association* 262 (1989): 943; A. R. Tarlov, J. E. Ware, S. Greenfield, E. C. Nelson, E. Perrin, and M. Zubkoff, "The Medical Outcomes Study: An Application of Methods for Monitoring the Results of Medical Care," *Journal of the American Medical Association* 262 (1989): 925–30.

125. W. E. McAuliffe, "Measuring the Quality of Medical Care: Process versus Outcome," *Milbank Memorial Fund Quarterly* 57, no. 1 (1979): 118.

126. A. C. Brewster, B. G. Karlin, L. A. Hyde, C. M. Jacobs, R. C. Bradbury, and Y. M. Chae, "MEDISGRPS: A Clinically Based Approach to Classifying Hospital Patients at Admission," *Inquiry* 22 (1985): 377–87; S. D. Horn, "Measuring Severity: How Sick Is Sick? How Well Is Well?" *Journal of Healthcare Financial Management Association* (October 1986): 21–32; W. W. Young, R. B. Swinkola, and D. M. Zorn, "The Measurement of Hospital Case Mix," *Medical Care* 20 (1982): 501–12; J. S. Gonnella, M. C. Hornbrook, and D. Z. Louis, "Staging of Disease: A Case-Mix Measurement," *Journal of the American Medical Association* 251 (1984): 637–46; S. Greenfield, H. U. Aronow, R. M. Elashoff, and D. Watanabe, "Flaws in Mortality Data: The Hazards of Ignoring Comorbid Disease," *Journal of the American Medical Association* 260 (1988): 2253–55; J. Daley, S. Jencks, D. Draper, G. Lenhart, N. Thomas, and J. Walker, "Predicting Hospital-Associated Mortality for Medicare Patients: A Method for Patients with Stroke, Pneumonia, Acute Myocardial Infarction, and Congestive Heart Failure," *Journal of the American Medical Association* 260 (1988): 3617–24.

127. S. F. Jencks and A. Dobson, "Refining Case-Mix Adjustment: The Research Evidence," *New England Journal of Medicine* 317 (1987): 679–86; S. F. Jencks, D. K. Williams, and T. L. Kay, "Assessing Hospital-Associated Deaths from Discharge Data: The Role of Length of Stay and Comorbidities," *Journal of the American Medical Association* 260 (1988): 2240–46; S. F. Jencks, J. Daley, D. Draper, N. Thomas, G. Lenhart, and J. Walker, "Interpreting

Hospital Mortality Data: The Role of Clinical Risk Adjustment," *Journal of the American Medical Association* 260 (1988): 3611–16; J. Green, N. Wintfeld, P. Sharkey, and L. J. Passman, "The Importance of Severity of Illness in Assessing Hospital Mortality," *Journal of the American Medical Association* 263 (1990): 241–46; R. W. Dubois, W. H. Rogers, J. H. Moxley, and D. Draper, "Hospital Inpatient Mortality: Is It a Predictor of Quality?" *New England Journal of Medicine* 317 (1987): 1674–80; H. S. Luft and S. S. Hunt, "Evaluating Individual Hospital Quality through Outcome Statistics," *Journal of the American Medical Association* 255 (1986): 2780–84; A. J. Hartz, H. Krakauer, E. M. Kuhn, M. Young, S. J. Jacobsen, G. Gay, L. Muenz, M. Katzoff, R. C. Bailey, and A. A. Rimm, "Hospital Characteristics and Mortality Rates," *New England Journal of Medicine* 321 (1989): 1720–25.

128. U.S. Congress, Office of Technology Assessment, *The Quality of Medical Care: Information for Consumers*, OTA-H-386 (Washington, DC: U.S. Government Printing Office, 1988).

129. Joint Commission on Accreditation of Healthcare Organizations, *The Joint Commission Guide to Quality Assurance* (Chicago: JCAHO, 1988); Joint Commission on Accreditation of Healthcare Organizations, *Primer on Indicator Development*.

130. See, for example, A. I. Mushlin, "The Analysis of Clinical Practices: Shedding Light on Cost Containment Opportunities in Medicine," *Quality Review Bulletin* 2 (December 1985): 378–84; Brewster et al., "MEDISGRPS"; A. C. Brewster, R. C. Bradbury, and C. M. Jacobs, "Measuring the Effect of Illness Severity on Revenue under DRGs," *Health Care Financial Management* (July 1985): 52–60.

131. R. H. Brook and K. N. Lohr, "Monitoring Quality of Care in the Medicare Program: Two Proposed Systems," *Journal of the American Medical Association* 258 (1987): 3138–41. For examples, see L. L. Roos, S. M. Cageorge, E. Austen, and K. N. Lohr, "Using Computers to Identify Complications after Surgery," *American Journal of Public Health* 75 (1985): 1288–95; J. E. Wennberg, N. Roos, L. Sola, A. Schori, and R. Jaffe, "Use of Claims Data Systems to Evaluate Health Care Outcomes: Mortality and Reoperation Following Prostatectomy," *Journal of the American Medical Association* 257 (1987): 933–36.

132. H. Krakauer in Heithoff and Lohr, eds., *Effectiveness and Outcomes*.

133. Lehmann, "Joint Commission Sets Agenda." See also Joint Commission on Accreditation of Healthcare Organizations, "Characteristics of Clinical Indicators," *Quality Review Bulletin* 15 (November 1989): 330–39; Joint Commission on Accreditation of Healthcare Organizations, *Primer on Indicator Development*.

134. W. Winkenwerder and J. R. Ball, "Transformation of American Health Care: The Role of the Medical Profession," *New England Journal of Medicine* 318 (1988): 317–19; A. S. Relman, "The Future of Medical Practice," *Health Affairs* 2, no. 2 (1983): 5–19.

Glossary

Acceptability. Degree to which health care satisfies patients.

Accessibility (Beneficiary Level). Ease with which health care can be reached by a beneficiary in the face of financial, organizational, cultural, and emotional barriers.

Accessibility (Market Level). The extent to which appropriate care is equitably received by a population.

Appropriate Care. Care for which expected health benefits exceed expected negative consequences.

Beneficiaries. Individuals who are entitled to receive services through a specific program.

Capitation. The method of paying for medical care by means of a prospective per person payment that is independent of the number of services received.

Coinsurance. A form of cost sharing whereby the insured pays a percentage of total cost (*see also* Copayment).

Comparative Criteria. Criteria derived from data recording the actual performance of a group of providers who were chosen as the standard for a given purpose; also called *empirical criteria*.

Competition. Situation in which health care providers compete to sell their services to health care consumers. Classical economic theory would predict that consumers would seek to buy the least costly acceptable care and that providers would therefore be given the incentive to perform efficiently.

Consumer. An individual in a population; used to include patients who are current users of health services and potential patients who are not current users of health services.

Copayment. A form of cost sharing whereby the insured pays a specific amount of the cost for each service used, e.g., $10 per visit (*see also* Coinsurance).

Cost Sharing. The general set of financing arrangements whereby the consumer must pay some out-of-pocket cost to receive care, either at the time of initiation of care, or during the time of the provision of health care services, or both.

Criteria. Predetermined elements of care against which aspects of the quality of a medical service may be compared.

Deductible. A form of cost sharing in which the insured incurs an initial expense of a specified amount within a given time period (e.g., $250 per year) before the insurer assumes liability for any additional costs of covered services.

Effectiveness. The probability of benefit to individuals in a defined population from a medical technology applied for a given medical problem under average conditions of use.

Efficacy. The probability of benefit to individuals in a defined population from a medical technology applied for a given medical problem under ideal conditions of use.

Efficiency. Maximization of the quality of a comparable unit of health care delivered for a given unit of health resources used.

Explicit Judgments. Judgments that require specifying in advance the criteria by which evaluations will be made.

External Review. Review in which criteria and standards of judgment are set by persons other than the provider or provider group that is being judged. External judges are commonly selected from those believed to be experts, but they may also be colleagues with similar expertise to those being judged.

Fee-for-Service. A method of paying for medical care on a retrospective basis by which each service received by an individual bears a related charge.

Health Care. All care delivered by health care professionals and staff of health care institutions.

Health Maintenance Organization (HMO). An organization that acts as both insurer and provider of comprehensive but specified medical services by a defined set of physicians to a voluntarily enrolled population paying a prospective per capita amount. Prepaid group practices and individual (or independent) practice associations are types of HMOs.

Implicit Judgments. Judgments that require choosing an individual whose ability is respected and asking him or her to use his or her own judgment.

Indicator Conditions. Discreet, identifiable health problems that serve as a convenient focus for evaluating and measuring the quality of health care. They are usually common, treatable conditions for which there is a consensus about appropriate management.

Individual (or Independent) Practice Association (IPA). A type of HMO whose physicians usually continue to practice in a private office on a fee-for-service basis. Members pay the umbrella organization capitation payments for covered services.

Internal Review. Situation in which providers themselves are involved in setting the criteria and standards by which they will be judged.

Interpersonal Competence. The degree to which a practitioner's behavior, when interacting with a patient, improves the patient's health and satisfaction.

Measurement. Assigning a quantity to an attribute by comparison to a standard.

Medical Care. Care delivered personally or prescribed by physicians.

Medical Technology. The drugs, devices, medical-surgical procedures used in medical care, and the organizational and supportive systems within which such care is provided. Medical technology includes ancillary, clinical, and managerial technologies.

Outcome Data. Information describing the health status of the patient as a result of the receipt of care.

Patients. Individuals who are receiving health care.

Patient Satisfaction. Judgment made by a recipient of care as to whether his or her expectations for that care have been fulfilled. It is a means of measuring acceptability of care just as health status outcome can be regarded as the means of measuring effectiveness of care. *See also* Acceptability and Effectiveness.

Peer Review. Evaluation of the performance of a professional by a fellow professional.

Peer Review Organizations. Organizations set up under the Tax Equity and Fiscal Responsibility Act (TEFRA) (P.L. 97-248) of 1982. These organizations are usually led by physicians. They are authorized by the U.S. government to review care for patients in the Medicare program in terms of necessity, appropriateness, and quality of care.

Practitioner. A health care professional who is permitted to prescribe and implement care for a patient that nonmembers of the profession may not prescribe or implement.

Prepaid Group Practice. A group practice that provides or arranges comprehensive covered services for enrollees who pay by capitation (*see* Health Maintenance Organizations).

Prescriptive Criteria. Criteria written by asking providers to decide what ought to be done in a given circumstance. Physicians writing such criteria have been found sometimes to specify care at an unrealistically high level. Also called *normative criteria. See also* Criteria and Explicit Judgments.

Process Data. Decisions made and actions taken on behalf of the patient by the provider and the providing organization, as well as information exchanged between patient and provider.

Professionals. Individuals who provide health care and who belong to a profession that assumes responsibility for the education and maintenance of standards of its members.

Profile. Set of data with regard to a particular variable aggregated over another variable, such as time or provider, and displayed in order to monitor some aspect of health care delivery. Profiles may be collected for providers or for patients. For example, a physician's prescribing profile displays the drugs prescribed by him or her for a particular population of patients over a chosen period of time. *See also* Profile Analysis.

Profile Analysis. Technique whereby aggregated statistical data are used to identify areas in which medical practices may be inappropriate, to focus other reviews, and to assist in the selection of topics for medical care evaluation studies. Additional purposes are to monitor the effectiveness of hospital review activities and to display local, regional, and national percentiles of utilization. Profile analysis involves review of provider profiles in order to detect changes in the patterns of care given over time or in order to make comparisons between providers to detect apparent aberrant patterns of care. Profile analysis does not, in itself, measure quality of care. Also called *profile monitoring*.

Provider. An individual or organization that provides personal health care to patients; used to refer to both physicians and hospitals.

Provider Competence. The ability of a health care professional or organization to coordinate available technology, skill, and judgment to improve the health of patients.

Quality of Health Care. The production of improved health and satisfaction of a population within the constraints of existing technology, resources, and consumer circumstances.

Quality Assessment. Measurement of the quality of care.

Quality Assurance. Process of measuring quality, analyzing the deficiencies discovered, and taking action to improve performance followed by measuring quality again to determine whether improvement has been achieved. It is a systematic, cyclic activity using standards for measurement.

Quality Management. A term used to cover three types of activities: quality planning, quality measurement, and quality improvement. These activities are commonly used in industry and are increasingly applied to health care.

Referent. The specific unit of health care to be measured and to which quality of care criteria apply.

Standards. Professionally developed expressions of the range of acceptable variation from norms of criteria. Commonly, all-or-nothing standards (e.g., 100 percent or 0 percent compliance required) are preferred. This is coupled with peer review of all cases that vary from the criteria.

Structural Data. Information on the quantity and characteristics of facilities, equipment, organizational arrangements, and personnel available to give care.

Technical Competence. The degree to which the practitioner coordinates judgment, skill, and available technology to improve health of patients.

Utilization Review (UR). Study of the appropriateness of the use of particular services and the appropriateness of the volume of services used.

Part **II**

Reflections on the Effectiveness of Quality Assurance

Avedis Donabedian

INTRODUCTION

It is important, from the start, to say what this work is intended to be and what it is not. I shall specify, therefore, the substance of my subject and the method to be used in addressing it. I will then describe how the text is organized.

The Subject

It is not sufficient to say that this discussion is about the effectiveness of quality assurance. "Quality," "quality assurance," and "effectiveness" have no fixed meanings that everyone accepts. A tailored definition has to be offered for each.

Quality of Care. The definition of quality to be adopted here is rather broad, but not so broad as to be crippling. Quality shall mean a judgment about the goodness of both technical care and the management of the interpersonal exchanges between client and practitioner. From time to time the amenities of care may be mentioned; these refer to the acceptability and pleasantness of the conditions under which care is provided.

The quality of technical care is to be judged by its effectiveness, which is the proportion of currently achievable improvements in health that any given instance of care, given the patient's situation, can be expected to attain. The standard of reference, therefore, is the efficacy of what we currently know and can do. The level of that efficacy is not a subject for judgments of quality as here defined, though in another context it might be.

The quality of the interpersonal exchange and of the amenities of care is to be judged by their contribution to the effectiveness of technical care, but only partly so. One must also consider the degree to which, independently of effectiveness, the properties of the interpersonal relationship and amenities conform to patient expectations and preferences, as well as to societal norms.

As to the relationship between cost and quality, I shall take the position that the purpose of care is to achieve the greatest improvement in health made possible by current knowledge, but that this should be obtained at lowest cost to the patient, and only as far as the fully informed patient is willing to allow. It is the patient's preferences that determine how the expected improvements in health are to be valued, and what amounts of effort or money are to be expended in the pursuit of what expected results.

The subject of scrutiny in the assessment of quality, as here defined, is the behavior of the providers of care. The behavior of their clients is also included, but only to the extent that the providers of care, be they practitioners or institutions, can be expected to influence that behavior. If providers, through their decisions and behaviors, can influence access to care, that shall be a proper subject for a judgment on quality. But, quite arbitrarily, the definition of quality to be adopted will exclude systemic or societal properties that influence accessibility, as it will exclude activities meant to alter client behavior, other than those legitimately under the control of caregivers. The definition of quality will also exclude judgments on the suitability of accepting lower levels of effectiveness in return for social gains, such as reductions in cost or greater equity in access to care.

The purpose of the foregoing exclusions is not to advocate a more modest (some would say impoverished) definition of quality. Rather, it is to trim the scope of quality assurance to a more manageable set of activities. To simplify my task still further, when I refer to practitioners I shall have in mind mostly physicians; and when I discuss institutions, it will be hospitals that, most of the time, I shall be thinking of.

Quality Assurance. A broad definition of quality assurance would include all that a society does to maintain and enhance the quality of care. More specifically, it would include two components: (1) system design, and (2) monitoring system performance.

System design refers to how the system for financing and delivering care is set up, and particularly to those of its properties that are capable of influencing access to services and the conduct of care. It is this relationship between system design and system performance that allows one to assess "structure" as an indicator, though indirect, of the quality of care. The amenities of care are more directly dependent on system design than is the conduct of care itself.

Monitoring system performance is achieved through obtaining information about how system participants behave and what they accomplish. In other words, monitoring is conducted mainly by obtaining information about the "process" of care and its "outcomes." It is possible to monitor "structure" as well (for example, by periodic checks to determine if the system continues to adhere to its prespecified design); but this is a subject of limited concern here.

It is useful to distinguish two kinds of monitoring, one informal and the other formal. Informal monitoring occurs through experiencing and sharing observations whenever colleagues work together to provide care. It engenders judgments, more or less well-founded, about the relative competence of coworkers. It is perhaps a potent regulator of conduct, at least for those who value the good opinion of others. Nevertheless, informal monitoring is not included here as a subject of inquiry, except to suggest that an ambience of watchfulness, or lack of it, may facilitate or impede the formalized system of performance monitoring.

The formal monitoring of performance is an established, organized (even bureaucratized) effort meant to collect, continuously and predictably, credible information about the process and outcomes of care, to interpret that information, and to act upon it in ways calculated at least to diminish the likelihood of past errors occurring again and, it is hoped, to motivate progressive improvement in quality.

Besides excluding from consideration the informal monitoring of structure, process, and outcome, as well as the formal monitoring of structure, I shall not, in this discussion, deal directly with the relationship between system design and system performance. One should remember, however, that a formal mechanism for monitoring quality is itself a feature of system design—a feature whose effectiveness is the matter to be addressed. The actions taken in response to the findings of formal performance monitoring are also, quite often, modifications in system design—modifications whose effectiveness defines what can be achieved in this way. It is also likely that other structurally determined characteristics of a system will influence how the formal mechanism of quality monitoring is set up, what actions it can most readily take, and how effective these actions can be.

To summarize, "quality assurance" will be taken to mean the formal monitoring of the process and outcomes of care. Rather arbitrarily, "monitoring" will connote not only the assessment of quality but also a set of activities that follow. These include (1) the "localization" of speci-fied levels of performance in time, person, and place, (2) the interpreta-tion of the findings in a manner that leads to a determination of causa-tion, or to hypotheses about causation, (3) the consideration of suitable interventions, (4) the execution of the selected interventions, and (5) the assessment of the consequences of intervention by continued monitor-ing of performance.

Figure 1 shows the basic components of formal quality assurance as conceived of here. The chief steps in the iterative cycle of monitoring are shown in Figure 2. The factors that influence effectiveness are to be sought in the nature of the activity being monitored, the properties of the monitoring mechanism itself, and the characteristics of the environ-ment in which monitoring takes place.

Effectiveness of Quality Monitoring. The effectiveness of care has been defined already as the degree to which the known efficacy of current health care is realized in practice. But "efficacy" is as yet undefined. To some it means what any given intervention can accomplish under the most favorable circumstances; under more ordinary, less favorable cir-cumstances what is measured is "effectiveness," it is said. But, because it is difficult to say what circumstances for testing any given interven-tion are the "best," and therefore suitable for calibrating "efficacy," it seems more reasonable to say that the efficacy of technology is what it can accomplish under carefully specified, reproducible circumstances. Even then, it is uncertain whether efficacy is measured by the improve-ment in health as compared to a specified baseline of ill health or by the degree to which a prespecified level of health is attained. If the latter is meant, one still needs to specify whether the referent is some idealized version of "perfect health" or a lower, more realistic goal—a goal that may even vary from situation to situation. Fortunately, these considera-tions need not concern us here because a prespecified level of efficacy can be assumed as a given, so the effectiveness of care can be judged relative to its efficacy, as already described.

It is quite legitimate to consider the monitoring of performance to be a technology or a complex of technologies, some organizational and others more material in nature. If so, monitoring is subject, first, to an assessment of efficacy under carefully controlled circumstances, and then, to an assessment of effectiveness in the everyday world. Mainly to simplify my vocabulary, I shall refer almost always to the effective-ness of monitoring, meaning by that its ability to alter care so that the

Figure 1   Components of Quality Assurance

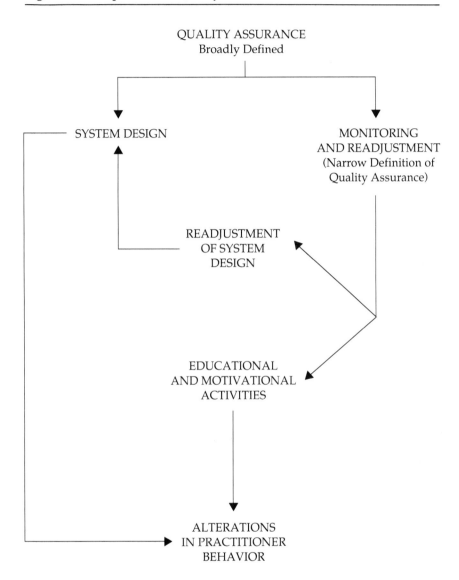

Figure 2   The Monitoring Cycle

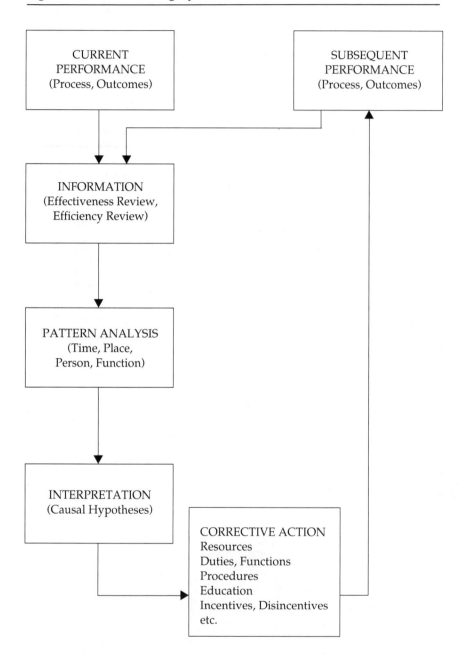

care becomes more effective in improving health and more conforming to individual preferences and social norms.

This twosome of effectiveness (of monitoring to alter care and of care to improve health) offers the possibility that monitoring may be very influential in altering clinical behavior, but that the alteration in clinical behavior has relatively little effect on health. It is even possible that the alterations in clinical behavior are inimical to health. Alertness to the possibility of this "countereffectiveness" is analogous to the attention paid to undesirable side effects in assessing the efficacy of drugs and biologicals, When system design (including administrative interventions such as monitoring) is assessed, "noxicity" could be the counterpart to toxicity. It is possible, for example, by adopting excessively rigid standards to seem to encourage care by rote, discouraging legitimate flexibility and innovation. It is also possible, by overemphasizing cost containment (perhaps because of administratively imposed constraints), to aim for levels of health improvement lower than those each patient would consider optimal.

Including the cost of care as a consideration relevant to the judgment of quality makes measuring the effectiveness of monitoring much more difficult. If monitoring reduces unnecessary but largely harmless care, there is an immediate reduction in cost. If potentially harmful care is given less often, there is a reduction both in immediate costs and in such direct and indirect costs as would have been subsequently incurred because of the harm that would have been suffered. If monitoring brings about useful additions to care, there is an immediate increase in direct cost, but possibly a compensating decrease, as well, because of early recovery. Improved health also produces subsequent benefits to the individual and to society. But if life is prolonged, illness recurs and new costs are incurred. Figure 3 depicts these several effects.

If, in addition to measuring costs, it is desired to compare the costs of care to its benefits, both as valued by the informed patient, one encounters the knotty problems of eliciting patient preferences and of placing a money value on states of health. Finally, the costs of the monitoring enterprise itself are to be reckoned in a manner that includes operating expenses as well as capital costs, the costs of compensated as well as uncompensated services, and perhaps even the psychic costs (and rewards) of participating in the monitoring enterprise as evaluators and evaluees. It is also conceivable that the monitoring enterprise and its consequences will alter an institution's market position and susceptibility to malpractice litigation, with attendant financial benefit or loss. Fortunately, since we have adopted a narrowly patient-centered ap-

Figure 3   Possible Effects of Monitoring on Cost

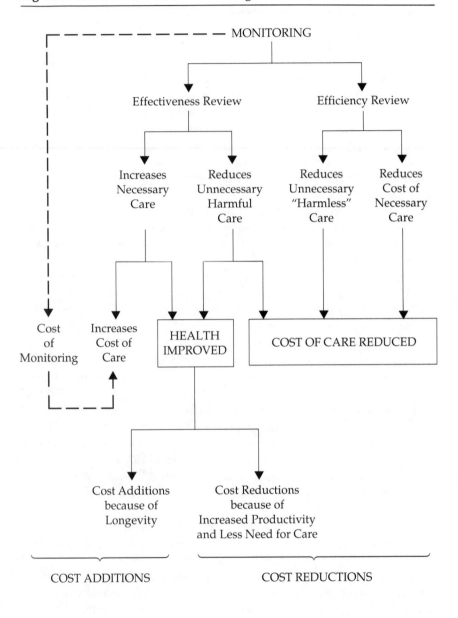

proach to evaluation, the costs of monitoring care become relevant only insofar as they are passed on to the patient as out-of-pocket expenses or as increases in premiums. But this increment may be difficult to identify and, in any case, it would reflect some estimate, however imperfect, of the net cost of monitoring to the institution, perhaps along the lines already described.

An evaluation of the consequences of monitoring would also face the problem of nonlinearities in the relationship between monitoring and its effects on care, and between these changes in care and their effects on health. For example, both the effects of monitoring on care and of care on health could depend on how bad or good the care was initially. Additions to either monitoring or care may have larger effects at first, and then have progressively smaller effects. There could be an optimal range in a continuum of situations, both monitoring and changes in care being less effective below and above that range. Even the postulation of smooth curvilinearities could be a highly conventionalized depiction of a reality in which effectiveness might manifest itself in rather sudden leaps of change, possibly associated with particular interventions, perhaps after a trial of other methods had failed. Catalysis and synergism are likely to characterize organizational systems as they do biological systems.[1]

These thoughts on the complexities of assessing the effectiveness of quality monitoring are offered mainly as a spur to more rigorous conceptual formulation and to empirical research. In a more practical vein, one would be more than content with observing what changes in clinical practice can reasonably be attributed to monitoring, and what changes in a patient's health and satisfaction can be attributed to changes in practice. But seeing how difficult it is to attribute causation, verifying the effects on clinical practice, let alone on health, would require rigorous research, including epidemiological observation and experimental studies. No wonder reliable information about effectiveness is so difficult to find.

The Method

Although credible information about the effectiveness and cost of monitoring is difficult to come by, the literature is not totally lacking in this respect. Many years ago, I reviewed the few studies then at hand and speculated on what they had to teach.[2] Since then, more information has become available, much of it reviewed by Eisenberg, with particular attention to educational interventions.[3] Still another review and interpretation of the literature might have served to extend and verify Eisenberg's observations and conclusions. By deliberate intent, this exposition is not that review. Rather, these are the reflections of one who, it is hoped, is a reasonably well informed student of the field. It is largely speculative in method, relying mainly on plausibility and coherence, rather than documentation, to gain acceptance. At best, it offers a set of hypotheses for subsequent empirical testing. At the same time, insofar as it is sound, it could serve as a framework for mapping and interpreting the literature on quality monitoring. No doubt, the empirical findings might also suggest changes or refinements in the analytic framework proposed here. Perhaps, in this way, this discussion can make a contribution to the iterative interplay of theory and empirical observation by which knowledge makes its often painfully slow advance.

Because there is widespread disenchantment with the effectiveness of quality assurance, this work might seem to be an exploration of the reasons for failure, a search for the obstacles to success. To some extent, this will be the case. But failure has not marked quality monitoring in every case. Every now and then, examples of reasonable, even remarkable, success are reported, though generally these have been in specific locations, during relatively short periods of observation. Accordingly, a more neutral analytic approach, one seeking to identify factors that may enhance or impede effectiveness, is perhaps more appropriate. I hope much of the time to take this more neutral position. Sometimes I may seem to stray from it, appearing to explain why the quality of care is not better than it is. If so, this is because there is an implied assumption that current deficiencies in quality reflect an inability or unwillingness to institute quality monitoring or to conduct it effectively.

Organization of the Text. I have not found a fully satisfactory way to organize a subject so broad and complex as this. Categories overlap and the contents interact. Yet, some degree of order, even if rather artificial, has to be imposed so one can begin to tease apart the tangled web.

My method will be, by and large, to proceed from the more general to the particular. I will begin with the characteristics of the all-embracing environment and move on to the attributes of more immediate contexts, meaning by the latter the formal organizations (particularly the hospitals) in which care is provided. Next I will deal with the characteristics of the medical profession, recognizing that only part of its work is conducted within formal organizations. This means that the attributes of the profession characterize both the general environment and the organizational environment in each particular context.

There will follow, in this order, a discussion of the nature of professional work, of the methods used to assess it, of the ways in which the monitoring of performance is organized, and of the methods by which changes in behavior might be obtained. A brief discussion of the role of consumers in quality monitoring will conclude my part of this book. Missing from this progression are strategies for bringing about political and organizational change. Although this is an area of vital importance, I must leave it to a more competent scholar on the subject.

THE LARGER ENVIRONMENT

An assumption fundamental to this discussion (although not put to a direct proof) is that properties of the environment influence whether quality monitoring will be attempted, in what ways it will be conducted, and how effective it will be. More specifically, I shall argue that incentives embedded in the health care system itself will be difficult to counteract by the monitoring of performance. Monitoring will be effective to the extent that its purposes correspond to dominant incentives and its methods conform to social and professional norms. Departing from this premise, I shall comment first on the social commitment to quality, and then consider in turn selected attributes of the organization of care, the organization of financing, and the legal environment.

Social Commitment to Quality

It is perhaps a fanciful exercise in futility to go searching in the deepest recesses of a society for the factors that influence the effectiveness of quality monitoring. Yet, one cannot avoid the conclusion that a health care system reflects the values adopted by a society and the ways in which it has chosen to conduct its affairs. Particularly relevant, one imagines, is the commitment of a society to providing quality care, as well as the way it has defined quality and assigned responsibility for safeguarding it. The balance of emphasis on quality, as compared to cost saving, is an important attribute of a society's general stance. So is the commitment, or lack of it, to care for particularly vulnerable populations: the very young, the very aged, the poor, those in rural isolation or urban confinement, and those discriminated against on the basis of persuasion, color, or ethnic origin. And so are the quality-relevant roles assigned to, or assumed by, the several levels and branches of government, the health care professions, the institutions that provide care, employers, labor unions, consumer organizations, and individual consumers.

The ways in which these and other attributes of the general environment influence the monitoring of quality are bound to be indirect and sometimes hard to discern. Much of this essay is an exploration of how, through the mediation of mechanisms increasingly closer to the monitoring enterprise itself, certain attributes of the general environment shape efforts to monitor quality, limiting or enhancing their effectiveness.

The Organization of Care

The organization of health care reflects values and forms fundamental to our society. Federalism, localism, pluralism, corporatism, and privatism all find their expression in how, as a society, we conduct our affairs, health care included. Of the many consequences of these societal attributes, I shall deal in this section with only two: the fragmentation of responsibility for care, and the low level of formal organization in a large sector of the health care system. Other consequences will be described in the sections on financing health care and on the nature of the health care professions, as well as elsewhere in this work.

Fragmentation of Responsibility for Care. The absence of centralized responsibility is manifested by lack of coordination and continuity in care, features widely believed to reduce its effectiveness and efficiency. There are corresponding effects on quality monitoring.

Without centralized responsibility it is difficult to adopt uniform standards and methods; or, if adopted, they are difficult to enforce. Information is not sought about entire episodes of care, irrespective of auspices or sites; or, the information is sought but is not available; or, if available, it is not uniform. Even if the needed information were gathered and used to assess quality, acting upon the findings would be exceedingly difficult. For example, the separation of hospital care from care before and after hospitalization not only prevents hospitals from monitoring entire episodes of care, it may actually encourage a narrow, self-serving enterprise—one that seeks effectiveness and efficiency during hospitalization without regard to the danger of inefficiency and lesser effectiveness after a patient has gone home or to a nursing care facility.

A commitment to localism and corporatism, including professional autonomy as a manifestation of the latter, leads to a dispersal of the monitoring function. This is clearly seen in the monitoring activities required by Medicare. These were assigned first to local agencies, the professional standards review organizations (PSROs) and then to state-wide agencies, the peer review organizations (PROs), with a preference accorded to those controlled by physicians. Under the PSROs, there was further delegation to individual hospitals.

At a more general level, our federal form of government separates responsibility for Medicare and Medicaid. This led to much conflict when the federal branch, using the PSROs as its agents, attempted to monitor the cost and quality of care in both programs. In the ensuing confrontation, federal authorities repeatedly gave ground. This un-happy experience perhaps explains the exclusion of Medicaid from the jurisdiction of the PROs, the agencies that replaced the PSROs. Now, each state must make its own arrangements if it desires to obtain the services of a PRO.

There is no evidence that would lead one to say that pluralism, decentralization, and delegation are most of the time inimical to the effectiveness of monitoring. Much could be said in their favor. For ex-ample, decentralization and delegation are said to make quality moni-toring more acceptable to physicians and hospitals. These features of a monitoring system might contribute to its effectiveness and efficiency by targeting the activity more precisely to local problems and needs. Similarly, pluralism and privatism permit a greater degree of choice by consumers, encouraging competition among providers.

But decentralization and delegation also expose a national quality-monitoring effort to the vagaries of local forces, including the nullifying influence of competing interests. The PSRO program, for example, ap-peared to reduce very effectively hospital use and costs in some areas, while remaining both ineffective and costly overall.[4] Allowing accredita-tion by the Joint Commission on Accreditation of Healthcare Organiza-tions (JCAHO) to substitute for more directly imposed requirements has attracted widespread criticism and disillusionment. Perhaps as a result, the JCAHO has embarked on a new initiative meant to enhance its effectiveness by requiring information on more precise indicators of the quality of care.[5]

As to competition among providers, it is not certain how much of it there is, or what forms it takes. Competition can be conducive to quality only if those who purchase care do so largely on the basis of clearly identifiable, valid indicators of quality.

Among the attributes that distinguish localities could be the availability of care at several levels of quality, credible information about these levels, and the ability to use that information. If information were available (for example, as a result of quality monitoring), it could conceivably be used by very knowledgeable consumers individually; it would be more likely to be used by group purchasers who can call on expert advice. Localities vary, one expects, in how sophisticated individual consumers are and how much care is purchased under group contracts.

Another feature by which locations could be distinguished is the balance of supply and demand. One of the most intriguing findings to emerge from evaluations of the PSROs is evidence of their apparent ineffectiveness in reducing hospital use during the second half of the year, when beds are plentiful compared to what is demanded, and their relative ineffectiveness during the first half of the year, when beds are in shorter supply.[6] This could be taken to suggest that delegating the monitoring of utilization to the hospitals runs the risk of having the objectives of monitoring nullified by the overriding need of the hospitals to fill their beds.

Low Level of Formal Organization. The degree to which a health care system is formally organized is another feature that can be expected to influence the institution of quality monitoring, the forms it takes, and its effectiveness. This is because formal, systematic monitoring, as well as the ability to take action based on its findings, cannot proceed unless there is an organized structure (in the delivery of care, its financing, or both) to sustain it. This explains, in part, why quality monitoring is most highly developed in hospitals, whereas the private office practice of medicine is signally lacking in this respect. The difficulty of instituting quality monitoring in nursing homes is perhaps another example, considering that most of these homes are small and poorly organized. But here the more fundamental deficiency could be the absence of a serious social commitment to quality in the care of the aged, chronically ill poor.

How and how fully care is organized are not attributes that stand alone. They are related to other attributes of the health care system and its societal environment, including some of the characteristics already described. There is also an affinity between more highly organized care and more organized, more controlled methods of financing and reimbursement. These, in turn, can influence the objectives of performance monitoring and its effectiveness, as I shall try to explain next.

The Organization of Financing

Organized financing, through governmental programs or private health insurance, can influence quality monitoring in at least two ways. First, the financing agency may institute and conduct a monitoring enterprise, with or without delegating some of its responsibilities and activities to the providers of care. Thus, the financing mechanism serves as the necessary alternative locus when those who deliver care are not sufficiently organized or motivated to undertake the monitoring task unaided. And when the providers are organized, the financing agency can still act as servant, partner, or even master.

Which of these roles is adopted depends to some degree on sponsorship and social location. Blue Cross and Blue Shield, during the many years of physician dominance, stood in a rather servile position relative to the providers of care, while commercial health insurance assiduously avoided any involvement in monitoring care. The earlier, physician-sponsored HMOs found it necessary to monitor at least the costs of care in partnership with their physician members. So did the Medicare program at first, becoming progressively more exigent (some would say dictatorial) as the more collaborative approach appeared to fail. Whether or not the more controlling approach will succeed remains to be seen.

A second way in which organized financing influences monitoring is by modifying the objectives to be pursued and the behaviors to be controlled. It is reasonable to believe that when financing is more highly organized, cost containment becomes a more pressing, even compelling, necessity. The behaviors to be controlled are influenced by the method of reimbursement. When payment is according to the cost of care, overservicing is the chief threat to quality. When reimbursement is per case or per capita, underservicing is the greater threat. The monitoring system is likely to be designed and operated accordingly; and its effectiveness would depend on the degree of congruence between objectives and incentives. It is difficult to reduce unnecessary care when it is rewarded with higher revenue, or to assure necessary care when providing it is financially disadvantageous. The former effect we observed in the experience of the PSROs. The latter effect would be expected to characterize the experience of the PROs, but the evidence bearing on that is not available as yet.

The Legal Environment

Quality monitoring reveals information and leads to activities material to the life and welfare of patients, and to the ability of physicians to practice their craft. Accordingly, the monitoring activity is extraordinarily sensitive to the provisions of the laws meant to protect both patients and practitioners, with due regard to the public interest. Three features of the legal environment seem particularly relevant: (1) the propensity of patients to seek redress through malpractice litigation and the need of providers to protect against it, (2) the exposure of those who conduct monitoring to liability for what they say and do, and (3) the requirements for due process. I shall deal briefly with each of these, after warning the reader that I am not qualified to offer legal opinions.

Malpractice Liability. There can be an extremely complex relationship between malpractice litigation and quality monitoring. First, the fear of malpractice liability can alter the properties of the care to be monitored. Second, the fear of liability to malpractice may in some ways hamper monitoring, while in other ways it can aid it. Third, the occurrence of malpractice suits and awards can itself become information subject to monitoring.

Much is said, but little proven, about the effects of excessive litigiousness on the practice of medicine. The inimical effects said to occur include (1) costly and potentially hazardous overinvestigation, (2) reluctance of physicians to undertake risky but justifiable procedures, (3) reduced access because physicians have avoided or withdrawn from specialties particularly liable to suit, (4) withholding of information from patients, and (5) mutual suspiciousness and latent hostility in the patient-practitioner relationship. Against these baleful consequences one could postulate the following possible contributions to better care: (1) a greater likelihood that hazardous procedures will be performed by qualified practitioners under appropriate circumstances, and only when justified by potential benefits, (2) greater attention to preventing harm to patients, in general, (3) more frequent involvement of patients in informed decisions concerning their own care, and (4) greater attention to improving the patient-practitioner relationship in other ways as well, considering that disgruntled patients are those thought most likely to sue.

Of all of these largely hypothetical effects on care, the practice of "defensive medicine," meaning the undertaking of unnecessary diagnostic investigations, has attracted the greatest attention. But because unnecessary intervention is a pervasive fault in clinical practice (as are all the adverse effects listed), excessive litigiousness can hardly be said to have added anything distinctive to monitoring by altering the practice of care in this way. The more distinctive consideration is whether or not, when care is monitored, an intent to reduce liability to malpractice suit shall be accepted retrospectively as a legitimate justification for having undertaken medically unnecessary interventions, or used prospectively in setting up the standards of care that guide the monitoring effort. These possible consequences can be regarded as a link between the alterations of practice attributable to the prospect of litigation and the more direct effects of litigiousness on the monitoring mechanism itself.

Just as the effects of litigiousness could be classified as harmful or beneficial to clinical practice, the more direct effects of litigiousness on quality monitoring can be grouped into those that might hamper and those that might aid the monitoring effort. On the negative side, there could be a reluctance to introduce monitoring or to operate it effectively because it is feared that the standards adopted for monitoring could be used to substantiate unacceptable care. Therefore, one would expect opposition to the formulation and publication of standards, unless they are offered as guidelines that permit considerable flexibility, as well as variability among localities.

It is also feared that the information amassed in the course of monitoring could be used by patients to sue hospitals and by hospitals to act against individual physicians. Such fears could lead to a reluctance to record or report, and in some cases even to find out (as when postmortem examinations are discouraged). One could infer, therefore, that the acceptability and implementation of monitoring would be influenced by the degree of clarity and consistency in formulating and interpreting laws that under some circumstances bar and under other circumstances allow access to information used for quality monitoring. In the absence of adequate safeguards, unavailability and adulteration of clinical information could be a noxious side effect of quality monitoring.

On the positive side, it can be argued that the fear of being sued for malpractice could be a spur to implementing more effective methods of monitoring. This would follow from an anticipatory, rather than a defensive, stance toward monitoring, based on an expectation that, through effective monitoring, deficiencies in quality can be prevented and both litigiousness and its rewards curtailed. This effect would be reinforced, no doubt, by holding a hospital responsible for the quality of care received by the patients in it, and by ruling that colleagues who participate in caring for a patient may share jointly in the liability for deficiencies in care. In this way, a collective responsibility is established, necessitating the monitoring of individual behavior by colleagues as well as by the organization in which they work.

The anticipatory efficacy of quality monitoring is predicated on the assumption that the probability of being sued, or sued successfully, is reasonably related to identifiable deficiencies in the quality of care in its technical or interpersonal aspects. If this were true, the simple occurrence of successful suits could become a useful method of monitoring in its own right, even though only a small proportion of deficiencies would be identified in this way. Unfortunately, the relation between quality and liability to being sued is not established.[7] One might suggest, therefore, that any reform that would link malpractice litigation more firmly to deficiencies of quality would strengthen the societal foundations for quality monitoring.

Protection for Those Who Monitor. The chilling effect of exposing participants in quality monitoring to being sued for slander or libel is too obvious to require elaboration. For that reason, over a number of years, more and more states adopted legislation that granted these participants either qualified or absolute privileges in court proceedings, provided they acted in good faith and according to established procedure.[8] Without such protection, formalized quality monitoring would have become next to untenable.

In 1986, the Health Care Quality Improvement Act extended the protection of limited immunity nationwide to all those who provide information to professional review bodies, as well as to persons and organizations involved in taking action against physicians on the basis of professional review, subject to having met the tests of reasonable belief, reasonable investigation, and due process. In return, there were requirements for reporting all malpractice claim settlements, for reporting all significant actions taken against physicians for reasons of incompetence, and for assuring that this information would be used by hospitals in granting staff privileges.[9] In this way, the act created an environment more conducive to quality-monitoring efforts, while also establishing monitoring activities of its own. It may have also contributed to the reluctance of professionals to act against colleagues, considering how dire the consequences could be.

Due Process. The requirements for due process make it inordinately difficult to take punitive action against those exhibiting an unacceptable pattern of clinical practice. For example, in attempting to impose a sanction, a PRO may have to undertake several reviews at progressively higher levels within the organization, after which a case may proceed in an upward climb through the office of the inspector general for the Department of Health and Human Services, to an administrative law judge, to an appeals council, and at last, to the courts.[10] It is a daunting prospect, and a reversal is possible at any stage. Nevertheless, it is a necessary protection. And while it discourages a recourse to sanctions, it could spur a search for other interventions that are less ponderous and possibly more humane and efficacious.

THE INTRAORGANIZATIONAL ENVIRONMENT

In this section I shall attempt to identify some features of the intraorganizational environment that could influence the effectiveness of quality assurance through monitoring. But before doing so I shall try to justify the separation of the environment into two compartments, one extraorganizational and the other intraorganizational, and comment briefly on the relevance of the latter to the subject of this discussion.

Distinctiveness

The separation of environmental forces into extraorganizational and intraorganizational is partly a matter of convenience. One expects to find within organizations a microcosmic representation of the forces at play in a society as a whole. In fact, it is through modifying the form and function of organizations that these forces have much of their effect. And it is through the capacity to undergo modification that organizations survive and flourish.

Yet organizations are also capable of being selective in their responses to external forces; they resist some while they respond to others—and the nature of the response can vary. These variations arise partly from differences in constituencies, of sponsors as well as of clients. Variations also represent specializations in function. It is quite legitimate, therefore, to regard the intraorganizational environment as having distinctive characteristics in addition to the attributes more uniformly shaped by sufficiently powerful external forces.

Relevance

Because quality monitoring is most likely to occur when care is provided in or through institutions or organized programs, the forms it takes, as well as its effectiveness, can be expected to reflect the characteristics of these organizations. It is widely acknowledged that organizational characteristics influence the quality of care provided.[11,12] But that is not our subject. We are interested, rather, in whether or not formal quality monitoring will be instituted, and with what effect.

It could be argued, of course, that the variations in quality that one observes when different kinds of organizations are compared are at least partly attributable to the presence and functioning of quality monitoring in some settings but not in others. There is reason to believe that this is the case insofar as informal monitoring is concerned. It appears that when care is made more "visible" to colleagues (possibly through sharing responsibility for care, consultation, teaching rounds, clinical conferences, and the like), the quality of care is likely to be higher.[13,14] Other advantages in quality have been attributed to controls over recruitment and staffing, to equipment and material resources, to direct supervision of professional work, or to more subtle attributes such as coordination, communication, and tightness of organizational control.[15-17] But the role of formal monitoring mechanisms, as a separable organizational feature, in influencing the quality of care provided is, to my knowledge, as yet unexplored. Therefore, much of what I say on the subject will be conjectural.

Features

Of the many features of the intraorganizational environment that might influence the implementation and effectiveness of quality monitoring I shall address the following: (1) ideology, (2) structural characteristics and resources, (3) incentives, (4) leadership, and (5) baseline performance.

Ideology. The roots of much that goes on in an organization are probably ideological. Insofar as quality monitoring is concerned, it is important to gauge the degree of importance accorded to quality, both in absolute terms and relative to competing objectives, particularly cost containment. Possibly the sources of the concern for quality also matter: whether, for example, the pursuit of quality is regarded to be a social responsibility, a professional imperative, a prudent yielding to coercion, or a profitable response to market forces. I would not be rash enough to insist that the particular motivation has a bearing on the success of quality monitoring. But I can suggest that it is easier to pay lip service to some motivations than others; and I can be reasonably certain that success in monitoring is more likely to ensue when all motivations impel in the same direction than when they are at cross-purposes.

One can perhaps expand the category of "ideology" so it includes, as well, the definition of quality that an organization adopts. In particular, it is important to know the relative importance given to technical care as compared to the interpersonal process, not simply in words, but also in corresponding actions. To some extent, the choice is ideological, reflecting the views of the organization's leadership, as well as the values and traditions of the major constituencies to which an organization is answerable. The choice is also influenced by the functions an organization serves. The quality of technical care is likely to be the dominant, even exclusive, concern of a major teaching center that has hardly any competitors in caring for the desperately ill. Responsiveness to the values and dictates of the academic community, to the nature of the task to be performed, and to the professional referral network, all conspire to make it so. In sharp contrast, a long-term facility under religious auspices is impelled by the values of its sponsors, by the nature of the care required, and by the need to elicit referrals from family members to emphasize the amenities and the interpersonal aspects of care, assuming the resources are available.[18] I do not wish to imply a preference for one over the other of these two orientations. I only wish to speculate on the possible origins of the orientations themselves, and to suggest that in the first instance the interpersonal process is at risk, whereas in the second situation technical care is in jeopardy.

Structural Characteristics and Resources. Quality monitoring, in order to succeed, needs resources, both material and human. Both are likely to be deficient. In particular, we have failed to understand how complex the task is, and how needful of specialized expertise. We insist that only a skilled mechanic can be entrusted with a car; yet we continue to act as if any health care practitioner, perhaps after only a rudimentary training, can master the intricacies of assessing professional performance and altering the behaviors of individuals and organizations.

The success of quality monitoring also depends on the presence of the appropriate organizational structure. The quality-monitoring enterprise is, of course, part of that structure. Accordingly, the effectiveness of the monitoring unit depends on the characteristics of its own internal configuration, as well as on the way it links with other units of the organization, or fails to do so. But it is equally important to examine how these other units are organized and how they interrelate. Of particular importance is the organization of the medical staff and the way in which it relates to the administrative apparatus and to the governing body of the organization.

All the foregoing observations on resources and organizational structure are preliminary. I mention them here because they characterize the internal environment of the organization. A more detailed discussion will follow in sections yet to come. But I do wish to mention here the importance of determining whether or not there is a clearly defined organizational site where responsibility for quality is assumed and exercised. In a hospital, according to the courts, that site should be the governing body of the institution. Yet, very often the members of that body are unwilling or unable to exercise that responsibility, having little knowledge of the subject and perhaps being overly deferential to medical expertise. It is important to know, therefore, what oversight of quality the governing body retains and what responsibility for quality it delegates, and to whom. The way responsibility is allocated among the governing board, the medical staff, and others in an organization can be expected to be critical, but we do not know as yet what particular configuration is most conducive to the effectiveness of formal monitoring.

Incentives. It seems obvious that physicians and other health care practitioners working in an organized setting would respond more favorably to formal quality monitoring if they saw it as a particular manifestation of the organization's more general commitment to recognizing and rewarding quality.

An organization can act most effectively through a built-in incentive system when practitioners are full-time employees and when there is a career progression that allows considerable scope for professional and financial rewards. What is needed, then, is credible, timely information about the aspects of practitioner performance that should be rewarded. Whether or not the quality-monitoring enterprise is the source of that information would be a critical determinant of effectiveness in monitoring.

Unfortunately, an organization's commitment to quality can sometimes be questioned. At least, that commitment can be vitiated by competing interests—keeping the institution solvent, for example. And even when the commitment to quality exists, the power to act effectively can be weakened in one or more ways. Relatively little can be done if health care practitioners are not full-time employees or not employees at all, if there is no significant career progression clearly linked to quality in performance, or if the quality-monitoring enterprise cannot provide the needed information. I shall have more to say about these obstacles to success a little later on in this text.

Leadership. Leadership is perhaps the component of the intraorganizational environment least amenable to structuring, the one most often dependent on serendipity and most often missing among the determinants of effectiveness in quality monitoring. To make quality monitoring work, leaders at the highest reaches of the organization should adopt it, become identified with it, and participate personally in it. The leader could be a member of the governing board or a senior administrator. But it seems that it is most important for health care practitioners to see a trusted and respected colleague at the helm of the monitoring enterprise, not merely as a figurehead but as a pilot and captain indeed. Some leaders derive much of their authority from their organizational rank. But the charismatic properties of the leader are perhaps more important to the members of an autonomous profession; and a combination of bureaucratic and charismatic leadership is perhaps the best of all.

We have had in the past anecdotal reports of the importance of leadership in implementing successful quality monitoring.[19-21] But we owe to Palmer et al. a more rigorous definition of leadership and a more precise measurement of its effects. Though the evidence is weak, it appears that quality monitoring is more effective in altering physician behavior when clinical leaders participate in it and alter their own behavior in response to the findings.[22]

Baseline Performance. The general level of clinical performance that characterizes an organization could be an important determinant of the perceived need for quality monitoring, of the design of the monitoring enterprise, and of its effectiveness. In this regard, the shared perceptions of the level of performance could be as important as the actual level, when more objectively assessed.

When the actual or perceived level of performance is exceedingly high, formal monitoring may seem redundant. When externally imposed, it is resented and, at best, perfunctorily performed. Major teaching institutions have often behaved in this way. I believe that cost control in response to per case reimbursement is more readily embraced in such settings than quality monitoring per se.

When actual performance is at an uncommonly low level, quality monitoring could be regarded as a threat to be countered. Should monitoring be introduced, it is unlikely to be effective, since the prevalence of poor practice is usually the consequence of deep-seated organizational pathology—a state of affairs not conducive to a healthy organizational response. It is likely, in particular, that the low expectations prevalent in such a setting will be translated to a corresponding set of criteria and standards that fail to challenge. Even when external criteria and standards are held out as an example, they are likely to be countered by a host of arguments seeking to show why the criteria do not apply to the peculiarities of the local situation.

It would be particularly difficult to bring about change if the perceived level of performance called for is much higher than the actual level. There is, then, no felt need to improve. Even if evidence of low performance were offered, it would not be believed, the method of assessment usually becoming the target of concerted attack. It is doubtful that there are many instances when perceptions of performance are lower than reality warrants. If they are, the prospects of improvement occurring would seem higher, unless the pessimistic perceptions were a symptom of resigned hopelessness.

Baseline performance is related to the effectiveness of quality monitoring also through the fundamental property of curvilinearity alluded to in a preceding section. Especially when performance is already at a high level, added improvements in care are likely to produce small improvements in health, and these improvements could come at a disproportionately high cost. For this reason, as well as the pattern of organizational response already described, one could hypothesize that quality monitoring is most likely to be effective when baseline performance is in the midrange of quality, being neither too low nor too high. But this generalization may not be of much value; it is excessively vague, and so many other factors are likely to nullify it.[23]

THE MEDICAL PROFESSION

Introduction

It is reasonable to postulate that the properties of professions in general, and of the medical profession in particular, influence receptivity to quality monitoring. I shall confine my attention to the medical profession not because the other health care professions are unimportant but because if I did not limit my task, I would stray into unfamiliar territory, adding to the burdens of an already difficult assignment. Perhaps if one were to understand how the properties of the medical profession influence its amenability to monitoring, we would have identified some of the categories we might use in a comparative study of other professions as well, both in the health care field and beyond. As an interesting by-product, we would be able also to assess more critically the rather common practice of using nurses to monitor the performance of physicians.

In a quite remarkable way, the properties of the medical profession permeate the entire universe of quality monitoring. As manifested in the social organization of the profession, these properties characterize the larger environment in which monitoring occurs. Through the organization of medical staffs they also characterize the intraorganizational environment. Furthermore, through the intermediacy of education, training, and socialization, professional properties are transformed into individual attributes—traits so deeply rooted in each physician that they seem features of personality. Perhaps self-selection, as well as screening for admission to medical school, serves to reinforce these traits. Whether, beyond this, there are idiosyncratic differences in personality that make some physicians more amenable than others to quality monitoring is something about which we know next to nothing. Perhaps we ought to find out.[24]

In subsequent sections I shall try to show how the properties of the medical profession influence efforts to monitor the performance of its members, making some initiatives acceptable or effective while others are not. I perceive this as a matter of fit: of the profession to monitoring and of monitoring to the profession. The more complete the fit, the more acceptable the monitoring. But it cannot be said that effectiveness requires perfection of fit right from the start; the profession itself may have to alter in order to accommodate more effective monitoring.[25]

Some General Features of the Medical Profession

The medical profession, in common with all others, functions under a social contract granting it privileges, but imposing obligations in return. The most precious of these privileges is self-governance. The most stringent of the corresponding obligations is stewardship of the public interest. Assuring the quality of care is the chief component of that stewardship.

In granting the medical profession primary responsibility for quality, society has recognized the special expertise required to determine what constitutes goodness in technical care. It has also designed to insulate physicians from interference by outside interests that might subvert clinical judgment contrary to the best interests of individual patients. At the same time, it has expected a reasonable degree of public accountability.

These are principles that have been largely adhered to by society and avidly embraced by the medical profession. There has been a difference of opinion, however, as to what societal requirements constitute interference with professional prerogatives, in contravention of an implicit social contract, or are a demand for accountability, according to the contract's provisions. In this tension between accountability on the one hand and professional autonomy on the other, one finds the origin of much that troubles quality monitoring today.

The desire of the medical profession to define quality and to control the means for assuring it have been recognized by delegation of the monitoring function outside hospitals to organizations (such as the PSROs and the PROs) controlled by or responsive to physicians, while within hospitals the organized medical staff is entrusted with that responsibility. The medical profession also controls the criteria and standards by which quality of technical care is to be judged. To some degree, this delegation is pursuant to a social contract whose purpose is to protect the public interest, as I have described. It is also a recognition of the formidable political power of the profession, including its ability to obstruct and disrupt.

As to the methods for implementing quality assurance, the medical profession has traditionally preferred to emphasize recruitment, education, training, and socialization. It has hoped in this way to produce a professional who is both technically competent and morally equipped to be self-critical and self-correcting. Monitoring of individual performance has been informal rather than formal; and individual conduct has been regulated indirectly through inclusion in or exclusion from the network of professional referrals, and by other more or less subtle indicators of professional approval. More formal review activities, such as the clinical pathology conferences or the reviews of deaths, are conducted for educational purposes only, according to an exquisitely orchestrated etiquette that avoids fixing blame on or attributing incompetence to individual colleagues.[26] And if individuals are found to have erred, "talking to" is the method favored for bringing about change.[27] Disciplinary action is to be taken only as a final resort, when clearly unacceptable behavior cannot be otherwise remedied, and that only when other physicians are both jury and judge.

It is these traditions that the medical profession would like to preserve and to see embedded in any new monitoring procedures that may need to be developed. Yet, how different this is from recent developments that physicians fear and oppose. True, there is still a marked preference, in more recent forms of monitoring, for delegating the enterprise to the physicians themselves; but this is almost more by sufferance than by right. Physicians are warned that if they will not do the job, others can be found who will. Moreover, what physician-directed review agencies do is more and more externally prescribed, often in painful detail. And both what is done and what is accomplished are subject to external verification.

It seems to physicians that the deepest purposes of the monitoring enterprise are often suspect. There appears to be little in what they are asked to protect that, according to their own traditions, they could call "quality." Also alien (and alienating) is the insistence by external controllers that monitoring should extend to the identification of individual malfeasance and should lead to disciplinary action. Some physicians claim, alluding bitterly to the disastrous experience of the Vietnam War, that the "body count" (meaning the number of physicians censured) has become the measure of success in federally prescribed performance monitoring. Worst of all, federal agencies have seen fit to bypass the medical professional altogether, releasing to the public information of dubious validity calculated to discredit the quality of care in many hospitals, and thereby creating mistrust and discord between physicians and patients.

If I am correct in my analysis, one could hardly say that there is a fit between recent developments in performance monitoring and the established professional culture. It is no wonder, then, that one can expect monitoring to be resisted and, when possible, weakened, perhaps to the point of nullification. It is only fair to say, however, that what physicians find most obnoxious in current federally required procedures was resorted to only after a system more in keeping with professional traditions seemed to have failed.[28] It remains to be seen whether more directive (not to say coercive) methods of monitoring will be more successful.

Studies of the PROs could tell us much about the factors that influence effectiveness. For though I have argued that congruence with professional traditions contributes to the effectiveness of quality monitoring, we must be prepared to find that this is not always the case. We have a possible parallel in studies tending to show that worker satisfaction is not regularly related to organizational effectiveness. But these studies have been mostly of nonprofessional workers in more highly bureaucratized settings.

Some Special Features of the Medical Profession

In addition to the awkwardness of the fit between some quality-monitoring mechanisms and the established culture of the medical profession, there are special features of the profession that create additional obstacles. I shall comment briefly on some of these under the following headings: (1) professional interdependence, (2) specialization and subspecialization, (3) unfamiliarity, and (4) federalism. Other peculiarities will be discussed in the next section, where the properties of professional work and its product are described.

Professional Interdependence. Quality monitoring, when it progresses to the point of identifying individual practitioners directly or by implication, requires that some physicians sit in judgment over others. This is something abhorrent to colleagues under any circumstances. It becomes even more difficult to do when the careers of physicians depend so much on the approval of colleagues who vouch for their competence by sending them patients and who, in many other ways, offer encouragement and support. The need for mutual support is intensified by the intrinsically uncertain and hazardous nature of clinical practice. It is generally recognized that every physician, at one time or another, is liable to be mistaken, sometimes with disastrous results. If, in such straits, one expects to be protected, consoled, and forgiven by colleagues, it is necessary that one extend the same consideration to them. It is particularly important to do so when all colleagues face the same hostile forces in the world at large, including among these dangers the litigiousness of the public and the unsympathetic scrutiny of external monitors. Thus, even though the participants in monitoring may be legally protected from reprisal, they are subject to other powerful motivators counseling caution.

Specialization and Subspecialization. Historically, specialization has been a spur to quality assessment and monitoring, beginning with the earliest initiatives under the leadership of the American College of Surgeons.[29,30] Specialists are in the happy position of benefiting personally while they also serve the public, by demonstrating that only persons with special qualifications should be permitted to provide certain kinds of care.

But specialization, especially when carried to an extreme, also results in considerable fragmentation in the patient's care, perhaps to the point where it is difficult to hold any one person responsible for the totality of what is done. This might permit each individual participant to evade the censure that the findings of monitoring would justify. The tendency in malpractice litigation to hold all caregivers individually and jointly liable is the legal response to the diffusion of responsibility.[31]

Unfamiliarity. Many formal monitoring initiatives are relatively new. Many physicians have neither learned about them nor participated in them during the course of their education and training. As a consequence, physicians have little appreciation for the social and professional imperatives that underlie the monitoring enterprise. Its methods, to the extent that they draw on epidemiological principles and statistical analysis, are also alien to most physicians. I suspect, therefore, that fundamental reform in medical education must occur before monitoring becomes fully acceptable and effective. Just as the Children of Israel were doomed to wander in the wilderness of Sinai until all who had offended the Lord had died, we may have to tarry until a new generation of physicians has matured before we can enter a Canaan where quality monitoring is a familiar, even sought-after, feature of professional life.[32]

Federalism. The state-by-state compartmentalization of the medical profession has impeded, in the past, the flow of information about physicians across state boundaries. Physicians censured in one state could move to another to set up shop again. One could suppose that state licensure has also impeded freedom of movement, perhaps limiting to some degree the harm that might attend such peregrinations. We wait to see what effect, if any, the recent consolidation of information about actions taken against physicians, and the requirements that the information be used, will have on effectiveness of quality monitoring.[33] Quality monitoring could become more effective or, paradoxically, the consequence of taking action against individual physicians could become so serious that such actions could be taken less often, or if taken, could be challenged more vigorously in the courts. But, as I have said before, a reluctance to be punitive may not be a bad thing altogether, assuming effective rehabilitative actions are taken instead.[34]

Some Features of Intrainstitutional Practice

Physicians bring to their practice within institutions the consequences of the general and special professional attributes that I have described already. The most important of these are the creation of a separate organizational structure and the continuation of private practice. Consequently, physicians continue to maintain a virtually complete corporate and economic identity only tenuously subject to control by the larger organization. I shall comment briefly on this phenomenon and on some of the forces that modify its effects.

The Organization of the Medical Staff. The presence of a separately organized medical staff in hospitals is in recognition of the profession's claim to self-governance in matters that pertain to professional practice. But since the boundary between "professional" and "nonprofessional" issues is vague, the territory that physicians can claim to control can be expanded almost at will. Consequently, there may be much in the hospital that administrators cannot, autonomously, command. Rather, it becomes necessary to establish a partnership through which competing interests are identified, differences negotiated, and a consensus established. This is particularly true of quality monitoring, a matter central to professional prerogatives. If, in this respect, the organized medical staff is at odds with the administrative apparatus, quality monitoring could languish, especially if only the administrators support it. But a well-organized medical staff can also serve as an instrument of quality monitoring, both on its own initiative and in collaboration with administrators.

Certain structural characteristics are likely to influence both the kind of monitoring carried out and its effectiveness. Perhaps the most critical structural feature is control over the granting and renewal of hospital privileges, particularly the use in such decisions of information about past clinical performance, as obtained from internal monitoring or from the outside.

Whether or not members of the medical staff sit on the governing board could also be relevant; and so could be the composition of the joint conference committee. The manner in which the members of the executive committee, the chief of staff, and the heads of departments are chosen, as well as the length of their tenure, could also be a factor. The key features to look for are the presence of opportunity for exchanges between the medical and nonmedical components of the organizational directorate, and the degree to which there is agreement on quality monitoring between the two. But the presence of individual leaders, as I described in an earlier section, could be the most important ingredient of all. The inability to command creates the opportunity to lead.

It should be recognized, however, that the opportunity to interact and to lead can also be inimical to quality monitoring. The nonphysician members of a governing board can be unduly deferential to medical expertise, being only too glad, when faced with unfamiliar issues pertinent to quality, to pass on the responsibility to a respected and persuasive leader of the medical staff—even one intent on emasculating the quality-monitoring enterprise. In such cases, the counterpoise could be one or more of the following: a competent, persuasive chief administrator; a well-informed governing board; a nonphysician leader of the governing board; and a set of external forces that put the entire institution at risk, should quality fail. In the happiest of circumstances, all these influences would act in consort to assure effective quality monitoring. If they are at odds, the effectiveness of monitoring is bound to suffer proportionately to the intensity of the internecine conflict.

Private Practice and Salaried Employment. Because most physicians who work in hospitals are in private practice, the hospital has little control over them beyond the regulation of hospital privileges. There is no orderly ladder of career advancement to which the results of quality monitoring can be linked. These weaknesses in organizational control can only potentiate the effects of collegiate interdependence, as already described.

Salaried employment is likely to alter the pattern of dependency on and control by colleagues. Salaried physicians are likely to be more dependent on the organization as a whole and more closely identified with its goals. They are, by the same token, less susceptible to reprisal should they monitor and pass judgment on colleagues. Here the role of a full-time department head is particularly important, since this position offers an opportunity not only to exercise bureaucratic controls but also to exhibit charismatic leadership. A competent, full-time pathologist, who is not constrained to euphemistic reporting, is another important figure in the hierarchy of quality monitoring. At the lower levels of the professional structure, the resident staff play an important role. Poor performance that physicians seem to ignore when they are informed of it can be corrected when the resident staff is appropriately instructed.[35]

Some External Modifiers. The effects of certain properties of the legal environment on some features of intrainstitutional practice have been described already. Another external factor, the supply of physicians, could also be relevant. Presumably, hospitals can be more stringent in admitting and advancing physicians when there are many candidates vying for hospital privileges. Responsiveness to quality control could perhaps be a factor to be considered in the choice of attending staff.

An environment in which hospitals are more ardent competitors could also encourage more effective quality control. But competition might also impose the necessity to attract patients and fill beds. In some circumstances this could lead to wooing physicians who are not noted for responsiveness to quality control but who have large, lucrative case-loads. The critical factor, I suppose, is the basis for competition, this being either cost or quality, or a balance of the two. Quality monitoring, if it were able to provide valid information that could be readily under-stood by consumers could be the prerequisite for making competition an instrument of quality enhancement. Competition and quality moni-toring could then be mutually reinforcing. They could also act at cross-purposes—unhappily a more likely event, at least insofar as technical quality is concerned. Competition would be more likely to enhance the effectiveness of information about the amenities of care—which would be desirable. But if this information were used to mask failures in techni-cal care, we could expect a substitution of the more readily appreciated amenities of care for the more subtle attributes of technical care whose effects are inapparent or delayed.

THE NATURE OF PROFESSIONAL WORK AND ITS PRODUCT

We have just seen how the organization of the medical profession, in the society at large and within institutions, may influence the effective-ness of quality monitoring. In exploring that subject, I suggested that the nature of professional work was itself a determinant of how physi-cians are organized and how they behave. In this section I shall develop that theme by amplifying my earlier comments on professional work and adding some comments on the science of technical care and the science of interpersonal care.

Professional Work

I have already suggested that the hazard and uncertainty inherent in medical practice necessitate a degree of group solidarity that individual physicians cannot afford to disrupt, considering how much they depend upon it for solace and protection. But if it is disruptive to criticize others, it is also debilitating to be too critical of oneself. Self-doubt, if carried too far, threatens the ability to act decisively, especially in a crisis. There is tension, therefore, between the self-examination that leads to professional alertness and growth, and the self-doubt that can produce at worst paralysis and at best a professional dawdling costly to everyone concerned.

Another kind of tension that quality monitoring needs to resolve is the incongruence of the general to the particular. It is the mission of clinical practice to particularize by adapting care to the special needs of each patient. Ideally, health care is a bespoken article, cut precisely to each patient's measure. Quality monitoring, by contrast, depends on criteria and standards reflecting the requirements of the average patient in any given category. The guidelines for monitoring prescribe most unequivocally the routines that apply to all. They are less able to capture the finer detail that makes each case, ultimately, distinctive. Therefore, in some cases physicians are genuinely uncomprehending of how the judgments that flow from monitoring can apply to their own individual patients. At other times, physicians understand the relevance of the judgment but seek, by appealing to the distinctiveness of each patient, an easy escape from accountability. We shall see in a subsequent section how the method of monitoring must adapt to the legitimate need to particularize, gaining as a result in its ability to persuade the genuinely skeptical and to restrain the merely evasive.

Still another attribute of clinical practice, especially in situations of some complexity, is its collaborative nature and its dependence on organizational support. Physicians, as a group, may be able to control only a part of what is done for patients; any one physician could control even less. I have mentioned already that, as a response to this fragmentation of responsibility, it has become customary to hold all participants in care, as well as the institution that harbors them, jointly liable for malpractice. Another consequence, noted by Palmer et al., is that physicians seem more able to improve their care in response to failures revealed by monitoring when the change to be made is more directly under their own control.[36]

The Science of Technical Care

Uncertainty in clinical practice is caused partly by the inability of physicians to assess precisely the almost unlimited variations in the cases they face, especially when clinical interventions have small probabilities of improving health. But much of the time uncertainty is rooted in the science and technology of medicine itself. Often there is no convincing evidence of the superiority of one course of action over another. Therefore, different schools of thought abound, and even individual physicians cling to their private predilections. Consequently, it may be difficult to formulate precise criteria of the goodness of care, or, if formulated, the criteria may be unconvincing.

Rapid advances in the science and technology of medicine can also cause a discrepancy between what the quality monitors require and what many physicians believe to be good care. Sometimes the criteria of monitoring incorporate advances as yet unheard of by many physicians. At other times the criteria are too slow to change. Under these circumstances quality monitoring must suffer in effectiveness, considering that its scientific foundations are subject to debate.

The antidote to "technological uncertainty" is a more mature science of medicine—one more supportable by convincing evidence and more capable of bringing about unquestionable improvements in health. The diffusion of knowledge should also be enhanced. As a result, quality monitoring would gain in credibility, and perhaps in effectiveness as well. And the monitoring enterprise itself could aid the diffusion of knowledge, heralding the new and ushering out the old. In the meantime, one can at least suggest that the effectiveness of monitoring is lessened when the scientific validity of its criteria is questioned, or when it advocates departures from established practice, even though that practice is contrary to the most recent knowledge. By contrast, monitoring is perhaps more effective if the practice it disapproves is already in a natural decline, a trend that quality monitoring can readily speed up.[37]

The Science of Interpersonal Care

The science of interpersonal care seems to be in even greater disarray than that of technical care. We seem unable to say how different styles of managing the interpersonal relationship compare in contributing to the success of technical care. As a further obstacle to easy answers, the style chosen could depend, in ways as yet to be elucidated, on the characteristics of the condition to be treated, as well as the attributes of both patients and physicians.

Lacking a scientific basis for preferring certain styles of management over others, we judge the interpersonal process almost entirely by its conformity to patient preferences and social norms. But social norms are not uniform across subsets of patients, different as they are in their origins and experiences. Individual patients are even more varied in their preferences. Patient preferences, furthermore, may not correspond fully to social norms, and neither may they correspond to the interpersonal style most likely to be effective.

These uncertainties hinder the formulation of criteria for managing the interpersonal process. Even if such criteria are formulated and accepted, there would be no readily available information about what goes on in the often subtle interaction between patient and physician.

There is, of course, a way around these obstacles: to question patients about their satisfaction with care. In a rather marvelous way, the degree of satisfaction is the patient's overall judgment on the quality of every facet of care, with subjective weights of importance having been attached to each. But expressions of satisfaction continue to be a little suspect, since patients often do not tell us what they really think, and when they do, they seem to adapt their expectations to their actual experiences, pardoning their physicians for ordinarily unacceptable, even reprehensible, behavior.

The hypothesis offered is that we have been handicapped in monitoring the quality of the interpersonal process by an inability to formulate, in advance, detailed criteria and standards of the optimal strategies to adopt. But perhaps, more fundamentally, we simply have not cared enough!

THE METHOD OF ASSESSING PERFORMANCE

It is reasonable to hypothesize that the effectiveness of quality monitoring would be influenced not only by the context whose characteristics have occupied us so far, but also by the attributes of the monitoring effort itself. It is to these more intimate properties that I turn my attention in this section and the two that follow, considering in turn the methods of assessing performance, the organization of the monitoring enterprise, and the methods used to change the behavior of physicians. The methods to be used to obtain organizational change, although vitally important, are not addressed in this work.

We know little about how the particular method used to assess quality influences the effectiveness of monitoring. As in the preceding parts of this text, I shall be offering hypotheses only, guided by the assumption that the preferred methods, besides being more efficient, are more effective because they produce information that is pertinent, credible, complete, and timely. Since we are limited in our ability to command, we aim to persuade; and even if we could coerce, we would perhaps prefer to rely upon the ability of persuasion subtly to command the professional self more thoroughly than any organizational imposition could.

The Definition of Quality and the Objectives of Assessment

The ability of quality monitoring to persuade could depend most fundamentally on the definition of quality that guides it. Physicians might regard some aspects of care to be unrelated to quality, or only peripheral to it. Other aspects they might consider to be outside the scope of their responsibilities or beyond their control. Information about such irrelevancies (as physicians would perceive them to be) cannot be expected to capture the professional mind or command the professional will. This does not mean that physicians are always right in what they consider to be aspects of care vital, rather than incidental, to quality. It only suggests that if monitoring is to succeed, important disagreements about the meaning of quality may need to be resolved in advance.

The link between quality and cost may be one of the subjects to be elucidated early on. One could hypothesize that physicians will not respond as readily to initiatives intended merely to cut cost, especially if they perceive that quality might be endangered. On the contrary, one might suggest that physicians will respond more readily if they are asked to alter behaviors that touch on matters, such as cost only, that do not infringe on more fundamental professional prerogatives. In other words, behaviors vital to quality, involving professional knowledge, judgment, or skill, the questioning of which would imply a failure in clinical competence, might be more zealously guarded against outside intervention.

As a third alternative, it is possible that neither of the above predictions will always come true because still other variables might influence the response. Whether monitoring is oriented to education or to punishment could be one of these mediating variables.

Approaches, Targets, and Timing

It is possible that the approach to assessment may itself influence the credibility and persuasiveness of information about the quality of care. Williamson has argued, for example, that one can expect physicians to be powerfully motivated to undertake reforms when they discover that the outcomes of the care they have given are significantly inferior to those they expected. But his own extensive testing of a method based on this principle has yielded rather discouraging results.[38] I know of no evidence that findings based on assessments of outcome are more likely to elicit behavior change than those based on assessments of the process of care, or vice versa. Presumably, much depends on the credibility of the information; and neither process nor outcome can be said regularly to yield judgments of superior credibility.[39] Still, it is what the recipients of the information themselves believe that motivates behavior change; and it is reasonable to expect that they might regard one approach to assessment to yield more credible judgments, on the average, than another.

The targets of assessment are the clinical entities whose management is being assessed. These include diagnoses (such as pneumonia), conditions (such as hematuria), surgical interventions (such as appendectomies), diagnostic procedures (such as electrocardiography), and treatments (such as the use of antibiotics). It is difficult even to speculate on whether or not the choice of target for assessment, in and of itself, influences the effectiveness of monitoring. If there is an influence, it is likely to derive from some related property, such as the accuracy and completeness of information regarding performance, the validity of the criteria by which quality is judged, the seriousness of the deficiency discovered, the relevance of physician behavior to that deficiency, and the ease with which the contributing behavior can be changed.

In their timing, assessments can be prospective, concurrent, or retrospective. Prospective assessments allow intervention to occur before care that has been planned is actually given. Concurrent assessments allow intervention while care is in progress. Retrospective assessments are meant to prevent repetition of error in the future; alas, whatever damage has already occurred cannot be recalled. It seems to follow that it is the effectiveness of the intervention (a subject to be discussed later) that sets the several timing strategies apart. One might also suggest that judgments on quality made promptly, while the events that led to them are still vivid in the physician's mind, are more likely to impress and motivate.

Particularization and Individualization

Particularization. By particularization I mean the degree to which assessments of quality have taken into account the peculiar characteristics of each case before arriving at a final judgment. I have already referred to the tendency of quality assessments to be based on what makes cases similar, and of clinical care to be almost obsessed with what makes them different. By appealing to such differences, whether legitimately or otherwise, clinicians deflect criticism, denying the need for change. The method of assessment must address this problem.

One way of doing so is to redesign explicit criteria so as to accommodate a larger number of case variants. This can be done by specifying in more detail when certain criteria apply and when they do not.[40] It can also be done by presenting the criteria as a decision tree that incorporates a variety of contingencies.[41] In most cases it is done by resorting to multistaged assessment. In the early stage, or stages, explicit criteria are used to separate cases into those that are likely to have been well managed and those that are not. All of the latter (and perhaps a sample of the former as well) are then subjected to detailed analysis. Experts are asked to judge each case based on implicit criteria or a combination of implicit and explicit criteria, using as much information about each case as can be assembled, including an interview with the managing physician if the situation warrants it. The more closely this final stage of clinical ascertainment reproduces the thought processes of actual clinical management, the more credible and persuasive its findings should be. But if this meticulous process of ascertainment is hypothesized to contribute to effectiveness, it can also be expected to contribute to cost. The design of the screening criteria to be used in the multistage approach is a critical element in determining the cost effectiveness of the procedure as a whole.[42]

Individualization. By individualization I mean the degree to which the actual perpetrators of poor quality are individually identified, a practice in contrast to only describing patterns of quality among providers as a group. The first step in individualization is perhaps the identification of particular hospitals, but I am more concerned here with the identification of individual physicians as compared to simply offering information about the medical staff of a department or of a hospital as a whole. Physicians abhor individualization, but this practice, as I shall describe in a subsequent section, could contribute to effectiveness if certain conditions are observed.

The Criteria and Standards of Quality

It would be surprising if the properties of the criteria and standards used to assess the quality of care were not related to the efficiency and effectiveness of monitoring. Perhaps the key determinant is the degree to which those to be monitored agree to be judged by the criteria and standards, having been convinced that they are valid and applicable to their particular situation.

When experts use implicit criteria to assess the quality of care, it is the stature of the assessors, based on personal qualifications and institutional affiliations, that determines credibility. Credibility can also be strengthened when more than one expert independently arrive at similar judgments, and when they undertake to explain the reasons for their judgments in a manner convincing to their audience.

When explicit criteria are formulated ahead of time by a panel of experts, the composition of the panel becomes critical with respect to both the qualifications of each member and the degree to which the composition of the panel reflects the relevant range of institutional affiliations and professional viewpoints.[43] Of course, when the criteria are made explicit, either from the very start or subsequent to an expert judgment, the criteria themselves can be assessed on their own merits, independently of their originators. In that case, the validity of the criteria can be judged most rigorously by their conformity to scientifically verified knowledge. When, as is often the case, our science is inadequate, validity is assessed, less convincingly, by the degree to which the criteria are supported by professional consensus.

The acceptability of the criteria is only partly based on judgments of their validity in a general sense. Another consideration is the applicability of the criteria to particular forms of practice in particular situations. Criteria formulated by experts who practice in academic settings may be considered inapplicable even to corresponding specialists who practice in other settings, and even more so to family physicians who deal with a different clientele under very different circumstances.[44] This is why the identity of the physicians responsible for the criteria and standards, either implicitly or explicitly, could be so important.

Criteria and standards are likely to be more acceptable if they are formulated by those who are to be judged by them. Partly, this may be regarded to confer greater relevance to the particular situation in which the criteria and standards are to be used. Partly, the experience of participation may itself create an identification with the criteria, motivating compliance. But none of this is certain. It is possible that a greater familiarity with the formulation of criteria breeds a little contempt, perhaps because one has seen how tenuous the evidence that supports some of them is, or perhaps out of a feeling that one who has participated in making a criterion has a certain license also to unmake. Similarly, it is possible that criteria formulated by external professional bodies of recognized competence and authority will be more likely to be accepted by everyone in a given setting than criteria formulated by colleagues with whom one might feel freer to disagree. Perhaps externally formulated criteria, somewhat modified for internal use, combine optimally the twin requirements of being authoritative and being acceptable—and that only in circumstances as yet not possible to specify. Clearly, we have much to learn.

With slightly more confidence one could hypothesize that to be most effective, criteria and standards would have to be pitched to a level of stringency not so high that almost everyone fails or so low that almost everyone passes. Either extreme would be more likely to discredit the criteria and the judgments they engender. Rather, the most effective criteria and standards could be those that begin by identifying the grosser deficiencies but are progressively made more demanding as the level of quality improves. Needless to say, many considerations, including the balance between the costs and benefits of care, enter the specification of the desired level of quality. But this is not the place to go into these.

If the cost of monitoring is an issue, as it always is, the efficiency of the screening criteria would also influence one's evaluation of quality monitoring.

Information about Care

The Achilles' heel of quality assessment is the questionable nature of the information about the process of care and its outcomes. To obtain information by direct observation, even if allowed, is costly; it is also said to alter the behavior being observed. Medical records, even in hospitals, are often incomplete, and the data recorded are not always fully accurate. There is little there about the interpersonal process, nor can one hope to find much information about the patient's condition subsequent to discharge.

The ability of quality monitoring to convince has been seriously weakened by these deficiencies. One hears, quite often, the accusation that the quality of the record, rather than the quality of the care itself, is being assessed. In the face of such skepticism, which is often merited, one should not be surprised when judgments on quality are disregarded. One can hypothesize, therefore, that the effectiveness of monitoring would be enhanced by improvements in recording, by instituting more direct status monitoring of patients, and by taking steps to assemble additional information when the quality of care is subjected to the final "clinical ascertainment" I have already described.

We should not expect that judgments suspected of being spurious will command respect or elicit self-motivated behavior change.

ORGANIZATION OF THE MONITORING ENTERPRISE

The intraorganizational apparatus to which the quality of monitoring role is entrusted has to perform a complex task vital to the success, even survival, of the organization. To perform it requires expertise and authority, as well as subtlety and tact. It is quite likely, therefore, that the manner in which the quality-monitoring function is staffed and organized will influence powerfully how effective monitoring will be.[45]

In this section I shall deal with some structural features of the intrainstitutional monitoring enterprise under the following headings: (1) organizational leadership and authority, (2) intraorganizational linkages, (3) internal structure of the monitoring function, and (4) extraorganizational linkages.

Organizational Leadership and Authority

I shall assume that the ability of the monitoring enterprise to act effectively will depend on the leadership it can directly or indirectly call upon, the expertise and resources at its command, its organizational location, and its linkages to the centers in the organization where policy is formulated and key decisions are made. Quite obviously, this is a set of interrelated factors, none of which can be considered separately from the others. Perhaps one way to proceed is to imagine the directorate of an organization in the act of considering how a quality monitoring unit is to be set up.

As I described in an earlier section, a key decision is whether the quality monitoring unit is to be merely the organization's barely sufficient response to external requirements or, on the contrary, the custodian of a function regarded as vital to the organization's social mission. If the former, the function is likely to be stripped to a minimum and assigned to a corps of lowly operatives capable of performing preassigned routines, perhaps supervised, part-time, by one or more junior clinicians who were unsuccessful in eluding the burden. One wonders how likely this form of organization is to generate information that commands attention. If, on the contrary, an organization's directorate are responding to a deeply felt need, the importance they accord the monitoring function would be reflected in whom they recruit to direct it and the resources, human and material, they assign the director. The expertise of the director and the director's senior associates would be a key issue.

This is not the place to spell out in any detail how expertise might be defined in an analysis of the factors that influence the effectiveness of monitoring. I could suggest, however, that one would look for clinical competence sufficiently advanced to command the respect of the clinicians to be monitored, specific knowledge of health care monitoring, knowledge of health care organization, and grasp of a body of methods that are essentially epidemiological in nature.

The organizational position accorded the director of the monitoring function would presumably correspond to the director's expertise. It would also signal the importance accorded that function by the organization's directorate—a signal the rank and file could not fail to notice. But the bureaucratic label of the director's post is not simply symbolic. With it goes a corresponding degree of access to the centers of authority and power in an organization.

The ability to lead depends partly on expertise and partly on organizational position, but there is more. The director may possess the additional, difficult-to-define attributes of leadership. Even if so, the degree to which other recognized leaders in an organization support, participate in, and are identified with the monitoring enterprise would be a factor to look for in any analysis of effectiveness.

Having identified the nature of expertise, organizational position, and leadership, it would be reasonable, next, to look for the structural links between the monitoring function and other related functions in the organization.

Intraorganizational Linkages

Perhaps the most important of these links, as I have already suggested, is the one between the monitoring system and the structure of incentives that is designed to direct and motivate the behavior of professional personnel. In ordinary circumstances the major mechanism by which hospitals control the behavior of physicians is through selective recruitment and the specification of hospital privileges. When, less frequently, physicians occupy salaried posts, the organization can also control progression up a ladder of increasing responsibility and rewards. Whether the one or the other situation prevails, the effectiveness of monitoring can be expected to depend on the degree to which its findings determine the intraorganizational careers of the medical staff, and of other professionals as well. The more general principle may be that effectiveness depends on the linkage to clearly visible, meaningful administrative action. If it has no such consequences, monitoring is quickly recognized to be impotent and futile.

Another linkage clearly related to behavior change, as I shall describe in the next section, is that to the apparatus of continuing education in an institution. One could also suggest that quality monitoring and risk management are two functions that, if structurally linked, could lead to greater effectiveness in reducing risks that are relevant to the quality of professional care. Because the functioning of equipment and the reliability, sterility, and purity of the materials used in providing care are relevant to success in the management of patients, one could argue that these functions also need to be related in some way to the monitoring enterprise. In fact, there is precious little in the operations of an institution that does not touch on quality in at least one of its aspects: technical care, the interpersonal exchange, or the amenities. It is unreasonable, of course, to expect a separate coordination mechanism for every possible interaction. In addition to establishing the key structural link between the quality-monitoring function and management at a very high level in the organization, one would look to the informal network of relationships that facilitates communication with other units in the organization, as the occasion arises.

Internal Structure of the Monitoring Function

The quality-monitoring function is, in itself, sufficiently complex to require careful structuring. Before a new, more comprehensive monitoring activity begins, a hospital is bound to have had some of the more traditional activities that are, in fact, forms of quality assurance through monitoring. Examples are tissue review, mortality review, infection control, and drug-use review. The monitoring of physician performance itself could be institution-wide or departmentalized. Other professional groups in an institution are very likely to conduct quality monitoring on their own. Then, there are other quality-monitoring activities in units that support patient care. There are, for example, activities pertaining to the clinical laboratory, pathology, radiology, biologicals and pharmaceuticals, equipment and supplies, and so on. How all these activities are to be coordinated or unified is an important issue in designing the overall monitoring enterprise. One could hypothesize that the degree of coordination achieved will influence the effectiveness of monitoring, but I have no opinion to offer about the relative contribution to effectiveness of alternative ways of structuring and coordinating the monitoring effort. This is a subject for further study.

Recently, two rather distinct approaches to monitoring have been recognized as starkly contrasting types.[46] In the first, responsibility for quality is concentrated in the upper reaches of the professional-managerial hierarchy. Criteria and standards are centrally determined. The purpose is to achieve adherence to the criteria. The method is identification of those who fail to comply, followed by some action, often punitive. In the second type of monitoring, responsibility for quality is to a great degree dispersed, much of it being vested in persons (professional and other) who are closest to where care is actually provided. The method used is to identify deficiencies in quality, to analyze the details of the process that accounts for the deficiency, and to redesign the process so the occasion for error is at least reduced and perhaps eliminated. The purpose is not to enforce conformance to criteria and standards but to achieve continuing improvement in quality through self-evaluating— and self-motivating—participation.

As yet we have not agreed on what to call these two contrasting types. I think it is both incorrect and offensive to refer to the first as the medical model and to the second as the industrial model, although I can appreciate that in some circumstances it would be politic or expedient to do so. Perhaps we could call the first model "managerial" and the second "participatory," but these words carry connotations of approval or disapproval, depending on who uses them. "Centrifugal" and "centripetal" seem to be more neutral, but they are perhaps overly mechanistic terms.

The problem of terminology, of course, is the least of our worries. First we need to consider whether, in the actual world of phenomena, there is indeed such a sharp division of types distinguishable by two totally separable clusters of attributes, or whether the two types are only intellectual constructs or idealized forms. The truth of the matter is perhaps somewhere in between; pure examples of the two types can actually be found, but most quality monitoring seems to combine features of both.

A second consideration is whether or not one must choose one or the other of the two forms, or whether it is possible, quite deliberately, to design a system that has features of both. I tend to favor the latter approach, believing that it would result in more effective monitoring under most circumstances. Yet, we could find that one or the other of the two pure types is more effective in general. We might also find that neither is clearly superior to the other; circumstances as yet undefined might determine which of the two types is likely to be more effective. These speculations are paradigmatic of the uncertainty under which we now must act as we attempt to monitor the quality of care.

Extraorganizational Linkages

The uncertainties that beset the design of internal monitoring systems extend to the ways in which such systems ought to relate to the activities of external monitors, so as to minimize effort and maximize effectiveness. It is generally believed that some degree of external instigation and oversight is necessary to motivate the institution and conduct of internal monitoring. What is not clear is precisely how external and internal monitoring are to be balanced so as to produce a mutually beneficial symbiosis rather than a mutually frustrating discord.

It seems to me that the foundation for effective collaboration is prior agreement on the purposes and methods of quality assurance through monitoring, based on as complete a mutuality of interests as it is possible to establish. If external monitoring is guided by a concept of quality alien to the providers of care, if its methods grate on professional sensibilities, or if its purposes are at variance with the best interests of the providers, an adversarial relationship is likely to develop. The internal monitors might then concentrate their energies on duping their external counterparts rather than on truly safeguarding the quality of care.

If the basic objectives, interests, and methods of the two parties are congruent, it should be possible to design procedures that enable the providers to generate information that serves, at the same time, their own internal monitoring requirements and the requirements of the external monitors. In this way, both efficiency and effectiveness would be enhanced.

I see in the relationship between external and internal monitoring a reenactment, on a larger scale, of the two types of internal monitoring I have already described: the managerial versus the participatory, or the centrally controlled versus the peripherally activated. Since the dissolution of the PSROs, we have moved toward greater external specification of what is to be monitored, in what ways, to achieve what goals. Will this be more effective? Or, even if effective in the short term, might we find, in retrospect, that it has imposed on the providers of care an inordinately prolonged and resentful adolescence, when the goal should have been a more mature self-directiveness in quality monitoring?

No doubt I betray my prejudices in posing the question thus. The more neutral statement is to say that the structuring of the relationship between internal and external monitoring is likely to influence effectiveness, and to suggest the relevance of congruence in objectives and interests, of adaptation to professional norms, and of the balance of centralization and delegation. I have no detailed typology of internal-external linkages to offer as a guide to further analysis. I do have, however, a rather elementary classification of methods for obtaining behavioral change, the subject next in line to be considered.

METHODS OF OBTAINING BEHAVIORAL CHANGE

The ultimate purpose of quality monitoring, as defined here, is to change the behaviors of providers (and through them, the behaviors of clients as well) in ways that safeguard and enhance the quality of care. There are two ways in which behaviors can be made to change: one is by altering organizations and their procedures; the other is by acting more directly on the practitioners themselves. The relative effectiveness of methods for obtaining organizational change will not be discussed in this exposition. I shall only deal with what is known or surmised about the effectiveness of some methods of modifying the behavior of practitioners. In doing so, I shall draw heavily on a review and assessment of the pertinent literature (especially that on educational methods) by John Eisenberg.[47] But since I shall rather indiscriminately mingle my own thinking with his, I ought to exonerate him in advance of all responsibility for the distortions I may introduce.

The methods I shall mention and discuss briefly are the following: (1) direct intervention, (2) reminders, (3) feedback, (4) education and training, (5) incentives and disincentives, (6) organizational adaptations, and (7) using consumers to influence practitioners.

Direct Intervention

There are forms of anticipatory or concurrent monitoring that offer opportunities to directly intervene in the process of care so as to halt or redirect it, using either financial or administrative means. Second surgical opinion programs are an example; certification and recertification of hospital admissions and stays is another.

Voluntary second opinion programs appear to be ineffective because relatively few patients take advantage of them. By contrast, mandatory programs are reported to be effective in reducing the incidence of elective surgery—more so for some conditions than others. They do this partly by persuading patients not to submit to surgery when the second opinion does not confirm the need for it. Additionally, these programs are said to have an indirect, "sentinel" effect, meaning that physicians who expect their recommendations for surgery to be reviewed are less prone to recommend it in the first place. At least one study has reported that the financial gains from such programs more than offset their cost.[48,49]

By contrast to the rather favorable experience with second surgical opinion programs, the national program for certifying hospital admissions and stays, administered by local PSROs (often with delegation to the hospitals themselves), was judged to have failed overall.[50] I have already commented on the possible interpretations of this experience. One can reasonably conclude that the characteristics of the setting in which a method is used are as important as the characteristics of the method itself, if not more so.

Reminders

It is believed that a considerable number of deficiencies in clinical performance result from inattention induced by the pressure of work and the complexity of the task. When clinical records are computerized, it is possible to program the computer to deliver messages alerting physicians of events they should have noted and dealt with. Examples include the concurrent use of drugs that either potentiate or counteract each other, the failure to monitor drug effects, the failure to order needed laboratory tests or to act upon abnormal test results, and the failure to initiate preventive measures when indicated. The procedures established require that clinicians enter a response, either accepting or rejecting the suggestions in the computer's message. Persistent nonresponse to repeated messages is calculated to trigger supervisory action.

Several studies have reported that computer reminders, often generated according to instructions that the medical staff itself has approved, are well received. They are also effective in bringing about appropriate actions, but only when the physician agrees with the recommendations offered. Reminders seem not to change the established opinions of physicians; rather, they appear to elicit actions physicians are already predisposed to take.[51] Similar reminders that do not depend on the use of computers could be as effective. It is possible, however, that the immediacy, impersonality, and relative privacy of the computer's message would give it an edge. In addition to verifying these speculations, an analysis of the effectiveness of reminders would look, perhaps, into how the criteria that generate the reminders were formulated, the nature of the action suggested, the manner in which the actions suggested pertain to the incentives that govern physician behavior in any given setting, and the nature of follow-up action expected when physicians ignore the suggestions carried by the reminders.

Feedback

In pure form, feedback is merely the conveying of information about the quality of care to those who have provided that care. In a broader application, it would also include providing such information to those who have received care or might receive it in the future. In this section I shall address only the former, returning to the question of informing clients in the final section of this text.

Feedback, when used in pure form, implies that physicians know what good care is, and that any deficiencies that may have been noted are the result of inattention or carelessness. It is, of course, difficult to divorce information on performance from the criteria and standards that produced the judgment on performance. To the extent that these are conveyed, either directly or by implication, feedback may be said to have an educational function as well. Furthermore, the legitimacy and acceptability of the criteria and standards are, no doubt, important determinants of the effectiveness of feedback.

Other attributes thought to influence effectiveness are (1) whether feedback involves a comparison to abstract criteria and standards only, or also to the actual performance of colleagues within an institution or in other institutions; (2) whether the feedback describes group performance without singling out individuals, or whether individuals are also told how they have performed compared to others; (3) whether the feedback is conveyed impersonally (for example, by a mailed tabulation) or personally, in a face-to-face meeting; and (4) whether or not the person conveying the information is a respected colleague with greater experience as well as higher rank. According to Eisenberg, feedback is more effective when it is provided face-to-face, by a respected colleague, based on comparison with peers.

Education and Training

Education is called for when insufficient knowledge or skill is at least in part the reason for deficient care. How often ignorance or ineptitude is a cause, and to what degree, is difficult to say. No doubt they are important, but their contribution to poor care can be expected to vary considerably from setting to setting.

Good education and training are regarded by the health care professions to be the foundation for good practice. Beyond a lengthy and rigorous initial experience, a lifetime characterized by continuous learning is the ideal. Professionals hold educational interventions to be the preferred method for obtaining behavioral change, especially if the method does not single out individuals for invidious attention.

I shall not attempt the Herculean task of assessing the effectiveness of initial or subsequent education in assuring the quality of care. Nor am I able to say whether or not the conveying of knowledge by education is more or less effective than the acquiring of manual or other skills through training. Eisenberg, after a review of the literature, reports that some studies have shown continuing education to be effective, others have shown it to be ineffective, while many others are inconclusive because of deficiencies in their methods or ambiguities in their findings.[52]

Guided by a review of the literature, and the principles of adult education, Eisenberg surmises that in order to be most successful in modifying the behavior of physicians the following conditions should hold: (1) a practitioner should have accepted (presumably on the basis of valid evidence) that he or she has a need to learn; (2) the educational content should be specific to the need already identified; (3) education should be conducted face-to-face; (4) if possible, it should be conducted one-to-one; and (5) it should be conducted by an "influential"—a person the practitioner trusts and respects. Presumably, many educational efforts fail because one or more of these conditions have not been met.

The conditions detailed above suggest the importance of establishing a clearly defined link between quality monitoring and continuing education, as typified by the "bicycle" model proposed many years ago by Brown and Uhl, and repeatedly advanced since.[53] The relative effectiveness of alternative ways of linking monitoring to education, and of conducting the educational effort itself, should be high on the agenda of research on the effectiveness of quality assurance through monitoring.

Incentives and Disincentives

Feedback and education are meant to appeal to the internalized values and to mobilize the personal resources of practitioners. There are likely to be, as I suggested in an earlier section, factors in the environment that potentiate or debilitate these efforts. Much depends on the implicit expectations and informal understandings by which a company of colleagues order their affairs. But a great deal may also depend, as I have emphasized already, on the provisions of a more formalized system of rewards and penalties. I am convinced that the relative impotence of quality monitoring to directly modify practitioner behavior is attributable to the absence of a clearly defined, consistently operative link between the results of monitoring and the career prospects of practitioners. The formal system of incentives and disincentives deserves particular attention in any analysis of effectiveness.

Incentives are rewards and disincentives are penalties; but the two can be confused because not receiving a reward when a system of rewards has been instituted can be construed as a disincentive, and not being penalized when a system of penalties has been established can be interpreted as an incentive. Yet, a system based on recognizing and rewarding merit could be quite different from a system based on ferreting out and punishing error. It is very likely to be different in acceptability to professionals, and perhaps also different in effectiveness. One might also hypothesize that a system having features of both approaches could be the most effective.

Rewards and penalties might also be distinguishable by whether they are professional, financial, or both, and by whether they are generalized or particularized. For example, a promotion connotes both professional and financial rewards that are not necessarily related to any particular meritorious action; rather, a general pattern of laudable behavior is being recognized. By contrast, withholding payment for an unapproved procedure is a financial penalty particularized to a specific misdeed. A proposal that physicians be awarded part of the savings that accrue from their maintaining a lower-than-average length of hospital stay would be an example of a positive financial reward related to a pattern of behavior, rather than a specific action.

I can no more than suggest that the distinctions I have proposed might in some way be related to effectiveness. It is a little more likely that the magnitude of the rewards or penalties would be. If penalties are to be used, another factor that might influence their acceptability, as well as the readiness to use them, is having a set of penalties graded by severity, so that the penalty can be matched to the seriousness of the offense.[54] Needless to say, the acceptability of penalties also depends on the credibility and legitimacy of the judgments that lead to them, and on the presence of procedural and legal safeguards against arbitrary action. But perhaps the most important prerequisite for effectiveness is clear evidence that penalties are used fairly and consistently, and that when the occasion demands it, they will be quite severe. Besides their more direct effects, such actions would serve notice that the quality-monitoring enterprise is more than a "paper tiger" that can be safely ignored. I find support for this interpretation in a nationwide study by Gertman et al. showing that hospitals that were able to shorten stays by Medicare patients were distinguished from those that were not by having imposed at least one termination of health insurance benefits upon admission during the period studied.[55]

After reviewing the pertinent literature, Eisenberg concluded that penalties do modify physician behaviors, but that they are deeply resented and may have unexpected or unwanted consequences—a "backlash," as he calls it. There is no doubt that a backlash would create political and administrative problems, but it is not clear what its effect on the quality of care might be.[56]

Some Organizational Adaptations

Though the emphasis in this section is on the more direct ways in which physician performance can be influenced, there are a few organizational adaptations so closely related to behavior that they might be included here. I shall describe these briefly under the following headings: (1) facilitation, (2) routinization, and (3) bypassing.

Facilitation. Under this title I would include actions taken by the organization to reduce resistance to modifying behavior by releasing time and providing equipment and other support. The introduction of computer-aided management might be another, more sophisticated, facilitating approach. The general idea is that the willingness to modify one's behavior is more easily translated to effective action when the effort necessary to do so is reduced through organizational adaptations. By contrast, obstacles to action can frustrate the best of intentions. Therefore, a study of aids and obstacles to behavioral change would be a reasonable adjunct to studies of the effectiveness of direct efforts to modify behavior.

Routinization and Guidance. The institution of routines that channel or direct behavior, or constrain it, is another method for potentiating the willingness to comply. Checklists for history taking, physical examination, or preventive interventions are one example.[57] The use of algorithms and protocols is another example of directiveness that has been reported to be effective, alone or in combination with feedback and education.[58] But not all activities are subject to routinization, nor are all practitioners equally amenable to direction. The proper role of routinization and guidance is a subject to be explored.

Bypassing. Strictly speaking, bypassing is not a method that potentiates modification of individual behavior. Rather, it is a stratagem resorted to when it is concluded that changing physician behavior is too costly of time and effort. It is easier to "bypass" the seeming intransigence of some physicians by assigning the task to others (for example, to nurses or the resident staff). A particularly striking example is the one reported by Williamson et al.[59] In this study, physicians were found to be refractory to several educational interventions meant to have them note and act upon abnormal laboratory findings. Only when house staff were subsequently employed was it possible to obtain a reasonable level of follow-up.

Using Consumers to Influence Practitioners

I believe not enough attention has been given to the ability of clients to influence physician behavior by telling them what problems they have experienced in receiving care and what improvements they would like to see. To make such exchanges more effective, it is important for physicians to accept responsibility for the care of an enrolled population, as in a health maintenance organization (HMO), and to meet not patients, who are often too vulnerable to be candid, but healthy plan members, who are not so inhibited. It might even matter whether the meeting is held in a medical facility (the doctor's domain) or in another place where clients might feel more at home.

These speculations, stemming from a conversation with the late George Rosen many years ago, lead me to the next and concluding section of this text. There, the possible role of consumers in quality assurance through monitoring will be somewhat more amply discussed.[60]

THE ROLE OF CONSUMERS

No discussion of quality assurance through monitoring can be complete without some recognition of the actual and potential role of consumers. To do so has become customary; it is expected. It demonstrates that one has the right attitudes, the approved values. Is it ever anything more? It should be, for consumers as individuals (and even more so as organized groups) have the power radically to alter the health care system, if only they could be mobilized and empowered. Theirs is the power either to heal or to hurt. That is why it is so important that consumers be invited to participate responsibly in quality monitoring.

I shall classify the roles consumers can and should play in quality assurance through monitoring according to their roles as (1) contributors, (2) targets, and (3) users.

Consumers as Contributors to Quality Monitoring

Consumers can contribute to quality monitoring in at least three ways: as standard setters, as evaluators, and as informants.

Consumers as Standard Setters. I have devoted much attention here to the definition of quality that, from the very beginning, must set the monitoring enterprise in motion and determine the forms it takes. At this fundamental level, consumers are participators in the definition of quality itself. Insofar as the attributes of the interpersonal process and the amenities are concerned, consumers should be nearly sovereign, subject only to dominant social values. Informed consumers should also participate as equals in specifying the health outcomes to be pursued by technical care, and the magnitude of the costs that it is reasonable to incur in doing so. It is no longer permissible for providers unilaterally to define the quality of care, either in general or in specific instances. If this principle is accepted, one has to consider by what methods consumers might bring to bear on the quality-monitoring effort their views of what quality should mean, and one must also study the effectiveness of these methods.

It is said that the governing board of an institution, since it is made up mostly of nonphysicians, is able to represent the consumer's perspective. More effective representation might result if one or more members of the board were to participate more actively in the monitoring enterprise itself. Administrators, especially if alert to marketing, could also play this part. But it could be argued, as well, that members of the governing board are hardly representative, in social origin or status, of an institution's customers. It is also likely that, after a prolonged association with health care professionals, members of the governing board, as well as administrators, drift into closer identification with clinicians than with consumers. More direct representation of the rank and file of consumers, on a rotating basis, could be a more effective mechanism. Devising and testing alternative methods of incorporating consumers into quality-monitoring activities is, obviously, a matter of high priority among studies of effectiveness. It is also important to find out more about how consumers define quality and what they expect of the physicians and institutions that serve them.[61]

Consumers as Evaluators. When consumers say that they are either satisfied or dissatisfied with the care they have received, they are, in effect, passing a judgment on the quality of care. Precisely what is being judged and with what degree of validity is less certain.[62,63] It is likely that consumers' judgments are heavily influenced by the nature of their relationships with practitioners and, to a lesser degree, by the amenities of care. I have already said that in these matters the consumer is indeed the expert; therefore, the consumer's judgment stands, unless there is compelling reason to question it.

The opinions of consumers about the process of technical care are more likely to be faulty. Their opinions about the outcomes of care should be more trustworthy, but consumers are probably more able to assess immediate effects on well-being and function than changes in physiological status that only have future implications. And their judgments on both immediate and remote effects are probably distorted by faulty expectations. In some cases these expectations could be unrealistically high; in others they might be unjustifiably low.

All these uncertainties notwithstanding, canvasing consumer opinion is an indispensable method of quality monitoring, especially if we wish to obtain information about the acceptability of the patient-practitioner interaction and the amenities of care. What is done with the information obtained, and how effectively, is something about which little seems to be known.

Consumers as Informants. In addition to passing judgments on the quality of care, consumers could be sources of information about what they experienced in the process of seeking and receiving care, and what the consequences to their health and well-being have been. This is not always objective information, but it could have much validity. Collecting and using such information systematically could add to the comprehensiveness of quality monitoring and contribute to its effectiveness in altering some aspects of clinician behavior. In any event, this is a subject worthy of study.

Consumers as Targets of Monitoring

Consumers can become targets of monitoring in two partly overlapping ways: as coproducers of care and as subjects or vehicles of control.

Consumers as Coproducers of Care. No one would question that the success of health care depends, in large measure, on the consumer's intelligent participation in that care. More is involved than the rather passive "compliance" with the physician's orders, as we used to say. The more accurate model is of a partnership in which patient and practitioner are coproducers of care.

This formulation is relevant to monitoring in at least two ways. First, because the manner of managing the personal interaction influences the patient's effective participation in care and the improvements in health that follow, these latter can be used as indicators of the quality of the former.[64,65] Second, the purpose of quality monitoring could be to assess not only what the practitioners do but also what the patients experience, including behaviors and consequences that practitioners can influence as well as those they cannot. If this is the objective of monitoring, it becomes necessary to consider what can be done to change not only practitioner behavior but patient behavior as well, and to study the effectiveness of measures meant to modify patient behavior. Perhaps many of the methods used to modify practitioner behavior would have a counterpart when the object is to alter the behavior of consumers.

Consumers as Subjects or Vehicles of Control. When it is difficult to control physicians directly, we have often resorted to controlling them indirectly through their patients—as a consequence restraining the patients as well.[66] I have already cited second surgical opinion programs and certification of hospital stays as examples. In these instances the consumer is the more direct target of control and the person on whom the sanctions, if any, more heavily fall. Yet, through the patient, the physician is also encompassed.

A more comprehensive discussion of direct and indirect controls on consumer behavior would take us too far afield.

Consumers as Users of Monitoring Information

Consumers could perhaps influence the effectiveness of quality monitoring most directly if they were informed of its confirmed findings. They could do so more immediately as regulators of the quality care. In time, they could function as better informed agents of political and social change.

Consumers regulate the quality of care mainly by choosing what care to seek, expect, and accept, and from whom. To do so intelligently and with good effect, they would need to know what constitutes quality and where it is to be found, especially insofar as technical care is concerned, since this is the aspect of care about which consumers know least. To choose prudently, consumers would also need to know not only what the prices are, but what the total cost of care is going to be. To speak of cost now would be a digression, so I shall confine my remarks to information about quality, as long as it is understood that this is only part of what needs to be known.

It seems to me that the effectiveness of information about the quality of care would depend on a large number of factors in an extremely complex configuration—a configuration that would reproduce the complexity of the health care system itself. As a summary, we might classify these factors under three headings: (1) the nature of the information itself, (2) the characteristics of the consumers who are to use the information, and (3) the properties of the system in which the consumers are to act, if possible according to the information. I can no more than touch lightly on each of these subjects.

I imagine that for information about quality to be effective, it needs to be available at the time when decisions on health care are being made, in a manner relevant to these decisions. It should be easy to understand and should emanate from a source perceived as trustworthy. Furthermore, if its effect on behavior is to be socially useful, the information needs to be true.

It seems to me that the information about hospital mortality that has been recently disseminated in our news media fails several of these tests. I believe the information to be useful as a starting point for further investigation of quality, but I do not see how the average consumer is to use it as a guide to action, even assuming that a clear message has emerged from the charges and countercharges the information has engendered. Still, it would be useful to find out by surveying consumers and providers what impact this information has had, if any.

In my opinion, we simply do not have at present the kind of

detailed information about quality that the average consumer could use in making rather specific choices about health care. This does not mean that an informed choice of providers will not raise the probability of receiving better care. It does mean that the information generated by quality-monitoring activities is neither available to, nor usable by, the general public.[67]

Large-scale purchasers of health care services (on behalf of government agencies, employers, employees, or other consumer organizations) are in a much better position to ask for more detailed information generated by quality monitoring, and to use that information, first to choose providers, and subsequently to regulate their behavior. It follows that the degree to which care is purchased collectively, the values that guide the purchasers, and the methods they use would be major determinants of how effective information generated by quality monitoring is going to be in enhancing the quality of care.

But it is not enough to have purchasers ready to act collectively in pursuit of quality. The system that provides care should be susceptible to consumer initiatives. In one way or another, the key properties of the system pertain to choice. It is important, of course, that consumers have the opportunity to choose. But the necessary counterpart to this is the presence of alternative sources of care that respond to choice by adjusting the quality of the services they offer, or their price, or both.[68] In the market for health care services, consumers sometimes may not be empowered to choose (as in some Medicaid programs, for example), or there may not be enough alternatives to choose from (as in some rural areas, for example, and for some special services in other areas as well), or, if there are alternatives, they may all be about equally suspect (as in some inner-city areas, for example). But, paradoxically, a plethora of possible choices might also be disabling. It has been proposed by several students of the subject that it would be easier to regulate both quality and cost through choice if more care were organized (for example, in hospital-based, prepaid group practices).

As we contemplate this seemingly newfound insight, we ought to pay tribute to those pioneers who many years ago reached the same conclusion.[69] But more importantly, we are reminded of how inseparable the monitoring of quality and the effectiveness of monitoring are from the structure and workings of the health care system and, indeed, from the way in which our society as a whole is organized and conducts its affairs.

In this larger context, informed consumers, through organized political action, can make the kinds of changes in the health care system that will make it more amenable to quality monitoring and more responsive to its findings. Toward this happy end, we would all, no doubt, be eager to contribute.

SUMMARY AND CONCLUSIONS

This work is not an assessment of how effective or ineffective the quality assurance enterprise has been. It is, rather, a search for factors that, based on some general principles, can be expected to enhance or reduce effectiveness. Its findings could be useful in interpreting the empirical data already at hand, in formulating hypotheses for future research, and, while we await more perfect knowledge, in guiding policy formulation and suggesting how quality assurance mechanisms might be designed.

In this exploration, both quality and quality assurance have been defined rather narrowly. Quality is judged by the ability of care to achieve the greatest improvements in health currently possible in ways acceptable to patients and conforming to social norms. Quality assurance is taken to mean a formally organized activity whose function is to obtain information about performance in pursuit of quality, to interpret that information, to pass on the findings to those responsible for taking appropriate action, and, if action is taken, to verify its effects. Effectiveness is judged, most immediately, by the ability to alter the behavior of health care practitioners in ways expected to safeguard and enhance quality, irrespective of whether behavior modification is accomplished directly (e.g., by education) or indirectly, by changing the settings and circumstances of the practitioner's work.

In searching for the factors that influence effectiveness, one has a choice of proceeding from the most general to the more particular or of doing the reverse. The former strategy was chosen for this discussion, the progression of subjects being as follows: (1) the larger environment, (2) the intraorganizational environment, (3) the medical profession, (4) the nature of professional work and product, (5) the methods of assessing performance, (6) the organization of the monitoring enterprise, (7) the methods of obtaining changes in practitioner behavior, and (8) the role of consumers.

Clearly, these subdivisions are neither mutually exclusive nor regularly progressive from the more general to the more particular. For example, forces at play in the larger environment pervade the intraorganizational environment as well; the attributes of the medical professions, besides characterizing both environments, large and small, are partly internalized to become attributes of the practitioners themselves; and consumers play a role, or could do so, at all levels. What emerges from the analysis, in fact, is an appreciation of the remarkable interdependence of the factors assigned to each level. It seems as if almost nothing can be viewed in isolation. Everything appears to depend for its existence, for the forms it takes, and for its effects, on everything else in this balanced, reverberating system. If there are some principles that emerge from this exploration, this would surely be the first: that the introduction of formal quality monitoring is a disturbance in the health care system, conditioned by the characteristics of that system and causing obvious or subtle readjustments in it. This is the principle of interdependency.

Quality assurance through formalized monitoring of care, followed by appropriate readjustments, is dependent, by its very nature, on the prior presence of formal organization in the health care system. It is in formal organizations that either finance or deliver care, or do both, that one encounters the necessity to monitor, the means for monitoring, and the capacity to institute change in response to what monitoring reveals. Organizational dependency is a second principle that emerges in this exploration. The principle reveals itself in the fragmented nature of the quality-monitoring effort, much of it being concentrated in hospitals, while other sectors that might need it even more have received much less attention. Within institutions, the principle explains the importance accorded to the organizational locus of the quality assurance enterprise, to the organizational linkages of its director, and to the resources at the director's command. But there is a consequence even more important than these.

The more fundamental observation is that our incomplete and dispersed mode of organization, coupled with the established values that shape our public life, are unreceptive to centralized, direct control. We must govern, if at all, by consent. But this is consent beyond passive acquiescence. Rather, a coalescence of views and interests is envisaged—a working alliance toward a common purpose. This is required, in particular, of the two centers of power and influence in our institutions: the administrative apparatus and the medical staff. In this more actively collaborative form, consensuality can be offered as the third principle that this exploration has highlighted. Much of what follows is a search for the sources of this consensuality.

Formal quality monitoring can be regarded as an innovation to be introduced in rather alien territory. True, the monitoring of clinical practice is not totally new, nor are the intended receivers completely unprepared. The medical profession has had an illustrious history of concern for quality and action to promote it. But the very presence of these antecedents suggests the importance of fit between the new and the traditional, especially because the rationale and methods of some forms of monitoring are largely unfamiliar, and their sponsorship by agencies external to the profession rather threatening. Therefore, new monitoring initiatives, as regards their objectives and methods, face the challenge of congruence with professional ideology, the organization of professional practice, and the nature of professional work.

New methods of monitoring are likely to be acceptable and effective if they benefit from, rather than upset, the interdependence among colleagues; reinforce rather than weaken group solidarity; and mitigate rather than exacerbate the real or imaginary hazards that professionals face in the course of their work. In particular, monitoring mechanisms need to strike that elusive mark between professional autonomy and accountability that acknowledges both, without slighting either. Congruence, therefore, is the fourth principle that conditions quality-monitoring interventions in the health care system.

A fifth principle is credibility; for those who are to be judged by the findings of a quality-monitoring enterprise need to believe that they are true. Credibility depends on many factors; among them are agreement on the concept of quality that drives the monitoring system, the completeness and accuracy of information about performance, and the scientific, as well as consensual, validity of the criteria upon which judgments of quality are based. Neither technological uncertainty nor dissension, whether professional or social, can provide a basis for credible quality monitoring.

There is a corollary to credibility that may deserve separate mention as a sixth principle in its own right. It is relevance—to one's perception of responsibility, one's own circumstances, one's patients in general, and each patient in particular. It is reasonable to maintain that the ability to particularize (to one's own patients and to one's own work) is a precondition to the ability to persuade and motivate.

The ability to motivate takes us, I believe, a big step beyond consent, credence, or cooperation. It implies a greater proximity to the mainsprings of professional behavior. It is served by at least two additional principles: ownership and self-interest.

Ownership, the seventh in our enumeration of the principles that might govern the effectiveness of formal quality monitoring, implies an identification with, rather than alienation from, the monitoring enterprise. It corresponds to a feeling that the enterprise is "ours" rather than "theirs." Many attributes of that enterprise contribute to it, attributes that, if one were aiming for a longer list, could appear as separate principles. Sponsorship is one; familiarity another; participation another still.

One could postulate that ownership is directly proportional to the closeness of the sponsors of monitoring to its targets. Governmental agencies, especially if federal, are most remote in their structural location, their culture, and their methods. Corporate enterprise is perhaps a little less so. To the extent that the practice of medicine can be viewed as a business, there might be a narrow strip of common ground. But the cultures of the professions and the business world are, in the main, widely apart.

Ownership, and legitimacy as well, might be said to begin with professional sponsorship: most remotely by one's own professional association, then by one's own specialty group, and, closest of all, by the leadership of one's own medical staff organization. But, at that final step, the progression might cease to be salutary if dissension has reduced confidence among colleagues.

Ownership is also acquired through early exposure to the workings of monitoring systems during the process of education, training, and socialization. Thus, the purposes and methods of monitoring come to be regarded as domestic and familiar rather than external and foreign. But, most of all, ownership comes about through personal participation in the quality-monitoring enterprise. Besides engendering a sense of ownership, personal participation also implies consent, congruence, credibility, and relevance; hence, the importance accorded to participation as a motivator when quality assurance systems are designed.

Perhaps self-interest, enlightened or otherwise, is the most powerful motivator of all. It can either obdurately frustrate or mightily aid the purposes of formal quality monitoring. This explains the importance given to incentives in the main body of this text. I have contended, for example, that the monitoring enterprise is not likely to succeed if it calls for actions contrary to the economic and professional interests of hospitals and doctors. And I have ascribed the seeming impotence of past monitoring efforts to the virtual irrelevance of their findings to the careers of individual health care practitioners. Success would follow, I have maintained, if the results of monitoring could consistently and continuously shape professional careers. A mutuality of interests, binding the monitors to the providers, is offered, therefore, as the eighth in this list of governing principles.

Mutuality of interests, if the rewards were sufficiently large, would overcome many obstacles to successful monitoring. But if the rewards are small, uncertain, or deferred, much would depend on the time and effort required to get the monitoring job done. Reasoning by analogy, one might postulate frictional impediments within organizations—impediments that require physical or psychic effort to overcome and that can be smoothed by adding resources or restructuring the task of monitoring. Facilitation can be offered, therefore, as a ninth principle pertinent to the design, operation, and effectiveness of formal quality monitoring.

A consideration of motivators and facilitators leads, naturally, to the subject of disincentives or punitive action. But these are subsidiary to a more general principle that, for want of a better word, I shall call coerciveness. There is much debate about the role of controls, regulatory or administrative, in promoting quality monitoring and contributing to its effectiveness. Quality monitoring must have teeth, we are told. I tend to agree, even though I have argued, so far, that monitoring, to be successful, must become an integral part of professionalism itself. There is, no doubt, an externally imposed imperative that all professionals face. Its origins, ultimately, are in the contract between society and the professions. The professions can neither ignore it nor unilaterally define its terms. It is necessary, therefore, for society, using a variety of means, to define its expectations and see to it that they are met. In that sense, the principle of coerciveness, the tenth on our list, can be said to undergird and envelop the quality-monitoring enterprise. The legitimacy and necessity of coerciveness are not at issue. It is only the nature and degree of its intrusions that need to be established.

It may have become obvious that the principles I have offered so far are not entirely distinct from one another, that they could be given different names, and that there are many others that could have been mentioned, more or less distinct from those I have identified. It remains to be seen whether the identification of these principles constitutes an adequate summary of the main arguments advanced in this text, and whether they have served to clarify, rather than to obfuscate, the subject. Having accepted these risks, I hope I shall not invite outright derision when I end with the last of my principles—one rather apart from the others, belonging perhaps in a different discourse altogether. It is the principle of virtue, personal and public, that I wish to advance as an addendum to this decalogue. For it seems to me that the pursuit of quality is, in essence, the moral dimension of professional life. A commitment to it allows almost any reasonably constructed quality-monitoring mechanism to succeed. Without it, the most ingenious of creations will surely fail.

ACKNOWLEDGMENT

The author is grateful to the Institute of Medicine for its support, but hastens to exonerate it of any responsibility for the views expressed in this work. These are the author's only.

NOTES

1. An example of rather sudden improvement in clinical performance is described in J. W. Williamson, M. Alexander, and G. E. Miller, "Continuing Education and Patient Care Research," *Journal of the American Medical Association* 201 (18 September 1967): 938–42. In this demonstration, intensive educational efforts of some duration failed to improve follow-up on abnormal laboratory tests by attending physicians in a hospital. Rapid improvement occurred when house staff were hired.

    An example of what could be analogous to synergy is offered by M. A. Moorehead, R. S. Donaldson, et al., *A Study of the Quality of Hospital Care Secured by a Sample of Teamster Family Members in New York City* (New York: School of Public Health and Administrative Medicine, Columbia University, 1964). The study shows that accreditation by the JCAH was seemingly associated with somewhat better quality in community hospitals but not in the proprietary hospitals of the day in New York City. The study is summarized in A. Donabedian, *Explorations in Quality Assessment and Monitoring, Volume III: The Methods and Findings of Quality Assessment and Monitoring: An Illustrated Analysis* (Ann Arbor, MI: Health Administration Press, 1985), 190–91.

2. A. Donabedian, *A Guide to Medical Care Administration, Volume II: Medical Care Appraisal* (New York: American Public Health Association, 1969). See pages 122–51 on "Effectiveness," and pages 151–52 on "Dangers."

3. J. M. Eisenberg, *Doctors' Decisions and the Cost of Medical Care* (Ann Arbor, MI: Health Administration Press, 1986). See, in particular, Part II, pages 87–142, on "Changing Physicians' Practice Patterns."

4. Health Care Financing Administration, *Professional Standards Review Organizations: 1979 Program Evaluation* (Washington, DC: U.S. Government Printing Office, 1980). On regional differences, see Table 2, page 8.

5. R. D. Lehmann, "Joint Commission Sets Agenda for Change," *Quality Review Bulletin* 13 (April 1987): 148–50.

6. Health Care Financing Administration, *Professional Standards Review Organizations: 1978 Program Evaluation* (Washington, DC: U.S. Government Printing Office, 1979). For seasonal effects, see Figure 1, page 20.

7. U.S. Congress, Office of Technology Assessment, *The Quality of Medical Care: Information for Consumers* (Washington, DC: U.S. Government Printing

Office, 1988). For material on the relation between malpractice compensation and quality of care, see pages 133–38.

8. A. F. Southwick and D. A. Slee, "Quality Assurance in Health Care: Confidentiality of Information and Immunity for Participants," *The Journal of Legal Medicine* 5 (September 1984): 343–79.

9. J. K. Iglehart, "Congress Moves to Bolster Peer Review: The Health Care Quality Improvement Act of 1986," *New England Journal of Medicine* 316 (9 April 1987): 960–64.

10. U.S. Congress, Office of Technology Assessment, *The Quality of Medical Care*, 1988. The procedure for applying sanctions is presented in schematic form on pages 128–29.

11. R. H. Palmer and M. C. Reilly, "Individual and Institutional Variables Which May Serve as Indicators of Quality of Medical Care," *Medical Care* 17 (July 1979): 693–717.

12. A. Donabedian, "The Epidemiology of Quality," *Inquiry* 22 (Fall 1985): 282–92.

13. D. Neuhauser, *The Relationship between Administrative Activities and Hospital Performance*, Research Series 29 (Chicago: The University of Chicago Center for Health Administrative Studies, 1971).

14. S. M. Shortell, S. W. Becker, and D. Neuhauser, "The Effects of Managerial Practices on Hospital Efficiency and Quality of Care," in *Organizational Research in Hospitals*, ed. S. M. Shortell and M. Brown (Chicago: Blue Cross Association, 1976), 90–107.

15. B. S. Georgopoulos and F. C. Mann, *The Community General Hospital* (New York: The Macmillan Co., 1962).

16. W. R. Scott, W. H. Forrest, Jr., and B. V. Brown, "Hospital Structure and Postoperative Mortality and Morbidity," in *Organizational Research in Hospitals*, ed. S. M. Shortell and M. Brown (Chicago: Blue Cross Association, 1976), 72–89.

17. A. B. Flood and W. R. Scott, "Professional Power and Professional Effectiveness: The Power of the Surgical Staff and the Quality of Surgical Care in Hospitals," *Journal of Health and Social Behavior* 19 (September 1978): 240–54.

18. R. A. Kane and R. L. Kane, "Long-Term Care: Variations on a Quality Assurance Theme," *Inquiry* 25 (Spring 1988): 132–46.

19. R. M. Sigmond, "What Utilization Committees Taught Us," *Modern Hospital* 100 (February 1963): 67–71.

20. S. Shindell, *Hospital Utilization Review—Western Pennsylvania* (New York: American Public Health Association, Program Area Committee on Medical Care Administration, 1966, mimeographed).

21. L. E. Weeks, ed. *C. Wesley Eisele in First Person: An Oral History* (Chicago: American Health Association, and Hospital Research and Educational Trust, 1988).

22. R. H. Palmer, E. J. Orav, J. L. Hargraves, E. A. Wright, and J. A. Hall, "Internal Leadership versus External Review for Ambulatory Care Quality Assurance," abstracts of the Program Proceedings of the American Public Health Association, 116th Annual Meeting, Boston, 13 November 1988, p. 177.

23. For some early observations on the relation between baseline level of performance and subsequent improvement in clinical performance, see Donabedian, *A Guide to Medical Care Administration, Volume II*, 149–50.
24. Mechanic reports that physicians in prepaid group practice express greater readiness to accept "peer review of medical work in the doctor's office" and to consider it appropriate for "government physicians to attempt to evaluate the quality of care patients receive," but he also points out that one cannot tell from cross-sectional studies if physicians who hold such views are more likely to join prepaid groups, or if these views are adaptations subsequent to working in prepaid groups. See D. Mechanic, "The Organization of Medical Practice and Practice Orientations among Physicians in Prepaid and Nonprepaid Primary Care Settings," *Medical Care* 13 (March 1975): 189–204.
25. For some time now, it has been noted that the medical profession is undergoing profound changes that, among other consequences, could make it more accepting of external controls. For a recent assessment, see a collection of papers on "The Changing Character of the Medical Profession" in *Milbank Memorial Fund Quarterly* 66, suppl. 2 (1988).
26. M. Millman, "Medical Mortality Review: A Cordial Affair," Chapter 4 in *The Unkindest Cut* (New York: William Morrow and Co., 1977).
27. E. Freidson and B. Rhea, "Processes of Control in a Company of Equals," *Social Problems* 11 (Fall 1963): 119–31.
28. U.S. Congress, Congressional Budget Office, *The Impact of PSROs on Health-Care Costs: Update of CBO's 1979 Evaluation* (Washington, DC: U.S. Government Printing Office, 1981). See also Health Care Financing Administration, *Professional Standards Review Organizations*, 1979 and 1980.
29. E. A. Codman, "Report of the Committee on the Standardization of Hospitals," *Surgery, Gynecology and Obstetrics* 18, suppl. (1914): 7–12; and 22 (January 1916): 119–20.
30. P. A. Lembcke, "Evolution of the Medical Audit," *Journal of the American Medical Association* 199 (20 February 1967): 543–50.
31. See U.S. Congress, Office of Technology Assessment, *The Quality of Medical Care*, 136.
32. Num. 32: 13.
33. Iglehart, "Congress Moves to Bolster Peer Review."
34. The possibility that requirements for reporting punitive action will create a reluctance to take such action was suggested to me in a conversation with Dr. David B. Siegel of the Health Alliance Plan of Michigan.
35. Williamson et al., "Continuing Education and Patient Care Research."
36. Palmer et al., "Internal Leadership versus External Review."
37. M. R. Chassin and S. M. McCue, "A Randomized Trial of Medical Quality Assurance: Improving Physicians' Use of Pelvimetry," *Journal of the American Medical Association* 256 (22–24 August 1986): 1012–16. In this trial, the effectiveness of intervention by a PSRO could have been enhanced by the decline in the use of pelvimetry in progress for some time before the trial was instituted.
38. J. W. Williamson, *Assessing and Improving Health Care Outcomes: The Health*

Accounting Approach to Quality Assurance (Cambridge, MA: Ballinger Publishing Company, 1978). The findings on effectiveness are summarized on page 150.

39. A. Donabedian, *Explorations in Quality Assessment and Monitoring, Volume I: The Definition of Quality and Approaches to Its Assessment* (Ann Arbor, MI: Health Administration Press, 1980). See Chapter 3, pages 79–122, for a comparison of the merits and drawbacks of assessing either process or outcomes.

40. C. M. Jacobs, T. H. Christoffel, and N. Dixon, *Measuring the Quality of Patient Care: The Rationale for Outcome Audit* (Cambridge, MA: The Ballinger Publishing Co., 1976). Examples of particularizing criteria by specifying "exceptions" are given on pages 52–69.

41. S. Greenfield, C. E. Lewis, S. H. Kaplan, and M. B. Davidson, "Peer Review by Criteria Mapping: Criteria for Diabetes Mellitus: The Use of Decision-Making in Chart Audit," *Annals of Internal Medicine* 83 (December 1975): 761–70.

42. J. O. McClain, "Decision Modeling in Case Selection for Medical Utilization Review," *Management Science* 18 (August 1972): B706–17.

43. R. H. Brook, A. Davies-Avery, S. Greenfield, L. J. Harris, T. Lelah, N. E. Solomon, and J. E. Ware, Jr., "Assessing the Quality of Medical Care Using Outcome Measures: An Overview of the Method," *Medical Care* 15, suppl. (September 1977): 1–165. The selection of judges is described on pages 39–40 and discussed on page 60. Also see A. Donabedian, *Explorations in Quality Assessment and Monitoring, Volume II: The Criteria and Standards of Monitoring* (Ann Arbor, MI: Health Administration Press, 1982). Studies on consensus are described on pages 301–31.

44. Donabedian, *Explorations, Volume II*, 170–80.

45. There is empirical support for this hypothesis in the findings of a remarkable nationwide study of programs for controlling hospital infections. See R. W. Haley, D. H. Culver, J. W. White, W. M. Morgan, T. G. Emori, V. P. Munn, and T. M. Hooton, "The Efficacy of Infection Surveillance and Control Programs in Preventing Nosocomial Infections in U.S. Hospitals," *American Journal of Epidemiology* 121, no. 2 (1985): 185–205.

46. D. M. Berwick, "Continuous Improvement as an Ideal in Health Care," *New England Journal of Medicine* 32 (5 January 1989): 53–56.

47. Eisenberg, *Doctors' Decisions*.

48. E. G. McCarthy, M. L. Finkel, and H. S. Ruchlin, *Second Opinion Elective Surgery* (Boston: Auburn House, 1981). The findings of a cost-benefit analysis are described in Chapter 5. Also see H. S. Ruchlin, M. L. Finkel, and E. G. McCarthy, "The Efficacy of Second-Opinion Consultation Programs: A Cost-Benefit Perspective," *Medical Care* 20 (January 1982): 3–19.

49. S. G. Martin, M. Schwartz, B. J. Whalen, D. D'Arpa, G. M. Ljung, J. H. Thorne, and A. E. McKusick, "Impact of a Mandatory Second-Opinion Program on Medicaid Surgery Rates," *Medical Care* 22 (January 1982): 21–45. The authors offer evidence concerning the "sentinel effect" and cost compared to benefit.

50. U.S. Congress, Congressional Budget Office, *The Impact of PSROs.*
51. C. J. McDonald, S. L. Hui, D. M. Smith, W. M. Tierney, S. J. Cohen, M. Weinberger, and G. P. McCabe, "Reminders to Physicians from an Introspective Computer Medical Record: A Two-Year Randomized Trial," *Annals of Internal Medicine* 100 (January 1984): 130–38.
52. Eisenberg, *Doctors' Decisions.*
53. C. R. Brown, and H. S. M. Uhl, "Mandatory Medical Education: Sense or Nonsense?" *Journal of the American Medical Association* 213 (7 September 1970): 1660–68.
54. B. C. Vladeck, "Quality Assurance through External Controls," *Inquiry* 25 (Spring 1988): 100–107.
55. P. M. Gertman, A. C. Monheit, J. J. Anderson, J. B. Eagle, and D. K. Levenson, "Utilization Review in the United States: Results from a 1976–1977 National Survey of Hospitals," *Medical Care* 17, suppl. (August 1979): 1–148. See page 99 for a summary of findings on effectiveness.
56. Eisenberg, *Doctors' Decisions.*
57. D. I. Cohen, B. Littenberg, C. Wetzel, and D. B. Neuhauser, "Improving Physician Compliance with Preventive Medicine Guidelines," *Medical Care* 20 (October 1982): 1040–45.
58. J. M. Orient, L. J. Kettel, H. C. Sox, Jr., C. H. Sox, H. J. Berggren, A. H. Woods, B. W. Brown, and M. Lebowitz, "The Effect of Algorithms on the Cost and Quality of Patient Care," *Medical Care* 21 (February 1983): 157–67.
59. Williamson et al., "Continuing Education and Patient Care Research."
60. The background for my conversation with George Rosen is described in I. S. Shapiro, "The Patient and Control of Quality in Medical Care," in *Proceedings, Tenth Annual Group Health Institute of the Group Health Association of America*, Columbus, OH, 24–26 May 1960 (Chicago: Group Health Association of America, 1960), 99–107.
61. Donabedian, *Explorations, Volume I*, 35–74.
62. J. E. Ware and M. K. Snyder, "Dimensions of Patient Attitudes Regarding Doctors and Medical Care Services," *Medical Care* 13 (August 1975): 669–82.
63. P. D. Cleary and B. J. McNeil, "Patient Satisfaction as an Indicator of Quality," *Inquiry* 25 (Spring 1988): 25–36.
64. T. S. Inui, E. L. Yourtee, and J. W. Williamson, "Improved Outcomes in Hypertension after Physician Tutorials: A Controlled Trial," *Annals of Internal Medicine* 84 (June 1976): 645–51.
65. S. H. Kaplan, S. Greenfield, and J. E. Ware, Jr., "Assessing the Effects of Physician-Patient Interactions on the Outcomes of Chronic Disease," *Medical Care* 27 (March 1989): S110–27.
66. A. Donabedian and J. C. Attwood, "An Evaluation of Administrative Controls in Medical Care Programs," *New England Journal of Medicine* 269 (15 August 1965): 347–54.
67. A recent search for valid information about the quality of care that might be made available to consumers demonstrates, in my opinion, how little we have to tell them. See U.S. Congress, Office of Technology Assessment, *The Quality of Medical Care.*

68. The conditions under which consumer choice could effectively regulate a market, or fail to do so, are elegantly described in A. O. Hirschman, *Exit, Voice, and Loyalty* (Cambridge, MA: Harvard University Press, 1970). For an update, see A. O. Hirschman, "Exit, Voice, and Loyalty: Further Reflections and a Survey of Recent Contributions," *Milbank Memorial Fund Quarterly/ Health and Society* 58 (Summer 1980): 430–53.
69. Committee on the Costs of Medical Care, *Medical Care for the American People* (Chicago: The University of Chicago Press, 1932); reprinted in 1970 by the U.S. Department of Health, Education and Welfare (Washington, DC: U.S. Government Printing Office, 1970).

Part **III**

What Does "Quality" Mean? Critical Ethical Issues for Quality Assurance

Gail J. Povar

INTRODUCTION

Perhaps the most critical issue in quality assurance is defining high-quality care. The task of quality assessment is to identify what level of quality is being delivered, while the task of quality assurance is to ensure that a given standard of quality is being met. In either case, a reference point is essential. Assessment efforts require "gold standards"; assurance efforts require goals.

In this volume, Donabedian and Palmer describe the state of the art in quality assurance and assessment, both in terms of what is, and, normatively, what ought to be, given certain assumptions about the structure and processes of health care. In addition, Palmer discusses in great detail the complex sociological and organizational interactions that must be accounted for in a quality assurance program. This discussion, too, will attempt to address a central question raised by both of the other authors: What is it that we are trying to assure with quality assurance? But I will use moral principles, rather than empirical data or theoretical constructs of health care organization, to guide my analysis. Refracting the meaning of the term "quality" through these moral prisms helps us to understand the choices we face in defining "quality" generally, and to identify the ethical problems that are of special concern for quality assurance in a socially funded health care insurance program.

The first section of this essay will review several fundamental principles widely used in the medical ethics literature. Examples of how such principles relate to the problem of quality assurance will demonstrate their pertinence to considerations of what is to be assured, and how.

The second section will expand on the material in the first part by examining the implications for a quality assurance effort of emphasizing a particular governing, or at least critical, ethical principle. Two issues in particular will be addressed: (1) How much weight should be given to subjective or individualized concerns, both in a definition of quality and as a focus for quality assurance? and (2) What role should concepts of justice play, if any, in modifying the definition of quality itself or in limiting the level of quality to be assured? Throughout, we will be asking how we should define "maximum" quality (best possible care), and how that standard should be altered, if at all, for a socially funded health insurance system.

The last section of the essay will move from a general analysis of the problem to specific proposals for quality assurance in Medicare. In brief, I hope to convince the reader that any definition of quality, for a socially funded program or otherwise, must: (1) identify a reference point on a continuum from totally subjective and individualized notions of benefit and burden to those based exclusively on an idea of net aggregate social benefit; and (2) account for the resources to be used to achieve the desired benefit/burden ratio. Furthermore, the responsibility for establishing the resource boundaries on a definition of quality should rest, I will argue, not with the medical professional or bureaucrat but with society as a whole. Finally, I shall conclude that there is a moral obligation to promote appropriate interpersonal as well as technical processes in health care, whether or not individualized perceptions of benefit and burden determine the goal of quality assurance overall.

MEDICAL ETHICS: A REVIEW

Medical ethics is a discipline that analyzes the conformity of medical care to specified philosophical principles and concepts. Such principles in turn should reflect a "justifiable portrait" of what medical practice, broadly conceived, ought to look like in its value dimensions. Historically, different principles have been dominant at various times and in various places. The oft-invoked Hippocratic oath and associated writings provide one perspective. Often described as paternalistic, this perspective places great responsibility on the physician to make decisions on behalf of patients, and assumes that the physician knows best what should be done. But this tradition has come under fire from both the consumerist and the social justice perspectives.[1-4] Late twentieth-century America, it seems, is especially concerned with assigning decision making to the patient, not to the physician. Nevertheless, there is today considerable diversity of moral viewpoint in the codes of ethics espoused by different health care professionals' organizations. It is not obvious, at least not without considerable analysis, which code should be considered preeminent for policy purposes. Even should we happen to agree as a society to adopt a particular code, the generalities in which such codes are written rarely provide more than the broadest guidance with regard to specific issues or circumstances.

At this point, one might be tempted to conclude that the pluralism of viewpoints characterizing contemporary medical ethics makes the discernment of "right answers" impossible. The preceding paragraph was intended as a cautionary note, however, not as an expression of nihilism. In fact, despite the variety of philosophical theories and beliefs about medicine that undergird debates in medical ethics, most commentators would be willing to support several core principles that describe the conditions of medical care.[5]

To clarify the following discussion, I will present a practical issue in medical care, which will then serve as the source of examples for the individual concepts.

The Case of tPA

For at least 20 years, data have suggested that blood clots (thrombi) superimposed on preexisting coronary artery narrowing (e.g., due to atherosclerotic plaques) played a major role in causing heart attacks (acute myocardial infarction, or AMI). During the 1960s and 1970s data accumulated that suggested that the use of naturally occurring enzymes could dissolve such clots, with as much as 20 percent decrease in mortality. Questions persisted about this work, however, until randomized controlled studies in 1980 confirmed that this therapy (thrombolysis) did indeed significantly improve blood flow to threatened tissue and even reduced the amount of heart muscle lost.[6] More recent studies have confirmed that thrombolytic therapy achieves substantial reductions in mortality from AMI.[7-9] The enzyme used for almost all the initial trials was streptokinase, derived from streptococcal bacteria. The major limitations of the therapy were the risk of major bleeding (5 percent in some series) with an associated mortality rate of 0.5 percent, and the fact that the enzyme appeared to lose effectiveness dramatically if it was not used within four, and preferably three, hours of symptom onset. The benefit seemed to be a significant improvement in coronary blood flow and a reduction in early mortality from heart attacks.[10]

In the early 1980s, a new enzyme became available as a result of advances in recombinant technology. Tissue plasminogen activator (tPA), evaluated in a large, multicenter trial, seemed not only somewhat safer but also more effective.[11] The possibility of increased safety was attributed to less interference in the body's natural clotting mechanisms and to a shorter "half-life." In other words, because tPA clears the body much faster than streptokinase, dosages are (at least in theory) more easily adjusted and side effects are minimized. In addition, streptokinase could cause allergic (anaphylactic) shock; tPA has not been shown to do so.[12,13] In terms of effectiveness, tPA achieved almost twice as much vessel-clearing as streptokinase in controlled trials and appeared to retain at least some effect even if administered beyond the three- to four-hour window limiting streptokinase.[14] Some studies suggested, however, that the initial dose of tPA must be followed by maintenance heparin therapy for the vessel to remain open.[15] Heparin is clearly associated with increased risk of bleeding. Both streptokinase and tPA may be administered intravenously (via the vein) without need for cardiac catheterization.

Despite recent evidence from two large, multicenter trials comparing tPA and streptokinase that the two therapies yield essentially equivalent outcomes both of lives saved and of incurred morbidity and mortality rates,[16,17] there continues to be substantial disagreement as to whether the two drugs are truly of equal value.[18] In particular, advocates of tPA argue that its superior performance in early reperfusion of cardiac tissue must inevitably correlate with better outcomes, and that studies failing to show this result are flawed because of the method used to administer adjunct heparin therapy.[19,20] In short, the issue of whether or not tPA and streptokinase are clinically equivalent for purposes of thrombolysis in the setting of AMI is far from settled.

In 1987, the cost of the therapeutic 100 mg dose of tPA, direct from the manufacturer, was $2,410. The therapeutic dose of streptokinase cost $256.48.[21] More recent cost estimates do not demonstrate a change in this cost differential.[22]

Should tPA represent the "standard of care" for patients with symptoms suggestive of AMI? By what criteria and under what circumstances? Does (should) the "standard of care" be different for individuals than for social groups? The ethical principles that undergird the answers to such questions will be considered in the next section.

Principles of Medical Ethics

Beneficence. The first and perhaps most familiar of these principles is beneficence. As usually understood, beneficence represents the duty of health care providers to do good and to prevent harm while keeping burdens to an acceptable minimum. The degree to which one has kept this moral duty is assessed in terms of the outcome intended and, ideally, in terms of the outcome achieved.

Beneficence can be understood at the level of the individual practitioner and patient as the effort to balance benefits and risks of diagnostic or therapeutic interventions. Very often, the duty to beneficence is interpreted to apply to medical benefits and medical risks, as apart from a more global assessment of benefits that incorporates the patient's values as well (see *autonomy*, below). Physicians considering thrombolytic therapy might well be persuaded that, for reasons of theoretical efficacy and greater flexibility of timing, tPA rather than streptokinase is the drug of choice for their patients with probable myocardial infarction. Indeed, they might insist that emergency rooms, and even their own offices, stock tPA to maximize the possibility of benefit by applying the treatment as close to symptom onset as possible.

Nonmaleficence. Nonmaleficence in health care is usually understood as complementary to beneficence; it refers to the health care practitioner's duty to do no harm. Indeed, one might choose to lump nonmaleficence and beneficence together, for they truly represent two sides of the same coin. Both address the intended or foreseeable consequences of a medical decision. Like beneficence, the duty to nonmaleficence is fulfilled to the extent that its goal (minimization of harm) is at least intended and, if at all possible, achieved. Using the example of thrombolytic therapy, nonmaleficence would dictate not using tPA or streptokinase in patients with contraindications, such as known bleeding disorders or active ulcer disease. This duty would also require that thrombolytic therapy be undertaken only in circumstances where the known serious side effects (i.e., bleeding) could be managed properly. Thus, physicians mindful of their duty to nonmaleficence should insist on the availability of rapid turnaround laboratory tests of blood-clotting status, and on prompt access to blood for transfusions, to ensure safe use of this therapy. The duty to nonmaleficence requires creating a safe context for use of a therapy, as well as selecting patients properly.

Together, the duties to beneficence and nonmaleficence form the justification for quality assurance efforts in the first place. To the extent that medical institutions, like those who practice within them, are responsible for patients' welfare, they share the moral obligations of the medical profession itself.[23] Quality assurance programs represent, then, the hospital's or the nursing home's or the ambulatory care center's

commitment to promoting good and to preventing as well as not inflict-
ing harm.

Autonomy. Autonomy is a complex concept that derives its power from
a variety of philosophical traditions. Respect for autonomy may be defined (broadly) as respect for persons. In addition, respect for autonomy, in the context of the "rights" language that underpins much of
our legal and political system, means respect for the rights of individuals to independent self-determination regarding the course of their lives
and the integrity of their own minds and bodies. A useful way to understand the relationship between a health care professional's duty to "respect for persons" and what we generally call "patients' rights" is that
professionals have a duty to respect their patients, which even the patients cannot renounce. On the other hand, patients *may* waive other
rights if they so choose (e.g., by assigning decision making to someone
else, even if they are competent to make the decision themselves).[24]

Respect for autonomy assumes that the patient is indeed capable
of self-determination. Many efforts have been made to define the
autonomous individual. In general, such a person must be capable of
reasoning, of understanding and integrating the information received,
and of communicating with others. Autonomous decision making also
reflects a relatively stable set of values (although reasoned changes in
viewpoint are obviously also consistent with capacity or autonomous
decision making). Patients may have selective decision-making capacity. For instance, a patient might be able to decide how much suffering
to endure but not how to allocate his or her estate. Capacity can even
vary by time of day—especially in the very elderly ill patient. Such
distinctions mean that capacity to make an autonomous decision in a
given situation can be assumed neither to be absent nor present based
on other kinds of decisions or behavior in other situations at other times.

With regard to tPA therapy, respect for autonomy would require
informing the patient of the risks and benefits of the therapy and ascertaining that the patient understood their implications for his or her own
life. In most instances, this duty would also entail formally obtaining
the consent of the patient before administering the therapy. This process is the familiar one of informed consent.

The concept of autonomy also modifies our understanding of beneficence; a "good outcome" from a medical encounter will be defined
not only in terms of medical outcomes (e.g., functional status or survival) but also in terms of the individual patient's assessment of that
outcome in light of his or her own life goals and values.[25] The decision-

analysis model of clinical decision making combines quantitated utility scores, intended to reflect patient values, with medical probabilities of particular outcomes (in terms of possible curative, palliative, morbid, or fatal events) in order to identify the best option for a given patient. In this model, the probability for a given patient of surviving a heart attack with or without substantial morbidity, of dying from the heart attack, or of suffering significant morbidity or mortality from throm-bolytic therapy would be combined with the patient's assessment of the importance of these various outcomes. The inclusion of patients' "utili-ties" in defining the best outcome is one effort to respect autonomy.

Clearly, when respect for autonomy and the duties to beneficence and nonmaleficence are brought together, benefits and burdens are no longer defined exclusively by empirical data, but by individual assess-ment of the implication of that data by individual patients. The obliga-tion to do good is then the obligation to further the patient's concept of the good; the duty to prevent harm is an obligation to protect the patient from the risks he wishes to avoid. From the above discussion, one can see that respect for autonomy and duties to beneficence/nonmaleficence understood in purely medical terms may come into conflict. Using the tPA example, a patient who especially feared a bleeding complication might refuse thrombolysis in spite of being an excellent candidate for it, and despite the physician's belief that it would substantially reduce the risk of extensive damage to the patient's heart muscle. Medical weigh-ing of risks and benefits would dictate using thrombolytic therapy; the patient's concerns direct otherwise. The difficulty for the physician in such circumstances is whether to attempt further negotiations (i.e., to dissuade the patient) or to accept the patient's decision as a valid expres-sion of autonomous decision making.[26]

An even more radical situation would occur if the patient's insur-ance provided only partial coverage for outpatient medications. For fi-nancial reasons, the patient might then defer treatment until it was possible to get to an emergency room (risking decreased benefit), rather than receiving the tPA in the doctor's office at a more optimal time relative to onset of symptoms. In such a case, the divergence in values and the reasons for the divergence make even clearer the potential conflict between beneficence and autonomy.

Of course, one should consider the possibility that the patient may have been "forced" to forgo something that he or she might otherwise have chosen (i.e., to be treated in the office) because of an externality—the lack of funds. Factors that limit autonomy are not exclusively related to competence or physical threat. In this last instance, the apparent conflict between beneficence and autonomy may really be between both of these values and a particular theory of justice. As we shall see shortly, respect for autonomy raises other potential conflicts with the principle of justice as well.

It is worth stating the obvious here: Patients are not the only persons for whom respect for autonomy is a concern. Professionals in general expect and enjoy a significant degree of self-government and freedom from bureaucratic oversight. Indeed, autonomy is one of the characteristics of their profession. Physicians, like patients, often claim considerable independence from direction or interference on these grounds. Resistance to review by anyone other than another professional is legitimated in part by the appeal to professional autonomy. But while a patient's autonomy is due respect in order that the patient may further his or her own ends, the professional is accorded such license because we believe it facilitates performing the professional function—in this case, patient care. Professional autonomy is respected, then, insofar as it promotes beneficence, or doing good. Like respect for patient autonomy, however, respect for professional autonomy may conflict with obligations to equity and justice in the distribution of health care.

Justice. Justice is a concept borrowed from principles of political philosophy that has increasing implications for medical ethics. There are two senses in which justice is invoked in health care. In the first instance, justice means equity: similar cases should be treated similarly. Equitable treatment of patients would forbid discrimination among individuals on the basis of irrelevant characteristics. Equity—treatment of like cases in like fashion—might also require that all those who have contributed to society in a particular way, and to a particular degree, be rewarded similarly. This is the idea of "just deserts." For example, an equitable system would assure that those who have made substantial social contributions are rewarded, without consideration of irrelevant characteristics such as their degree of political power or their likability. Medicare can be envisioned as an effort to take care of those who deserve our concern by virtue of their age (and our duty to respect the aged) or because of what they have contributed to society during their productive years. For Medicare, "entitlement" means that the only characteristic that matters is age—and achieving a particular age entitles one to participate.

For the individual physician, the duty to justice as equity would require taking care of those patients he or she is medically competent to care for, without regard to race, age, or (some would say) ability to pay. In our tPA case, one might argue that the duty to justice means that the patient must (ideally) receive tPA or streptokinase on grounds of medical risk/benefit and the patient's own values, not on the basis of class, or even on the basis of insurance coverage.

The second sense in which we use the term justice is in reference to the moral basis for the distribution of goods among members of society. Adherence to the concept of distributive justice means that resources must be distributed according to a morally defensible system. In other words, such distribution ought not to be arbitrary or capricious. There currently exist many competing concepts of "just distribution" in our society. They range from frank egalitarianism, meaning that no one may have more (or less) care than all may have,[27] to strongly libertarian views, implying that medical knowledge and ability are "owned" by the medical profession. Under libertarian views, no one can claim a right to care because the profession gives it out of compassion and concern, not out of duty.[28] An egalitarian viewpoint might require allocation of sufficient resources to Medicare to cover "the best there is" (excluding amenities) without regard to cost, for each individual. A strict social egalitarian could also argue, however, that if Medicare's resources were so limited as to prohibit coverage of a particular service, no one 65 years old or older ought to be able to obtain that service at all, even if they had the independent resources to do so. In either case, one kind of egalitarian position argues for identical treatment for the population in question: either everyone should have the best or everyone should have something less. Alternatively, Medicare might be considered a base, a fair or adequate level of coverage beyond which, it is acknowledged, some may choose to go by investing their own resources. Such a system might be considered fair and equitable—providing what is due—but certainly would not be egalitarian since many levels of care might be possible for patients of the same age with the same disease. Whether Medicare's obligation is envisioned as guaranteeing equal access to the best quality available, as affording equal access to adequate, acceptable quality, or as assuring access to the only quality available to anyone will depend on the ideal of distributive justice invoked.

Distributive justice, irrespective of which system one adopts, entails thinking about goods from the perspective of society, not just from the viewpoint of the individual. When resources are limited, even if only moderately, the concern for justice raises questions about trade-offs between different kinds of goods (guns versus butter). Some segments of society may be better served by investments in housing, for instance, than investments in tertiary care medical technologies, even though they will come to need those technologies in part because of their environment. If another, well-housed segment of society requires the medical technology, a moral question is raised as to whether society ought to invest (i.e., whether to distribute money) in housing or in the technology, if we cannot provide both. Assuming we purchase the technology, how accessible it is to different members of society—geographically or by ability to pay—also raises issues of distributive justice.

Justice and the tPA Case. Again, consider tPA. Let us suppose that everyone agreed that this represented ideal therapy for patients presenting with symptoms of acute myocardial infarction (AMI). Suppose further that the limits of the manufacturing process resulted in demand (as determined by extant treatment algorithms) exceeding supply. Cost became high, and a black market developed.

One concept of justice would say that it would be unethical for wealthier patients to obtain tPA for marginal indications (for instance, chest pain possibly consistent with AMI without EKG changes), while poorer patients were unable to receive it, even in the face of the most clear-cut evidence of AMI by symptoms and by EKG. Such a system of justice (based, let us say, on "objective medical criteria") would perhaps demand a revised algorithm, in the face of limited available tPA, that would be more selective in terms of eligibility for tPA so that anyone meeting the eligibility criteria could be treated. In other words, the "demand" scheme would be altered to meet the supply in order to ensure equity. The relevant similarity would be objective evidence of AMI, and individual financial resources would not be considered. The distributive scheme is egalitarian—none may receive tPA for an "objective" indication unless all with that indication may receive it.

An alternative scheme of distributive justice, based on a first-come, first-served criterion, would maintain the more inclusive algorithm for use of tPA in all treatment facilities until tPA ran out. Such a system would be defended on the grounds that treating anyone who could benefit as long as the drug was available is better than denying the drug to the first person in line (who might benefit to some extent) in favor of someone down the line who would meet the "objective" criteria of a more selective system precisely. In other words, such a system considers the moral claim of the present patient to be more powerful than that of a future patient, even if the latter's needs might turn out to be somewhat more compelling from a purely objective point of view.

Both these allocation schemes operate in medicine today. Intensive care unit (ICU) beds provide a good example. Often, the ICU is filled on a first-come, first-served basis until the facility is full, within certain medical algorithms. Once it is full, however, debate often ensues about whether to discharge someone who just hours before was an "appropriate admission" in order to make room for a sicker (or younger, or more salvageable, or more important) patient.[29]

In some hospitals, other less ideal settings (e.g., the surgical recovery room) are recruited for new patients to preserve the original algorithm *and* the first-come, first-served entitlement. In others, the "appropriateness for ICU admission" algorithm is designed to change as the demand begins to exceed supply. Patients who only recently came in become candidates for discharge to less heavily staffed units.[30]

Returning to tPA, we see that justice may conflict with other values. If society has multiple demands on its financial resources, both within and outside the medical care system, one might ask whether the additional cost of covering tPA therapy in a socially funded program is justified by the somewhat decreased incidence of unpleasant complications and increased "window" of effectiveness. In other words, although beneficence for individual patients might dictate using tPA, the social perspective suggests that more good might be accomplished if streptokinase were the thrombolytic therapy of choice: the money saved could be used better elsewhere. When possible therapies for a given condition differ markedly in cost and less markedly in their benefits, the conflict between beneficence and justice is apparent, especially when society as a whole is footing the bill.

A note of caution is warranted here. Cost-effectiveness analyses of the sort referred to above assume that utilitarian judgments (net social good is the moral objective of justice) are appropriate.[31] Effectiveness, however, reflects not only the characteristics of a therapy but the context in which it is applied.[32] A therapy may be less effective if the patients are sicker, more dangerous if the care is not as closely monitored. Such conditions often exist for individuals from socioeconomically disadvantaged groups. For instance, the investment to provide either tPA or streptokinase may have to be far greater in a public hospital requiring a whole new lab to monitor clotting times than in a new suburban institution with all the latest laboratory facilities. The concurrent illness rates of recipients of thrombolysis in an inner-city hospital might render the savings in mortality quite modest as compared to suburban populations. An aggregated analysis might conclude that society is better served in terms of life-years saved for a given investment by treating with tPA only suburbanites at their new hospital, while using streptokinase in the inner city. Such a conclusion, however, might offend our understanding of justice as equity, especially if both groups' care was paid for in full by the same socially funded system.

Autonomy and justice can come into conflict as well. Just as beneficence for an individual patient might conflict with justice (i.e., we would be willing to subject a few patients to the experience of hypotension from streptokinase to save the costs of tPA), so individual preferences would be subjugated to the social decision to invest in streptokinase as opposed to tPA for thrombolysis. The patient's choices would be limited by the availability of a particular agent.

Physicians may feel that their professional autonomy is impinged upon as well, to the detriment of their patients, if limits are placed on the therapies they may choose, even if those limits are justifiable from a fiscal perspective. (Consider, for example, physicians' reactions to drug formularies.) Professional autonomy, they might argue, demands the freedom to act in accordance with medical judgment and to be unrestrained by financial concerns. In the absence of such freedom, beneficence for the individual patient, it would be argued, is undermined.

Patients may also perceive a conflict. Consumerist language regarding "rights" often does not dovetail with social needs to distribute resources among competing claims. Thus, patients may claim a right to "the best" (assume tPA) and feel cheated if their insurance (Medicare) does not pay for it in order to make other services more broadly, or less expensively, available. Such patients might argue that they ought to be able to waive their claim to tPA for personal reasons (perhaps even due to a personal desire not to spend the common resources unnecessarily) but that the option to use it should be protected. Obviously, what is happening here is not only conflict between autonomy and justice, but a conflict over what a just distribution of resources ought to be. It has been observed that patients want to see resources conserved, but not at their own expense.[33]

Fidelity. A last principle that many philosophers include in their list is fidelity. In the health care field, fidelity refers to the duty to keep promises. It also represents the commitment to the relationship between patient and professional. Physicians take this to mean that they must always place the individual patient above all other considerations. A commitment to fidelity enhances the duty to beneficence, assuring that it is the good of that one patient that is foremost in the doctor's mind.

One can see immediately that fidelity, as defined above, and justice can come into conflict. Indeed, some might wish to argue that duty to both fidelity and beneficence will virtually preclude individual physicians from thinking about the duty to justice in the clinical situation.[34-37]

Not everyone agrees on such sharp distinctions between the obligation to the individual and the obligation to the community.[38-41] But those who do see the issue this way believe that doctors ought not to think in terms of cost effectiveness, but only in terms of risk/benefit.[42,43] In such a view, when weighing tPA against streptokinase both for individual patients and for all patients, the physician should only consider the medical risks of bleeding and the benefits of reperfusion (improving blood flow through the coronary arteries). Criteria for use would be on such grounds, with consideration of patient preferences. The profession's fidelity to its promise of beneficence—that is, to its promise to consider the patient first—some would argue, requires rejecting any consideration of the fiscal implications of therapeutic choices when caring for patients. Even those who wish that physicians would take costs into account must identify a "point of vanishing returns," a point at which the marginal investment far exceeds the expected marginal gain.[44] Even in such models, however, an individual physician's fiscal responsibility does not appear to extend to the point of withholding or recommending against a procedure of significant likely benefit to an individual patient in order to preserve the resources of the group.

Fidelity also demands that the medical professional stay with his or her patients. Abandonment is a violation of the promise to care. Of course, the physician may make arrangements for the patient's care to be transferred, if the relationship is for some reason impossible to continue. But the justifications for doing so are open to discussion. For instance, a physician may feel incompetent to care for a given disease. Or, the physician and the patient may have reached an impasse in style and communication. Or, the patient's insurance may no longer be accepted by the provider. Which of these constitute legitimate grounds for breaking the bonds of the relationship depends on one's concept of the acceptable trade-offs between physician autonomy (exercised in either the physician's or the patient's best interest) and the duty to fidelity.

The Case of Prostatic Surgery

Prostatic surgery for benign prostatic hypertrophy (BPH) has recently received considerable attention, in part because of a significant degree of variation in the rates of the procedure.[45] It is useful to examine the subject for two reasons. First, symptomatic BPH is increasingly common as men reach the sixth decade and beyond, so it is of particular relevance to Medicare. Second, unlike thrombolysis, prostatic surgery for BPH is for the most part elective, performed primarily to ameliorate symptoms. Although evidence of gradual or acute urinary obstruction and signs of infections are indeed indications to operate, the kind of procedure used, the precise timing of the procedure, and the criteria used to recommend the procedure have recently been closely questioned.[46–49]

Widely accepted indications for prostatic surgery (excluding cancer, which will not be addressed here) include one or more episodes of acute urinary retention attributable to prostatic enlargement, severe urinary tract infection (UTI), and biochemical evidence of obstructive impairment of kidney function, which can convincingly be attributed to an enlarged prostate.[50] Symptoms that frequently prompt patients to seek relief include increased frequency of urination, difficulty starting the stream, dribbling, and similar complaints.[51] There is remarkably little correlation, however, between such symptoms and prostatic size.[52]

Two approaches to prostatectomy are in common use: open prostatectomy and transurethral prostatectomy (TURP). The former requires an abdominal incision above the pubic bone and incision of the bladder wall to gain access to the prostate. The latter involves insertion of a flexible tube through the penile urethra; the prostate is then removed using instruments inserted via the tube. No abdominal incision is necessary. In Washington, DC, an uncomplicated TURP requires three to four hospital days, whereas uncomplicated open prostatectomy involves about a week of hospitalization.[53] In addition, some urologists argue that TURP has lower rates of mortality and morbidity than open procedures,[54] although recently this assertion has been challenged. TURP also seems to be associated with higher rates of reoperation compared with the open approach.[55] Finally, TURP is associated with a postoperative impotency rate of less than 5 percent, while open prostatectomy should not affect potency at all.[56]

The Principles Revisited

In the tPA case, beneficence entailed treating the patient with indications of AMI to reduce the extent of ischemia. Analogous indications for prostatectomy would be to prevent recurrent complicated UTIs, recurrent acute urinary retention, and reduced renal function. The principle of beneficence may require the relief of symptoms in addition to intervention in potentially life-threatening disease. Indeed, most medical care for the elderly has more to do with achieving control over troublesome symptoms than saving lives. In the case of prostatectomy, the alleviation of such symptoms as hesitancy, nocturnal urinary frequency, or burning on urination may be legitimate goals.

A model of beneficence based on empirically and objectively measurable variables might well address these symptoms in terms of their quantifiable characteristics—seconds of delay in starting stream, force of stream, frequency of nocturia, and so on. Treatment algorithms could then be defined in terms of symptom severity sufficient (on objective grounds) to yield enough improvement from surgery (objectively) to offset the risks of surgically related morbidity and mortality. Such risks would be assessed solely in terms of loss of life or degree of illness requiring hospitalization (e.g., postoperative infection or stricture formation with subsequent reoperation). Beneficence and nonmaleficence would both appear to be served.

Treating for symptoms, however, introduces additional complexity into the assessment of the quality of care. As several authors point out, how severe the symptoms of BPH are is highly subjective.[57,58] In fact, one study points out that the quantity of symptoms does not necessarily correlate with the patient's perceptions regarding the severity of the symptoms.[59] The indications for surgery may therefore vary greatly from one patient to the next. For instance, the patient who is very embarrassed by post-void dribbling may seek surgical correction. A sympathetic surgeon may do the procedure, but another may object on the grounds that the patient has experienced neither infections nor medically significant obstruction.

Like benefit, risk can have idiosyncratic meaning for patients. The fact that postoperative impotence is very uncommon does not necessarily suggest that patients will consider the risk to be minor. A recently married older man, anticipating increased sexual activity, might be particularly concerned about such sequelae. Just as the patient in the tPA case might, for personal reasons, choose to forgo tPA when medical benefit seems highly likely, so might a man balk at prostatectomy altogether, despite a "clear medical indication" such as worsening renal function. Alternatively, this patient might insist on open prostatectomy, with its reduced risk of subsequent impotence. The potentially increased perioperative mortality might prompt his physician, on grounds of nonmaleficence, to strongly prefer TURP for this patient. In addition, the medical profession as a whole, or this doctor in particular, may judge the patient's concern about impotence to be excessive. The patient's and the physician's weighing of the risks and benefits conflict.

Here, again, the principle of autonomy (respect for persons) as well as beneficence must be considered. Resolution of the question of whether or not to do a prostatectomy, and which approach to use, will depend heavily not on the external evidence of symptoms, signs, or risk but on the patient's assessment of such information in the context of his own life. His values are essential to the decision-making process.[60-63]

One might ask, Couldn't a decision-analysis model that assessed the outcomes over a broad range of utilities (the numerical value assigned to a patient's evaluation of the desirability of a particular event) tell us which variables are likely to alter the decision? If fear of impotence does not predict a change in choice of approach, why bring it up? Aren't we incorporating patients' values if we focus on those variables the model identifies as critical?

The answers to these questions lie in how strictly one wishes to observe the obligation to consider each individual as absolutely unique. A model that accurately predicts behavior for 95 percent of people will miss 5 percent. In any case, predictions derived from the study of populations cannot account for individual differences within that population.[64] Strict adherence to the principle of autonomy requires discussion of the risk of impotence, which each patient must weigh for himself.

It does not follow from the above discussion that the patient's choice should be accepted uncritically. Consider again the patient who is very anxious about dribbling. Serious attention to respect for that patient, as well as the duty to do good (provide appropriate therapy) and to avoid harm, would require close examination of the patient's complaint. What, for instance, seems to be at the root of the patient's (in the surgeon's opinion, excessive) concern? The patient may not really be interested in surgery per se, but in control of embarrassing leakage onto his clothes. Information about the use of an absorbent insert might well be greeted with relief and gratitude.

Strict definitions of informed consent, which are rooted in the tradition of autonomy, limit the physician's obligation to providing information and to ascertaining that the patient understands it in an atmosphere that provides for free choice. A broader understanding of the physician-patient relationship and of respect for persons would require the physician to explore the reasons for a patient's complaint and to make explicit the rationale for both the physician's and the patient's preferences.[65] Iterative decision making would seem more likely to identify the appropriate interventions.

Beneficence and autonomy are thus both important to the decision-making process. Objective measures of the severity of symptoms before and of complications after procedures, combined with models that demonstrate which of these symptoms or complications will be most troublesome to patients, will provide the physician with an a priori means of identifying the beneficent act. The physician can then recommend this to the patient and explain why. Respect for the patient should then trigger an exploration of the patient's reasons for accepting or rejecting that advice.[66] The obligations to beneficence as well as to respect for autonomy require this, particularly since patients' expressed preferences may appear to be incongruent with their apparent values.[67] A patient may express a strong desire to avoid renal failure and to be relieved of discomfort, yet repeatedly refuse a relatively minor intervention (e.g., TURP) to relieve urinary obstruction. Only probing discussion will reveal the profound fear and expectation of impotence because of the vivid example of a recent friend's bad outcome. Such a process takes seriously the expertise of the physician and avoids reducing the physician to a source of information. It also ensures that the values of the patient will be reflected in the final choice of therapy. The physician has met the duty to explore, with the patient, alternative conceptions of "the good" to be sought, but leaves the patient responsible for choosing among them.

Even if we can reconcile beneficence, nonmaleficence, and autonomy, we must still address the principle of justice. In the tPA case, if the patient's preferences and physician's obligations to beneficence were incorporated into a sound plan for treatment, that plan might still run afoul of considerations of distributive justice. Individual choices regarding prostatectomy may not in all instances coincide with options for which a socially funded program ought to pay. An ethically justifiable allocation of a social program's resources may inevitably limit individual choice, at least to the extent that some individuals might not be able to purchase care that is not covered.

Let us first assume that prostatectomies are sufficiently beneficial and safe that they survive a general risk/benefit criterion for payment. (A procedure like carotid endarterectomy might not.) Let us assume further that a payer making decisions about appropriate care will consider the need to limit expenditures. Finally, let us accept the argument that a principle of egalitarian access for its enrollees *ought* to govern a social insurance program.[68] Assuming increasingly strained resources, one might wish to argue for strict criteria for prostatectomy in order to (1) reduce the costs to Medicare of covering the procedure, while (2) preserving equal access to the procedure for all Medicare enrollees with a particular constellation of indications. Together these goals might dictate that only reduction in the rate of potentially life-threatening events would justify payment by Medicare for prostatectomy. In fact, if one defined quality only on such strictly "medical necessity" criteria, one could narrow the gap between high-quality care (the goal of beneficence) and that which the social insurance system covers.[69] It is only possible in this case to reconcile beneficence with distributive justice by altering the definition of beneficence so that it corresponds to available resources.

The payer would wish to see an analysis of the costs of "preventive" surgery versus surgery only after complications of prostatism, broken down by costs of hospitalization for UTIs or acute retention, costs of following symptomatic patients with appropriate physical and laboratory evaluation, and similar concerns. A risk/benefit analysis would attend to differentials in such variables as renal function, and mortality and morbidity from UTIs. In theory, of course, one could choose to be guided by symptoms and quality of life, rather than mortality rates. This would inevitably expand the caseload (thereby increasing expenditures) while being more difficult and more costly to measure. To disregard mortality rates would also be inconsistent with the widely accepted notion that preventing premature death is the first priority of patients and physicians alike.

One can see, then, that the *fact* of limited resources and the *ethic* of egalitarian distribution almost inevitably yield different interpretations of the obligation to beneficence. "The good" becomes what we can do within given funding levels and a particular view of just distribution. Neither a physician's assessment of a patient's disability nor the individual patient's assessment of symptom severity would alter what would be covered by insurance. A social policy based on very tightly limited indications is even more likely for prostatectomy than for use of tPA, given the immediate threat of death presented by myocardial infarction (contrasted with prostatic obstruction). Placing budget and justice issues before individual beneficence or autonomy could radically alter the justifications for and the performance of prostatectomy.

Whether the physician should express primary fidelity to the more restrictive or the more inclusive indications for prostatectomy clearly is problematic, once the above restrictions on payment are accepted. If the physician encourages patients to make unconstrained choices, based on symptoms, the patients may then be angry or disappointed to learn that their preference will cost money they may not have. A physician who espouses a "medical beneficence" model—one that is accepted both by other doctors and, as it happens, by the payer—may be accused of placing fiscal concerns over duty to the patient.[70]

In other areas of preference, rationing by ability to pay is clearly acceptable in our society; one does not encounter arguments based in justice that all families should be able to purchase a Mercedes-Benz or a Volvo, despite their somewhat increased margin of safety in a collision. All cars, however, are expected to meet some minimum standards of safety—for instance, they all must have seat belts. Within health care, we clearly tolerate differentials in ability to pay as well. But the car dealer is not expected to perform as an advocate for the car purchaser. The physician is unquestionably expected, on the basis of fidelity, to help the patient achieve whatever care is deemed necessary. The physician is expected to behave as though the distribution of health care is based on an egalitarian model, considering and recommending to the patient the technical medical care that any patient with a like illness would receive, and tailoring the care to the preferences of the individual patient.

The question then becomes how this understanding of the physician's obligations to fidelity and beneficence relates to the payment mechanism—to the distribution of social monetary resources to purchase health care. This subject is so complicated as to require a book in itself, but a brief analysis suggests that, in our system, either our concept of "good" health care, as determined exclusively by combined attention to beneficence and autonomy, or our understanding of just distribution will be forced to change. In health care, and in Medicare in particular, patients may accept differentials in access to amenities, or to certain services (cosmetic surgery), but not to care for medical complaints. The dual American assumption seems to be that (1) once one is inside the health care system at all (by virtue of insurance), technical care and competence should be identical for all, and (2) such care should reflect the latest in medical technological development applied to individualized goals.[71,72] It has been argued that this view of just health care is one of the reasons that the resources consumed by health care will continue to expand almost infinitely unless our society reexamines our concept of the good to be achieved by medical care.[73]

IMPLICATIONS FOR QUALITY ASSURANCE IN MEDICARE

How one ranks these ethical principles and applies them to quality assurance for a socially funded insurance program has significant implications. This section explores some of these ramifications, again drawing on tPA and prostatectomy as examples.

Beneficence and Nonmaleficence

If one strongly supports the principles of scientific or medical beneficence and nonmaleficence, then one will base one's quality assurance activities on empirically measurable and objective good outcomes—minimized morbidity and mortality, and maximized survival or functional ability. (Quality of life would not serve as a criterion because, while frequently based on such phenomena as functional status, it incorporates the subjective assessment of the value of that function to one's existence.) Veatch refers to this as the "infectious disease" model of quality assessment—the right antibiotic is the one that cures the infection.[74] Some have argued that solving the scientific issues will also resolve the question of what makes good care.[75] Furthermore, if a utilitarian understanding of benefit is the model of beneficence (sometimes called full beneficence) adopted, one will measure the aggregate good and bad outcomes for the group as a whole, rather than focus on each individual case. The standards to be assured would no longer include following the diagnostic or therapeutic path most preferred by the individual patient, or even seeking the patient's idea of the "best outcome." Instead, the criterion for quality would be that the group would experience the best aggregate outcome; some individual cases would be managed less ideally in order that the overall benefit/harm ratio was maximized so as to achieve the most benefit consistent with an acceptable level of harm for the population. Such an approach reflects a social epidemiology approach to health care.[76]

Again, consider the use of thrombolytic agents. If the criteria of beneficence/nonmaleficence for the individual are to be met, then each case must be assessed in terms of whether thrombolytics were appropriate, and if so, whether tPA or streptokinase was the better choice in terms of projected risks and benefits. If, on the other hand, "full beneficence" is the goal, then the experience of whole populations with thrombolysis and with the specific thrombolytics is the relevant measure. Depending on the data, criteria for high-quality care might dictate the use of tPA in such circumstances for everyone, even if, in individual cases, streptokinase might be perfectly acceptable therapy with a high likelihood of identical results.

Finally, nonmaleficence would dictate looking at the consequences of care in such a way that making thrombolysis available in some settings (e.g., rural hospitals without the ability to manage a subdural hematoma quickly) might constitute poor quality because the side effects cannot be managed. Beneficence and nonmaleficence coincide here; justice, taken as access to care, may conflict. Does our definition of quality, what we will assure, mandate upgrading rural care so that everyone can benefit from thrombolytic therapy (with all the costs that it would entail)? Or do we take the position that since we cannot practically or fiscally provide rural victims of heart attacks with ideal management of complications from thrombolysis, we must not, on grounds of nonmaleficence, offer such patients this potentially beneficial therapy?

Autonomy

What if we adopt respect for persons and for individual preferences as important concerns, even as essential modifiers of our understanding of beneficence and nonmaleficence? One effect would be that quality assurance would look at other parameters of structure, process, and outcome than those that contribute strictly to morbidity and mortality experience. Respect for persons calls for examining the conditions that preserve privacy and dignity for patients and that allow for adequate time and information to make decisions. It would impose the obligation to examine how well patients were informed and whether their values and goals were respected.[77–79] Physician behavior in interviews, the quality of medical decision making, and the tests or consultants used would all become foci of a quality assurance effort that employed assessment criteria identifying good and bad quality in this aspect of care.

Putting a priority on the values of the individual patient has other implications as well. The "right therapy" no longer reflects only the likelihood of survival, morbidity, and functional status. It now includes highly individual reasons, perhaps difficult to discern.[80] Is the patient glad to have survived, even with a certain degree of disability? Would he or she have *chosen* to do so? The patient was fearful of thrombolysis but was advised and thus agreed to have it immediately. But having suffered a hemorrhagic right cortical stroke, the patient is dubious about the value of having maximized survival of cardiac tissue. Would the outcome have been different if the decision making had been more attentive to the patient's particular concerns? Perhaps death from a heart attack would have been more acceptable than life as a hemiplegic. Of course, no therapeutic choice guarantees either freedom from complications or achievement of the sought-after objective. The critical question in this case is what likelihood of hemorrhagic complication the patient would have willingly accepted to maximize the chances of recovery from AMI. How well were these probabilities explained and the patient's understanding of them explored?

Even given exemplary explanations, a few patients may make choices that appear irrational but are nevertheless consistent with their own priorities.[81] Consider the patient with debilitating arthritis who would rather take an anti-inflammatory drug than continue on a post-tPA heparin drip to prevent further coronary occlusion. Electing tPA and heparin means the patient must give up anti-arthritics throughout the therapy, for the risk of bleeding would otherwise be unacceptable to both patient and caregivers. But the patient is unwilling to forgo the symptomatic relief these medications offer, even for a period of several days. Such a choice may not be congruent with our usual expectations of patients, but may nonetheless make sense to this particular patient. Varying perceptions of symptoms and risks may also account in part for the variable rates of prostatectomy. Different surgeons may be more or less willing to respond to different patients' tolerance of dribbling or hesitancy. In such cases, one is forced to ask whose values should prevail and why?

Diligent attention to autonomy raises such questions for quality assurance. It means that the process of decision making must be examined as carefully as the procedures performed and the outcomes achieved. Even outcomes might require a different kind of analysis. Usually, increased death rates for a given diagnosis trigger fears that care in a particular institution has deteriorated. In fact, an increased death rate due to pneumonia in Hospital X may reflect better care. In this hospital, every effort is made to respect terminally ill patients' choice to receive comfort care only. Such patients might survive a given hospitalization if treated aggressively for pneumonia, but the burden of treatment might be, in their view, disproportionate to the quality of their remaining life. In this case, the increased mortality reflects attention to the principle of autonomy, rather than the failure of physicians to institute proper medical therapy.

Justice

Justice issues create particular difficulties for quality assurance in two extreme approaches. In one case, the quality assurance staff reviews each and every case (on whatever grounds of beneficence, nonmalefi-cence, and autonomy are adopted) to ascertain if acceptable care was given. The cost of either the care or the process of assuring it are not considered. In the opposite case, the budget drives the definition of both quality (the best that x dollars will buy) and how to assure it (look only at easily collected data from large populations). The former option strives for "the best of everything for everyone"; the latter is a minimal-ist approach that seeks "only what our current budget will buy, irre-spective of what would be good or better."

Attention to the principle of justice requires deciding whether one of these poles is appropriate or whether something in between is prefer-able. If our concept of quality is independent of current budget con-straints (that is, we hold out a standard that may exceed current or future fiscal capabilities), then we are forced to admit that, for some populations or some conditions, we will pay for good care but not ideal care. Our justification for falling below the ideal standard would be that doing so allows us to purchase more care of other kinds or more care for larger numbers of people.[82] "Social optimum" care (as opposed to ideal) would be the most efficient and effective care possible, given fiscal constraints.[83] Such a standard would be arrived at by an institution (e.g., a health maintenance organization) or by a social insurance sys-tem. Individual practitioners and their patients could accept the social optimum as ideal as well, if they felt they ought to further the justice concerns of the larger entity. Indeed, it might be plausible to argue that physicians and patients are obligated to think of themselves as sharing the "commons" of the larger community.[84] Such an attitude would re-quire patients and doctors to revise their concept of beneficence so that it does not pressure the community to commit resources to health care at the expense of other needed goods.[85] The autonomous patient, in this vision of society, would make choices that reflect concern not only for his or her own goals but for those of the society as a whole.

It is more likely, however, that there would continue to be tension between ideal care, as espoused by doctors and patients, and the social optimum, as defined by an institution or insurance system. It has been argued that this tension is important, for it holds institutions and insur-ers to the obligation to justify policies that limit access to ideal care.[86]

In the case of tPA, the marginal increased risk and decreased effec-tiveness associated with streptokinase might be accepted as "good enough" given the markedly decreased costs of therapy; then money saved could be used to purchase other goods. Such a decision by a hospital might result in its being labeled as giving "second class care" (such accusations sometimes arise in arguments over the relative quality of care in public versus private and rural versus urban facilities). Alternatively, if an insurer decided to cover streptokinase but not tPA, it might be accused of discriminating unfairly in favor of the well-to-do, who could in theory choose to purchase ideal therapy. Less wealthy enrollees in the insurance plans would not have that choice. Underlying such disagreements would be assumptions about the acceptability of a multi-tiered system based on ability to pay.

Similarly, strict restrictions on coverage for prostatectomy would both reduce expenditures and make quality assurance easier, but they would also effectively ration prostatectomy for symptom control on the basis of ability to pay. The autonomy of choice might be the same for both the well-to-do and the poor, if physicians informed both groups of available options without mentioning limitations of coverage. The autonomy of action, however, would clearly be restricted for those who have no discretionary funds with which to act on their preferences.

Another way of understanding the conflict between particular views of distributive justice and the goals of beneficence, nonmaleficence, and autonomy would be to ask the medical profession to redefine standards in terms of the latter three principles, and in economic terms as well.[87,88] The criteria for "quality" (and hence the goal of quality assurance) could range from "parsimony"—meaning the best care achieved as inexpensively as possible[89,90]—to more finely balanced concepts of cost and benefit, which would accept "optimum" rather than "ideal" care as the quality standard. Parsimonious care reflects the ideal objective of providing individualized care designed to achieve the best outcome for the patient. It is elegantly and efficiently designed so as to avoid any extraneous incurred expense. Tests ordered for purposes of defensive medicine, for instance, have no place in parsimonious care.

As used in this section, the word "optimum" takes its meaning from economics: that point at which the benefits for the costs are maximized in light of possible alternative uses for the same resources.[91,92] Once economic efficiency becomes part of the definition of quality, then again the parameters used to measure quality of care must necessarily be altered. The goal might be the best value for the dollars spent. The unit of measurement will usually be groups of individuals rather than the individual case, although not always.[93] Once again, we would have to ask whether efficiencies would have to be realized irrespective of other conditions, or whether the social optimum would take into account vulnerable populations for whom the cost of achieving even modest benefits might be very high. In any event, what degree of departure from ideal care will be acceptable must be determined not only by the professions and the payers but by society as well.[94–96] In either case, autonomy—as expressed in terms of patient preferences for more certainty (which might affect the parsimonious approach), or in terms of rights to select treatment, irrespective of cost to the system (which might challenge the application of social optimum standards)—might conflict with quality assurance efforts that must take into account the resources available to provide care.[97,98]

Fidelity

Finally, fidelity raises additional issues for quality assurance efforts. First, the issue of conflict for providers: if the "system" adopts a criterion of quality that is either parsimonious or optimizing, should the physician within it always be the loyal opposition, in the name of fidelity? Some have argued that physicians must always advocate the ideal—for instance, by informing the patient of "ideal options" that are not covered and the implications of that policy for the patient.[99] Should the physician's care be evaluated with respect to how seriously he or she takes this obligation to educate patients about inequality in the system? Would failure to do so suggest that the doctor has been excessively "coopted"? Alternatively, should fidelity be defined as a dual obligation to the community of patients and to preservation of their aggregate health (the optimum)? In that case, "outliers" would be those doctors who consistently recommended levels of care (and generated costs) that exceeded the social optimum; the ethical concern about the failure to achieve the ideal would be moot. It has been argued that clinical algorithms do tend to adapt to available resources.[100] Put in the extreme, use of tPA under such criteria might be seen as antisocial or unprofessional, if streptokinase were available.

On a different note, the obligation to fidelity, like the duty to autonomy, raises the need to look at parameters that are not simply those of outcome, minimization of risk, or maximization of benefit for individuals. The duty to fidelity requires attention to whether institutions keep their promises (for instance, in the area of confidentiality). Fidelity, as well as adherence to principles of justice, might require examination of transfer policies from the emergency room, or particular physicians' refusal to accept patients. Certain processes of care that represent affirmation of the relationship of both institutions and practitioners to the patient would thus become the focus of quality assurance efforts.

WHITHER QUALITY ASSURANCE FOR MEDICARE?

The previous sections of this text have attempted to provide a perspective on the concept of quality from the viewpoints of commonly acknowledged ethical principles. The intent has been to demonstrate how these principles can drive the definition of quality in different directions. Which principle takes preeminence will have a significant influence on the role a quality assurance effort will play in shaping the delivery of medical care for Medicare recipients.

Although all of the issues addressed here are relevant to quality assurance in a social insurance program, several questions stand out. First, what definition of quality should be adopted by the quality assurance effort within a socially funded insurance program? Second, who should participate in setting the standard of quality to be assured? Third, what elements of health care should be the concern of this quality assurance effort? And finally, where should responsibility for such a quality assurance effort be situated?

What Do We Mean by Quality?

From the foregoing discussion, it seems that quality can be defined along three important dimensions: the goals desired, the risks involved, and the resources to be used. Two standards of care have been discussed in the preceding sections: the "ideal care" standard (i.e., the best that money can buy, given individual preferences) and the "social optimum" standard (i.e., the most efficient means to provide whatever level of care society wishes to guarantee to participants in the program). Which of these standards ought a socially funded insurer adopt?

Some have argued that attempts to set standards for anything short of "doing everything of even marginal benefit" would prove extremely difficult.[101,102] The goal is to maximize individual preferences, if possible, with an acceptable level of risk. Resource limitations, perhaps even those of the patient, ought not to confine the recommended course of action. Others would encourage all physicians to become clinical economists, not only to achieve parsimony but also to decide when the point of diminishing returns has been reached.[103] Even the best quality of care cannot be delivered without an awareness of the resources used.

It is, of course, fairly obvious that frivolous expenditures reflecting lack of knowledge or inattention to detail are antithetical to ideal care. Unnecessary tests cost money and risk harm to the patient. The more difficult case is presented when we ask how much we wish to spend to make a given result possible. After all, since we believe that early detection of breast cancer is critical to cure, we might wish to argue that mammograms in elderly women should be done twice or thrice yearly, rather than once. Surely doing so will detect some small number of cancers at an earlier stage. And just as surely, some patients would be enormously reassured by more frequent testing. But such a policy would render the cost of finding those few additional tumors astronomical.

This example simply illustrates that ideal care standards implicitly assume a threshold of resource use to achieve a given end.[104] Every investment in a given level of health care reduces the investment in an alternative social good; at some point, the cost of more care is judged to be excessive. Our definition of quality is therefore never free of considerations of the investment needed. It is the role that cost plays in the definition, not whether it is present at all, that should concern us.

From a practical perspective, a quality assurance effort will be forced to take account of the resources available. Otherwise, it risks creating unrealistic and ultimately unachievable demands on providers of care. Unless fiscal resources are allowed to expand to meet the infinite demand for care, some version of the social optimum will inevitably be adopted. The difference between ideal care and social optimum care is really not a difference in kind but a difference in degree. The real distinction between the two levels is the difference between affording a great deal of individual attention and choice to each and every participant, and accommodating fewer individual preferences and needs. Our educational system provides an instructive example. Private schools, at substantial cost, offer much in the way of tailored programs and individual attention. Public education, which grew out of the service rather than insurance tradition, offers access to the general population, but at some reduced level of flexibility in the face of a given student's learning style, maturity, and so forth.[105] Each community identifies its social optimum by trading off the cost of meeting the private school standard against both the marginal benefit to be gained and the alternative use of the tax dollars that would be needed. If school boards were to insist on assuring a standard of student/teacher ratios for the schools that precludes the community's investing in roads and police departments, we would consider it at least foolish and at worst unjust. Socially funded health insurance, in like fashion, cannot adopt a quality standard that outstrips either its own or external resources.

If it is the case that a definition of quality inevitably implies a particular level of resource use, then our underlying assumptions about a fair distribution of resources become increasingly important. A standard that asserts egalitarian access to individualized care within an insurance scheme might quickly exceed our willingness or ability to pay the costs. Alternatively, a quality standard that attempts to maximize efficiency and full beneficence would potentially allow quality assurance efforts to overlook high morbidity or mortality rates in certain subsegments of the insured population, since such an efficiency or cost-effectiveness standard might preclude treating certain populations or conditions. The quality of care for all enrollees might, in this case, differ substantially from the individualized model for some but not for others. Yet a third definition of quality would articulate the goal not in terms of "net social benefit" but in terms of "adequate" or "decent" care for each enrollee, because its distributional assumption would be to afford access to all services for all enrollees, but (given limited funds) on the basis of less fully individualized and subjective criteria. Any effort to balance responsiveness to individual medical/technical preferences, on the one hand, and fair access to medical care, on the other, is an effort to find a social optimum definition of quality.

Arguably, then, the social optimum approach is the only morally acceptable definition of quality for a social insurance system such as Medicare to adopt; for any standard that utterly outstrips the ability of the insurance system to pay could also tacitly support rationing by ability to pay for even an adequate level of care.[106–108]

A commitment to, for instance, provide an expensive "rescue technology" such as bone marrow transplants plus high-dose chemotherapy for all patients with refractory metastatic breast cancer (a substantial number of women over 65) could, without expansion of the total budget, preclude coverage of some other care (e.g., screening flexible sigmoidoscopy for colon cancer). Although it is difficult to imagine such a trade-off taking place in reality, the point is that new technologies will routinely emerge and inevitably will exceed the ability of the budget to expand. Without clear guiding principles to choose which interventions to cover, and for whom, benefit decisions may fail to meet the moral demands of distributive justice: allocation of resources on morally defensible grounds. It is difficult to imagine how one could justify such a situation to Medicare enrollees.

At the same time, accepting financial restraints is not the same as being driven by budget. I am not suggesting that, as in Great Britain, the budget should be set before discussion ensues regarding fair allocation. The definition of those processes and outcomes, which will become the criteria of the social optimum, should proceed independently of, but remain sensitive to, budgetary constraints.

In fact, failure to identify a just standard independent of the fiscal process could lead to budget-driven decision making by default. A similar phenomenon will occur if failure of political will results in reluctance to acknowledge that something less than everything will be assured. If the quality assurance program adopts the same unrestrained advocacy position in the macro environment that physicians are often enjoined to adopt in the micro context, then allocation is likely to occur not in light of a rational goal but according to the strength of competing historical commitments and political and medical pressure groups. This is, of course, one possible allocation scheme, based perhaps on the argument that the market will reveal the appropriate goals through such competitive forces. Such a system may even claim that it is meeting the duty to beneficence, on the grounds that the competing interests are looking out for the needs of Medicare enrollees. However, each organization will define beneficence differently, and the quality assurance effort as a whole will be at pains to explain to the public its rationale for choosing option A over option B. If quality assurance mechanisms share obligations to beneficence with the physician, then surely they, like physicians, ought to be obliged to explain their recommendations on the grounds of both data and coherent values.

The quality assurance mechanism may find itself advising reductions in expenditures for some services and increases in expenditures for others. It may even, at least in theory and depending on how the social optimum is defined, suggest that too much is being spent on medical (versus social) care.

As Medicare competes for a piece of the budgetary pie, the definition of quality to which it holds itself accountable will be crucial. That definition must encompass an explicit articulation of the goals to be achieved, the risks to be avoided, and justifiable marginal thresholds for investment of social resources.

Who Should Define the Social Optimum?

The definition of the social optimum should not be the sole responsibility of health care professionals and bureaucrats. Obligations to respect for persons, in aggregate, would require that enrollees have considerable voice in the process. It is likely that the public will, at least initially, resist anything short of the "more is better" theory of allocation.[109] The public must be educated well to understand the uncertainties and limits of medical care so that technical fireworks are not substituted for quality, and so that the real choices are identified. As discussed earlier, enrollees will have to grapple with their beliefs about distributive justice, which will inform choices about what ought to be provided to whom, and how. This moral reference point will require public discussion if the quality assurance program is to be susceptible to moral evaluation by the public it serves. In any event, for the quality assurance mechanism's standard to be defensible, its clients must participate in—and be accountable to—the decision-making process.[110,111]

What Elements of Care Are Critical?

We take it for granted that a quality assurance effort should attend to technical competence: If one is going to do a procedure, one ought to be able to do it in such a fashion as to achieve the expected benefit at an acceptable level of risk. We do *not* assume that a quality assurance effort should assert the need for amenities that are aesthetically appealing but neutral with respect to the outcome of care. To date, we have not routinely identified the interpersonal processes of care as a focus for quality assurance efforts.

The decision to adopt a social optimum instead of an ideal care basis for characterizing quality of care for Medicare patients does not and, in my view, should not preclude attention to the central principle of autonomy and respect for persons. A system that demurs from an obligation to tailor care to each patient's preference profile is not exempt from a standard of respectful communication and compassion. Of course, just as notions of what constitutes "beneficence" will be altered by the trade-off between ideal beneficence and justice, so idealized conceptions of respect for persons may have to be adjusted to fiscal reality. There may be ideal and adequate levels of privacy, maintenance of confidentiality, and the like. Of all precious resources, time may be constrained most of all by economic considerations. There may well need to be a search for more labor-efficient means of informing patients and helping them to reach decisions; perhaps computers or interactive videos will further this goal. Having stated all that, however, it is still the case that willingness to listen and elicit the patient's concerns, and reflect them insofar as possible in the treatment plans, are central values in health care that currently are not often the focus of quality assurance efforts.[112,113]

The fact that the range of options may be limited does not mean that a discussion of those options should be avoided (or permitted to be carried out badly) or that the patient's evaluation of those options becomes irrelevant. The decision-making process can and should be held to criteria that derive from both beneficence and autonomy. Respect for the resources and medical needs of the population as a whole does not preclude respect for the individual patient.

It might be tempting to rely on measures of patient satisfaction as a proxy for assessment of respect for autonomy, on the assumption that patients who were mistreated would complain. Such an approach, however, may not suffice, for patients who have not been offered participation may not expect it. Equitable treatment would be reflected in respectful address of people of every background and socioeconomic status. But some elderly inner-city patients may have become resigned to impersonal or even demeaning treatment. An individual accustomed to assembly-line clinic care may find acceptable a level of respect that would infuriate a well-to-do college graduate. A patient in a large, rushed clinic may be as startled by an invitation to offer his or her opinion of a proposed treatment plan as an upper-middle-class patient would be annoyed to be excluded. In this sense, satisfaction may reflect expectations as well as the actual standard of care. To assure that interpersonal processes meet an adequate criterion of respect, descriptions of encounters as well as responses to them may be important data. Establishing a goal of satisfaction alone could actually reinforce inequities in ethical treatment of patients.

The process of decision making and the humaneness of the physician-patient relationship as a reflection of beneficence and autonomy are not impossible to evaluate.[114] Retrospective chart review can promote both documentation of the decision-making process (thereby enhancing continuity) and set standards for the content of the process itself. Checklists can be created to assure that certain elements that promote the patient's values are present in the chart (for instance, a durable power of attorney or a living will). Physicians' understanding of their obligations to informed consent and decision making at the end of life could be assured in part by required attendance at conferences dealing with these issues. Continuing medical education credits in ethics would be essential to privileges. Finally, observed or videotaped physician-patient interactions, now required by the American Board of Internal Medicine as part of residency training, could be adopted for attending physicians and nurses as well. In sum, it is quite feasible to assess respect for autonomy, as well as beneficence, in medical practice.

He Who Pays the Piper Calls the Tune

At first blush, one might be tempted to suggest that the payer (Medicare) should also be responsible for the quality assurance effort. Arguments in favor might appeal to the need to make sure that "one hand knows what the other is doing" and to the ease of information flow. Whether such arguments, which are based in practicality, have empirical validity would need to be demonstrated.

Against such a unified approach are arrayed a host of ethical concerns. It has been argued that the payer's concern is or should be waste, while the concern of quality assurance should be harm.[115] When a laudable medical goal is costly to achieve it is "harmful" to the payer, certainly, but not in the sense of quality of care. Such a distinction can be lost, however, when the payer must watch for two kinds of harm at once. Just as the concept of quality assurance and utilization review can become confused in managed care, so can they be confounded by the administrators of Medicare. The fidelity of the quality assurance program is owed to the patient. The fidelity of the payer is owed to the taxpayer. These are not necessarily the same people at the same time.

A quality assurance program has ethical obligations overlapping those of the health care professional: to prevent harms (nonmaleficence), to promote good care (beneficence), and to consider first its clients (fidelity to patients). Increasingly, experts point out that physicians in both fee-for-service and prepaid settings are in a position of inherent conflict of interest when their income depends on how they execute the duty to beneficence.[116–118] It would seem unwise to expose a quality assurance program for Medicare to similar conflicts. Yet if the organization responsible for guarding Medicare's coffers assumes responsibility for quality assurance as well, such conflicts could be unavoidable. Virtually any payment mechanism has the potential to produce conflict of interest at the level of doctor and patient. It is not hard, however, to imagine creating a quality assurance system for Medicare that is independent of the budgetary and payment apparatus.

CONCLUSION

Beneficence, nonmaleficence, autonomy, justice, and fidelity are fundamental principles of medical ethics. They represent widely divergent concerns with regard to the goals of medical practice, and they often come into conflict. The difficult decisions faced by individual practitioners and policymakers with regard to what constitutes "the right care" often require examination of the implications of these principles.

For quality assurance efforts in general, and for those directed to care for Medicare enrollees in particular, several ethical issues are of special concern. A discussion of quality would, from the outset, be meaningless without careful articulation of the goals of care—the good to be achieved and the harms to be prevented. The principle of respect for persons also demands that careful attention be paid to the processes of decision making, and to the quality of caregiver-patient communication. Reliance on "objective" measures of morbidity and mortality may seriously undermine the role of patients' values in the selection of diagnostic or treatment alternatives. The evaluation of outcomes will have to reflect not only the technical and resource inputs but also the effect of patients' preferences on the patterns of care.

Although respect for persons and an individualized notion of beneficence are important principles, they are not the only determinants of good quality where Medicare is concerned. A "social optimum" vision of quality will only coincide with an individual patient's evaluation of benefit and burden if the choice that results does not place an undue claim on available resources. Society will have to participate actively in a discussion of the points at which additional marginal investment in medical care is no longer appropriate. It will also have to develop mechanisms to ensure that the demands of equity are met—that vulnerable and often politically less powerful populations are not neglected medically in the allocation of limited funds.

Ultimately, a socially funded insurance mechanism like Medicare cannot ignore, in its definition of quality, the principle of justice. A standard of quality that enjoins each physician to behave as if there were no limits on available resources creates unrealistic pressure on both Medicare's budget and on providers of care. A sound definition of quality, and a defensible goal for quality assurance, should instead acknowledge the inevitability of limited resources and provide an explicit account of the acceptable balance between self-determination for individual patients and fair access to health care for the community as a whole.

ACKNOWLEDGMENTS

I would like to thank Dan Brock, Richard Riegleman, L. Gregory Pawlson, Jacqueline Glover, Joanne Lynn, and David DeGrazia for their substantial criticism and advice. Molla Donaldson and Kathy Lohr of the Institute of Medicine also reviewed each draft of this work and made invaluable suggestions. In addition, my husband, Lawrence Bachorik, and two children, Alexandra and Justin, put up with my long hours at the computer and offered warmth and support when my energy waned.

NOTES

1. R. M. Veatch, *A Theory of Medical Ethics* (New York: Basic Books, 1981), 79–107.
2. R. M. Veatch, "Patient's Rights and Physician Accountability: Problems with PSROs," *Bioethics Quarterly* 3 (1981): 137–85.
3. G. Mooney, "Medical Ethics: An Excuse for Inefficiency," *Journal of Medical Ethics* 10 (1984): 183–85.
4. N. Daniels, *Just Health Care* (Cambridge: Cambridge University Press, 1985), 135–39.
5. T. L. Beauchamp and J. F. Childress, *Principles of Biomedical Ethics* (Oxford: Oxford University Press, 1983).
6. S. Sherry, "Thrombolytic Therapy in Acute Myocardial Infarction: A Perspective," *Drugs* 33, suppl. 3 (1987): 1–2.
7. GISSI-2 (Gruppo Italiano per lo Studio della Sopravvivenza Nell'Infarto Miocardico), "A Factorial Randomized Trial of Alteplase versus Streptokinase and Heparin among 12,490 Patients with AMI," *Lancet* 336 (1990): 65–71.
8. The International Study Group, "In-Hospital Mortality and Clinical Course of 20,891 Patients with Suspected AMI Randomised between Alteplase and Streptokinase with Heparin," *Lancet* 336 (1990): 71–75.
9. J. L. Anderson, "Recent Clinical Developments in Thrombolysis in Acute Myocardial Infarction," *Drugs* 33, suppl. 3 (1987): 22–32.
10. Ibid.
11. Ibid.
12. Sherry, "Thrombolytic Therapy."
13. Mark Abramowicz, ed., *The Medical Letter on Drugs and Therapeutics* 29 (1987): 107–9.
14. E. J. Topol, D. C. Morris, R. W. Smalling, R. R. Schumacher, C. R. Taylor, A. Nishikawa, H. A. Liberman, D. Collen, M. E. Tufte, E. B. Grossbard, and W. W. O'Neill, "A Multicenter Randomized, Placebo-Controlled Trial of a New Form of Intravenous Recombinant Tissue Type Plasminogen Activator (Activase) in Acute Myocardial Infarction," *Journal of the American College of Cardiology* 9 (1987): 1205–13.
15. D. Collen, "Coronary Thrombolysis: Streptokinase or Recombinant Tissue-Type Plasminogen Activator," *Annals of Internal Medicine* 112 (1990): 529–38.
16. GISSI-2, "Alteplase versus Streptokinase."
17. The International Study Group, "In-Hospital Clinical Course."

18. Collen, "Coronary Thrombolysis."

19. GISSI-2, "Alteplase versus Streptokinase."

20. Collen, "Coronary Thrombolysis."

21. Abramowicz, *Medical Letter on Drugs and Therapeutics.*

22. Collen, "Coronary Thrombolysis."

23. G. Povar and J. Moreno, "Hippocrates and the Health Maintenance Organization: A Discussion of Ethical Issues," *Annals of Internal Medicine* 109 (1988): 419–24.

24. D. Brock, "The Ethical Work-Up," presentation to the Society for General Internal Medicine, 28 April 1988.

25. D. Patrick, M. Davis, L. Southerland, and G. Hong, "Quality of Life Following Intensive Care," *Journal of General Internal Medicine* 3 (1988): 218–23.

26. D. W. Brock and S. A. Wartman, "When Competent Patients Make Irrational Choices," *New England Journal of Medicine* 322 (1990): 1595–99.

27. A. Gutman, "For and Against Equal Access to Health Care," in *Securing Access to Health Care: The Ethical Implications of Differences in the Availability of Health Services* (Washington, DC: U.S. Government Printing Office, 1983), Vol. II: 51–66.

28. H. T. Engelhardt, "Health Care Allocations: Responses to the Unjust, the Unfortunate and the Undesirable," in *Justice and Health Care*, ed. E. Shelp (Dordrecht, The Netherlands: Reidel, 1981), 121–37.

29. A. G. Mulley, "The Allocation of Resources for Medical Intensive Care," in *Securing Access to Health Care: The Ethical Implications of Differences in the Availability of Health Services* (Washington, DC: U.S. Government Printing Office, 1983), Vol III: 285–311.

30. Ibid.

31. J. LaPuma and E. F. Lawlor, "QALY's: Ethical Implications for Physicians and Policy Makers," *Journal of the American Medical Association* 263 (1990): 2917–21.

32. A. S. Detsky and G. Naglie, "A Clinician's Guide to Cost-Effectiveness Analysis," *Annals of Internal Medicine* 113 (1990): 147–54.

33. R. J. Blendon and D. E. Altman, "Public Attitudes about Health Care Costs: A Lesson in National Schizophrenia," *New England Journal of Medicine* 311 (1984): 613–16.

34. Veatch, "Patient's Rights and Physician Accountability."

35. N. Daniels, "The Ideal Advocate and Limited Resources," *Theoretical Medicine* 8 (1987): 69–80.

36. H. Brody, "Cost Containment as Professional Challenge," *Theoretical Medicine* 8 (1987): 5–17.

37. Veatch, *Theory of Medical Ethics*, 155–71.

38. Mooney, "Medical Ethics."

39. Daniels, "Ideal Advocate and Limited Resources."

40. J. Eisenberg, "From Clinical Epidemiology to Clinical Economics," *Journal of General Internal Medicine* 3 (1988): 299–300.

41. A. Donabedian, "Quality, Cost and Clinical Decisions," *Annals, AAPSS* 468 (1983): 196–205.

42. E. D. Pellegrino, "Rationing Health Care: The Ethics of Medical Gatekeeping," *Journal of Contemporary Health Law and Policy* 2 (1986): 23–45.
43. Donabedian, "Quality, Cost and Clinical Decisions."
44. Eisenberg, "Clinical Epidemiology to Economics."
45. J. E. Wennberg, A. G. Mulley, D. Hanley, R. P. Timothy, F. J. Fowler, N. P. Roos, M. J. Barry, K. McPherson, E. R. Greenberg, D. Soule, T. Bubolz, E. Fisher, and D. Malenka, "An Assessment of Prostatectomy for Benign Urinary Tract Obstruction: Geographic Variations and the Evaluation of Medical Care Outcomes," *Journal of the American Medical Association* 259 (1988): 3027–30.
46. N. P. Roos and E. W. Ransey, "A Population-Based Study of Prostatectomy: Outcomes Associated with Differing Surgical Approaches," *Journal of Urology* 137 (1987): 1184–88.
47. M. J. Barry, A. G. Mulley, F. Fowler, and J. Wennberg, "Watchful Waiting vs. Immediate Transurethral Resection for Symptomatic Prostatism: The Importance of Patients' Preferences," *Journal of the American Medical Association* 259 (1988): 3810–17.
48. P. Graversen, T. C. Gasser, J. H. Wasson, F. Hinman, R. C. Bruskewitz, "Controversies about Indications for Transurethral Resection of the Prostate," *Journal of Urology* 141 (1989): 475–81.
49. F. Fowler, J. Wennberg, R. P. Timothy, M. J. Barry, A. G. Mulley, and D. Hanley, "Symptom Status and Quality of Life Following Prostatectomy," *Journal of the American Medical Association* 259 (1988): 3018–22.
50. M. M. Christensen and R. C. Bruskewitz, "Clinical Manifestations of Benign Prostatic Hyperplasia and Indications for Therapeutic Intervention," *Urological Clinics of North America* 17 (1990): 509–16.
51. Fowler et al., "Symptom Status and Quality of Life."
52. Christensen and Bruskewitz, "Benign Prostatic Hyperplasia."
53. P. Gross, personal communication.
54. P. E. Krumins, S. D. Fihn, and D. L. Kent, "Symptom Severity and Patients' Values in the Decision to Perform a Transurethral Resection of the Prostate," *Medical Decision Making* 8 (1988): 151–68.
55. Roos and Ransey, "Population-Based Study of Prostatectomy."
56. Gross, personal communication.
57. Fowler et al., "Symptom Status and Quality of Life."
58. Krumins et al., "Symptom Severity and Patients' Values."
59. Fowler et al., "Symptom Status and Quality of Life."
60. Veatch, "Patient's Rights and Physician Accountability."
61. Barry et al., "Watchful Waiting."
62. Krumins et al., "Symptom Severity and Patients' Values."
63. L. B. McCullough, "An Ethical Model for Improving the Patient-Physician Relationship," *Inquiry* 25 (1988): 151–68.
64. A. Laupacis, D. L. Sackett, and R. S. Roberts, "An Assessment of Clinically Useful Measures of the Consequences of Treatment," *New England Journal of Medicine* 318 (1988): 1728–41.
65. McCullough, "Ethical Model."

66. Ibid.
67. Brock and Wartman, "Competent Patients."
68. R. Bayor, D. Callahan, A. Caplan, and B. Jennings, "Toward Justice in Health Care," *American Journal of Public Health* 78 (1988): 583–88.
69. T. C. Schelling, "Standards for Adequate Minimum Personal Health Services," *Milbank Memorial Fund Quarterly* 57 (1979): 212–33.
70. R. Blendon, "The Public's View of the Future of Health Care," *Journal of the American Medical Association* 259 (1988): 3587–92.
71. Ibid.
72. D. Callahan, *What Kind of Life: The Limits of Medical Progress* (New York: Simon and Schuster, 1990).
73. Ibid.
74. Veatch, "Patient's Rights and Physician Accountability."
75. P. Elwood, "Banking on Quality," *HMO Practice* 2 (1988): 101–5.
76. B. Abel-Smith, "Minimum Adequate Levels of Personal Health Care: History and Justification," *Milbank Memorial Fund Quarterly* 56 (1978): 390–401.
77. McCullough, "Ethical Model."
78. G. E. Steffen, "Quality Medical Care," *Journal of the American Medical Association* 260 (1988): 56–61.
79. M. E. Kapp, "Enforcing Patient Preferences," *Journal of the American Medical Association* 261 (1989): 1935–38.
80. M. Danis, D. L. Patrick, L. I. Southerland, and M. L. Green, "Patients' and Families' Preferences for Medical Intensive Care," *Journal of the American Medical Association* 260 (1988): 797–802.
81. Brock and Wartman, "Competent Patients."
82. L. Breslow, "Quality and Cost Control: Medicare and Beyond," *Medical Care* 12 (1974): 95–114.
83. A. Donabedian, "Quality and Cost: Choices and Responsibilities," *Inquiry* 25 (1988): 90–99.
84. D. J. Murphy and D. B. Matchar, "Life Sustaining Therapy: A Model for Appropriate Use," *Journal of the American Medical Association* 264 (1990): 2103–7.
85. Callahan, *What Kind of Life*.
86. Donabedian, "Quality and Cost."
87. Eisenberg, "Clinical Epidemiology to Economics."
88. Krumins et al., "Symptom Severity and Patients' Values."
89. Pellegrino, "Rationing Health Care."
90. Donabedian, "Quality, Cost and Clinical Decisions."
91. Veatch, "Patient's Rights and Physician Accountability."
92. Donabedian, "Quality and Cost."
93. J. Sabatini, "Ethics and Economic Appraisals in Health Care," *Social Science & Medicine* 21 (1985): 1199–1202.
94. Veatch, "Patient's Rights and Physician Accountability."
95. Povar and Mareno, "Hippocrates and the Health Maintenance Organization."
96. Bayor et al., "Toward Justice."

97. Povar and Mareno, "Hippocrates and the Health Maintenance Organization."
98. Blendon, "The Public's View."
99. Donabedian, "Quality and Cost."
100. J. Feinglass, "Variations in Physician Practice and Covert Rationing," *Theoretical Medicine* 8 (1987): 1199–1202.
101. Schelling, "Standards for Personal Health Services."
102. Abel-Smith, "Levels of Personal Health Care."
103. Eisenberg, "Clinical Epidemiology to Economics."
104. Sabatini, "Ethics and Economic Appraisals."
105. Abel-Smith, "Levels of Personal Health Care."
106. Daniels, "Ideal Advocate and Limited Resources."
107. Bayor et al., "Toward Justice."
108. Feinglass, "Variations in Physician Practice."
109. Blendon, "The Public's View."
110. McCullough, "An Ethical Model."
111. C. Inlander and L. V. Backus, "Consumers, Physicians and Payors: A Triad of Conflicting Interests," *Theoretical Medicine* 8 (1987): 61–68.
112. Steffen, "Quality Medical Care."
113. Kapp, "Enforcing Patient Preferences."
114. Ibid.
115. Schelling, "Standards for Personal Health Services."
116. Povar and Moreno, "Hippocrates and the Health Maintenance Organization."
117. Pellegrino, "Rationing Health Care."
118. Donabedian, "Quality, Cost and Clinical Decisions."

Index

Abandonment, 143

Ability to pay, rationing by, 149

Acceptability, 54

Accessibility of care: beneficiary level, 54; definition of, 18–19; market level, 54

Adequate care standard, 158

American Association of Retired Persons (AARP), health care lobbying of, 20

American College of Surgeons, Hospital Standardization Program, 36

Appropriate care, 54

Autonomy, xix, 136–38; and beneficence, 136–38; importance of, in decision-making process, 147; and justice, 142; and medical ethics, 136–38, 146, 147; and quality assurance in Medicare, 151–52

Baseline performance, and effectiveness of quality monitoring, 83–84

Behavioral change, 106; bypassing, 112; and computer reminders, 107–8; direct intervention in, 106–7; education and training in, 109; facilitation in, 111; feedback in, 108; incentives and disincentives in, 110–11; and intraorganizational linkages, 103; routinization and guidance in, 112; using consumers to influence practitioners, 112

Beneficence, xvii; and autonomy, 136–38; definition of, 134–35; importance of, in decision-making process, 147; in medical ethics, 134–35, 144–45, 146, 147, 149; obligations of physician to, 149; and professional autonomy, 138; and quality assurance in Medicare, 150–51

Beneficiaries, 54

Bioethics, central precepts of, xviii–xix. *See also* Medical ethics

Blue Cross and Blue Shield, and monitoring of costs, 75

Bypassing, and behavioral change, 112

Capitation, 54

Clinical behavior, effectiveness of quality monitoring in, 67

Clinical decision making, analysis model of, 137

Clinical efficiency, 12

Clinical pathology conferences, 86

Clinical practice: collaborative nature of, 93; dependence on organizational support, 93

Coinsurance, 54

Comparative criteria, 54

Competition, 54

Computer reminders, and behavioral change, 107–8

Concurrent assessments, 97

Congruence, 120

Consensuality, and quality monitoring, 119

Consumer(s), 54: as contributors to quality monitoring, 113–15; as coproducers of care, 115; and definition of quality, 22–24; as evaluators, 114; influence on practitioners, 112; as informants, 114–15; role of, in quality assurance, xviii, 19–22; as standard setters, 113–14; as subjects or vehicles of control, 115; as targets of quality monitoring, 115; as users of monitoring information, 116–18

Copayment, 55

Cost, link between quality and, 62, 67, 96

Cost-benefit analysis, and health care, 9, 67, 69

Cost containment, 14–18

Cost-effectiveness analyses, and justice, 141

Cost sharing, 55

Credibility, and quality monitoring, 120

Data: outcome, 56; process, 57; in quality measurement, 28–30; structural, 58

Deaths, reviews of, 86

Decision-analysis model, 146

Decision-making process, 147

Deductible, 55

Defensive medicine, 76–77

Diagnosis-related groups (DRGs), 39

Direct intervention, in behavioral change, 106–7

Disincentives, and quality monitoring, 122

Distinctiveness, of quality monitoring, 79

Distributive justice, xix, 139–40; and patient rights, 142

Due process, and quality monitoring, 78–79

Economic efficiency, and quality, 154

Education and training, and behavioral change, 109

Effectiveness, 55; factors that influence, 118

Efficacy, 55; definition of, 10, 64

Efficiency, 55; and cost/benefit analysis, 12

Empirical criteria, 54

End-Stage Renal Disease Program, 10

Ethics, and quality assurance, xvii–xx

Evaluators, consumers as, 114

Explicit judgments, 55

External review, 55

Facilitation, and behavioral change, 111

Federalism, 89

Feedback, role of, in obtaining behavioral change, 108

Fee-for-service plans, 16, 55

Fidelity, xviii, 142–43; conflict between justice and, 142–43; definition of, 142; in medical ethics, 142–43, 149; obligations of physician to, 149; and quality assurance in Medicare, 155; and risk/benefit analysis, 143

Financing: organization of, 75; and quality monitoring, 75

Government: role of, in defining quality, xiv–xv, 8–9, 11–13

Health care, 55; balancing of supply and demand in, 74; cost-benefit analysis of, 67, 69; cost-containment strategies, 14–18; critical elements in, 160–61; defining accessibility of, 18–19; defining quality, 131; fragmentation of responsibility for, 72–74; information about, 100–101; organization of, 74; physician perspective on, 4–7; public funding for, 5–6; standards in, 156–58

Health care distribution, 5–6; evidence for inefficient, 13–14

Health Care Financing Administration (HCFA), and cost containment, 15–16

Health Care Quality Improvement Act (1986), 26, 78

Health care technology, defining appropriate use of, 10–11

Health costs, concerns over rising, xi

Health insurance plans, development of private, 5

Health maintenance organization (HMO), 55–56; and monitoring of costs, 75

Heparin, 134

Hippocratic oath, 132

Hospital stays: certification of, 115; failure of program for certifying, 107

Ideology, and quality monitoring, 80–81

Impaired physicians programs, 25

Implicit judgments, 56

Incentives: and behavioral change, 110–11; and quality monitoring, 82–83

Indicator conditions, 56

Individualization, 98

Individual practice association (IPA), 56

"Infectious disease" model of quality assessment, 150

Informants, consumers as, 114–15

Informed consent, 146, 161

Institute of Medicine study, xi–xx

Internal review, 56

Interpersonal care, science of, 94–95

Interpersonal competence, 56

Interpersonal exchange, quality of, 61–62

Intrainstitutional monitoring enter-prise, 101; extraorganizational linkages in, 105–6; internal structure of the monitoring function in, 103–5; intraorganizational linkages in, 102–3; organizational leadership and authority in, 101–2

Intrainstitutional practice: external modifiers in, 91–92; features of, 90–92; medical staff organization, 90–91; private practice in, 91; salaried employment in, 91

Intraorganizational environment, 79; baseline performance in, 83–84; distinctiveness of, 79; features of, 80–84; ideology in, 80–81; incentives in, 82–83; leadership in, 83; relevance of, 80; structural characteristics and resources in, 81–82

Joint Commission on Accreditation of Healthcare Organizations (JCAHO), 73; hospital standards of, 31; redesigned structural standards, 36

Justice, xix; and autonomy, 142; conflict between fidelity and, 142–43; and medical ethics, 138–40, 147–49; and professional autonomy, 142; and prostatic surgery case, 147–49; and quality assurance in Medicare, 152–55; and tPA case, 140–42

Leadership, in quality monitoring, 83, 101–2

Long-term facility, and quality of care, 81

Malpractice: crisis, 21, 24–25; liability, and quality monitoring, 76–78

Managed health care plans: choices in, 15–16; and fee-for-service plans, 16

Manufacturing-based definition of quality, 29

Market strategy for health care, 15–16

Medicaid, 8

Medical care, 56. *See also* Health care

Medical ethics, 132–33; and autonomy, 136–38, 146, 147; and beneficence, 134–35, 144–45, 146, 147, 149; definition of, 132; and fidelity, 142–43, 149; and justice, 138–42, 147–49; and nonmaleficence, 135–36; and prostatic surgery case, 143–44; and tPA case, 133–34, 140–42, 147

Medical profession, 85–88; federalism in, 89; professional interdependence in, 88; public accountability of, xvii; quality, responsibility for, xvi–xvii, 85–86; quality assurance methods, 86–87; quality monitoring, 84–92; specialization and subspecialization in, 88–89. *See also* Physician

Medical records, and quality assessment, 100

Medical staff, organization of, 90–91

Medical technology, 56

Medical Treatment Effectiveness Program (MEDTEP), 38

Medicare, 8; and entitlement, 138; quality assurance in, xi, 132, 150–55, 156–62

Medicare Peer Review Organization (PRO) program, xii

Monitoring information, consumers as users of, 116–18

National Center for Health Services Research, 38

Nonmaleficence in health care, xviii; and medical ethics, 135–36; and quality assurance in Medicare, 150–51

Omnibus Budget Reconciliation Act (1986), xi–xii

Omnibus Budget Reconciliation Act (1989), 38

Organizational dependence, and quality monitoring, 119

Outcome data, 56

Ownership, and quality monitoring, 120–21

Parsimony, defined, 154

Particularization, 97–98

Patient care, fragmentation in, 89

Patient rights: and distributive justice, 142; physicians' fiduciary responsibility to, 26–27; and self-determination, 136

Patients, 56; and definition of quality, 22–24. *See also* Consumer(s)

Patient satisfaction, 56; in defining quality of care, 23

Pattern analysis, 35

Pattern monitoring, 35

Peer review, 57; desirability of, 25–26

Peer review organizations (PROs), 57; program of, 19–21; responsibility of, 73; and sharing of information on, 26

Performance, method of assessing, 95–101

Physician: consumer influence on, 112; fiduciary responsibility to patients, 26–27; impaired, programs for, 25; obligations of, 149; quality of care and, xiv, xvii, 7–8; role of, in setting standards, 4–6; supply of, 92; traditional perspective of, 6–7. *See also* Medical profession

Physician satisfaction, 24–27

Prepaid group practice, 57

Prescriptive criteria, 57

Private practice, 91

Process-based measures, 37

Process data, 57

Process measurements, 36

Product-based definition of quality, 29

Production efficiency, 12

Professional autonomy: and beneficence, 138; and justice, 142

Professional standards review organizations (PSROs), 9; impact of, on costs, 14–15; program, 9; responsibility of, for health care, 73

Profile analysis, 35, 57–58; hospital use of, 40–41

Profile monitoring, 35

Prospective assessments, 97

Prospective payment system (PPS) for Medicare hospitalizations, 19

Prostatic surgery medical ethics case, 143–44; and autonomy, 146; and beneficence, 144–45, 146; and justice, 147–49; risk-benefit analysis in, 145–46

Provider competence, 58

Public accountability, of medical profession, xvii

Quality: criteria and standards of, 98–100; definition of, xii, xiii–xv, 27–28, 61–62, 118, 156–59; and economic efficiency, 154; expansion of the consumer's role in defining, 19–22; expansion of government's role in defining, 8–9; government perspective of, 11–13; link between cost and, 62, 67, 96; manufacturing-based definition of, 29; patient and consumer definitions of, 22–24; physicians' definitions of, 7–8; product-based definition of, 29; responsibility of medical profession for, 85–86; scrutiny in assessment of, 62; social commitment to, 71–72; social optimum vision of, 163; standards setting, 4–6, 113–14; user-based definition of, 29–30

Quality assessment, 58; "infectious disease" model of, 150

Quality assurance, xv, 58; barriers to, xvi–xviii; definition of, 62–64, 118; effectiveness of, 70; ethical considerations of, xviii–xx, 162; interventions, 33–35; and Medicare, 132, 150–55, 156–62; methods for implementing, 86–87; new approach to, xii–xiii; responsibility of, for Medicare, 162; role of consumers in, xviii; strategies for, 40–41

Quality measurement, 28; bi-directional relationship between technology assessment and, 10–11; data for, 28–30; examples of, 36–40; PSRO techniques developed in the 1970s, 35; standards for, 31–33

Quality monitoring: baseline performance in, 83–84; consensuality of, 119; consumers and, 113–15; credibility of, 120; disincentives in, 122; distinctiveness of, 79; and due process, 78–79; effectiveness of, 64, 67–69; financing and, 75; formal/informal, 63–64, 119–20; ideology of, 80–81; incentives in, 82–83; influence of financing on, 75; informal, 63; internal structure of, 103–5; leadership in, 83; legal environment of, 76–79; and malpractice liability, 76–78; methods of assessing performance in, 95–101; organizational dependency, 119; and organization level in health care system, 74; ownership, 120–21; and professional work, 92–93; protection for participants in, 78; purpose of, 106–12; relevance of, 80, 120; sciences of, 93–95; and self-interest, 121–22; structural characteristics and resources, 81, 82

RAND health insurance experiment, 17

Referent, 58

Regional Medical Programs, 8

Reimbursement, and quality monitoring, 75

Relevance of quality monitoring, 80, 120

Responsibility, fragmentation of, for health care, 72–74

Retrospective assessments, 97
Retrospective chart review, 161
Risk/benefit analysis, and fidelity, 143
Routinization and guidance, and behavioral change, 112

Second opinion programs: surgical, 115; voluntary, 107
Self-determination: patient rights in, xix, 136
Self-interest, and quality monitoring, 121–22
Services, evidence for inefficient provision of populations, 13–14
Social optimum: definition of, 159–60; standard for, 156; vision of quality, 71–72, 163
Specialization, medical, 88–89
Standard setters: consumers as, 113–14; physicians as, 4–6
State government, cost-containment programs of, 9
Structural data, 58
System design, relationship between performance and, 62–63
System performance: monitoring, 63; relationship between design and, 62–63

Teaching center, and quality of care, 81
Technical care: quality of, 61, 81; science of, 93–94
Technical competence, 58
Technology, cost/benefit analysis of, 9
Technology assessment, bi-directional relationship between quality measurement and, 10–11
Tissue plasminogen activator (tPA) case, 133–34; and autonomy, 136; and beneficence, 135; and justice, 139, 140–42, 147; and nonmaleficence, 135–36
Title V programs, 8
tPA. *See* Tissue plasminogen activator

User-based definition of quality, 29
Utilization, of geographic variations, 13–14
Utilization efficiency, 12
Utilization review (UR), 35, 58, 162; hospital programs of, 15, 40–41

Voluntary second opinion program, 107

About the Authors

R. Heather Palmer, M.B., B.Ch., S.M., has been a full-time faculty member at the Harvard School of Public Health since 1976. She currently teaches a course on evaluation of quality of health care and has recently taught short courses on quality assurance in Milan, Italy, and Madrid and Murcia, Spain. She is also director of the newly established Center for Quality of Care Research and Education (QCaRE) in the School's Department of Health Policy and Management.

Board certified in pediatrics, Dr. Palmer has a Master of Science degree in health services administration from the Harvard School of Public Health. Dr. Palmer's research concerns the evaluation of quality of health care, primarily in ambulatory settings. She was principal investigator for a randomized, controlled trial of the effectiveness of quality assurance in 16 primary care group practices. She was also principal investigator for a project to develop and evaluate computerized reminders to physicians in ambulatory care and a study of quality differences among primary care practitioners.

Dr. Palmer is currently chairperson of the Board of the American Medical Review Research Center and a member of the Board of the National Committee on Quality Assurance. She recently served on the Advisory Committee on Quality Assessment in Ambulatory Care Settings of the Blue Cross and Blue Shield Association, the Planning Committee of the National Demonstration Project on Quality Improvement in Health Care, the advisory panel to the Office of Technology Assessment's study on "Quality of Medical Care: Information for Consumers," the Joint Commission on Accreditation of Healthcare Organizations' Ambulatory Standards Task Force, and the General Accounting Office Expert Panel that gave advice on quality assurance to the Pepper Commission on Comprehensive Health Care.

Avedis Donabedian, M.D., M.P.H., is the Nathan Sinai Distinguished Professor Emeritus of Public Health at the University of Michigan. Dr. Donabedian, who received his M.D. from the American University of Beirut and his M.P.H. from the Harvard School of Public Health, taught previously at the American University of Beirut, at the Harvard School of Public Health, and at New York Medical College.

Dr. Donabedian's work has consisted largely in systematizations of knowledge in various areas of health care organization, especially quality assessment and monitoring, but also assessments of needs and resources for health care, and the design of program benefits. His contributions, comprising six books and many other publications, have been recognized by membership in the Institute of Medicine of the National Academy of Sciences, in the American College of Healthcare Executives, and in the American College of Utilization Review Physicians. His publications have won the Dean Conley Award of the American College of Healthcare Executives, the Norman A. Welch Award of the National Blue Cross Association, and the Elizur Wright Award of the American Risk and Insurance Association. He has also received the Baxter American Foundation Health Services Research Prize and an Award in Recognition of a Distinguished Career in Health Services Research from the Association for Health Services Research.

In 1990, the Fundación Avedis Donabedian para la Mejora de la Assistencia Sanitaria (the Avedis Donabedian Foundation for the Improvement of Health Care) was established in Barcelona, Spain, "to continue the scientific and informational work that has characterized the professional life of Professor Donabedian."

Gail J. Povar, M.D., M.P.H., is Associate Professor of Health Care Sciences and Medicine at the George Washington University Medical Center in Washington, D.C., where she is a practicing internist as well as a medical educator and scholar. She has been a Visiting Scholar and is currently a Fellow of the Kennedy Institute for Ethics at Georgetown University.

Dr. Povar received her B.A. from Cornell University and her M.D. from the University of Vermont. She earned her M.P.H. degree in Medical Care Organization at the University of Michigan. She is a member of the American College of Physicians, the Society of General Internal Medicine, and the Society for Health and Human Values. She has served on the governing board of the American Public Health Association and as chair of its Forum on Bioethics.

Dr. Povar's research concerns issues in clinical ethics as well as ethical problems for health policy. From 1985 to 1989, as the recipient of a Kellogg Fellowship, she researched the problem of defining "quality" in health care in England, Sweden, Ecuador, Brazil, Canada, and the United States. She is currently serving as a consultant to the Institute of Medicine for its Clinical Guidelines Project.